THIS BOOK IS ABOUT HEFFERS

*This book is dedicated to the memory of
my dear Aunty Winnie*

Miss Winifred Anstee (1918-2005)
worked for Heffers from 1947 to 1973.

THIS BOOK IS ABOUT

HEFFERS

THE BOOKSHOP
THAT IS KNOWN
ALL OVER
THE WORLD

Julie E Bounford

Gottahavebooks,
16 Middle Street, Great Gransden,
Cambridgeshire SG19 3AD, UK
sales@gottahavebooks.co.uk

ISBN 978-0-9933781-3-3
First edition published 2016 by Gottahavebooks

1 3 5 7 9 8 6 4 2

Cover and page layout design by Bounford.com
(The cover is based on an original Heffers bookmark design – *see page 74*)

CONTENTS

Heffers in the nineteenth century.

Heffers in the twenty-first century.

FOREWORD

Not long after I became Chairman of Heffers in 1984, I attended a course specifically for heads of family firms. What was rapidly apparent was that although many firms succeed in passing the mantle from father to son, very few make it to a third generation and only one or two had their hands raised, as I did, to indicate a move into a fourth generation. To be part of a large family, all who lived in the same city, had children who grew up together, and many of whom worked together, was an extraordinary experience. I can still remember, as a very young child, a visit to the bookshop in Petty Cury, helping open the post with my father and grandfather (Reuben and Ernest) and starting my stamp collection with some of the foreign stamps which came in on orders sent from all over the world. I also recall the excitement of going into the closed bookshop, some years later, to hang flags out of the windows for the VE celebrations the following day.

The expansion of Heffers as a family firm drew very much on the strengths of those members of the family who chose to work in it, ensuring that they had the correct training or experience first, before directing them into the most appropriate branch of the firm. When I joined the business, I was one of seven family members working in it at that time. In its heyday, Heffers had ten shops in Cambridge as well as the printing works. However, the nature of retail business changed enormously towards the end of the twentieth century, and by the end of my working life, I had been the sole member of the family working in the firm for fourteen years. At that point, it was obvious to the family that Heffers was not the right size to continue to withstand the pressures of the twenty-first century and another chapter in the firm's existence began.

In this book, Julie Bounford has very successfully managed to combine meticulous research into the Heffer family, and the history of the growth of that family business, with a rich tapestry of anecdote and illustration from so many of those who once worked for or who are still working for Heffers, and without whom Heffers would never have become the success it was. Many of them came straight from school and remained loyally there for their entire working lives. Many others gained invaluable experience there but went on to success elsewhere. Some were as eccentric as some of our customers and others played an essential role in the less visible parts of the business. I am glad to have this opportunity to pay tribute to the invaluable contribution made by all those members of Heffers staff, past and present, who are all a part of this story.

Nicholas Heffer
France
August 2016

APOTHEOSIS AT THE SIGNING TABLE

Looking ahead for places to sit down,
Come spring I might, one last time, limp downtown
And into Heffers, into Waterstones,
In either order, haul my creaking bones,
To stand, with a long-practised half-lost look,
Somewhere beside the stack of my new book
Until I'm asked to sign. As if surprised
I'll sit down, slowly, seeming paralysed
By sheer humility as they bring stock
Of books that I forgot I wrote. I'll sign
Each tempting title-page with my by-line
Like a machine for hours on end. The clock
Will seem not to exist. My signature
Will grow, however, steadily less sure,
Until, the felt-tip quivering in my grasp,
I scrawl the hieroglyphs of my last gasp.
A final short sip from my cup of tea
And I will topple, croaking tragically.
Slumped on the carpet, I will look around,
And all the walls of books in the background,
More splendid even than they were before,
Will seem to hear my small voice from the floor.
'Heffers or Waterstones, this is goodbye,
But I rejoice that I came here to die,
So one day those who know my books may say
That this is where he signed his life away.'

Clive James, 2016
(Heffers regular for many years)

TIMELINE

1843 William Heffer is born at Exning, Suffolk, the eighth child of Charles, an agricultural labourer, and his wife Phoebe.

1863 William Heffer and Mary Crick marry on 28th May at All Saints' Church in Jewry, Cambridge. William is working as a groom for Mr Adams in Sidney Street, Cambridge, at the time and later has a stint running the Sir John Barleycorn and the Forester public houses before going back to being a groom.

1876 William takes up the tenancy of a small shop and house at 104 Fitzroy Street, Cambridge, assisted financially by the vicar of St Andrew the Less, the Reverend Edward Tucker Leeke. He sells stationery and educational supplies, as well as hymn books. He becomes a newsagent and later opens a sub Post Office at the same premises in 1886.

1889 First book published by Heffers; *A Jubilee Memorial of the Consecration of Christ Church, Cambridge: Which Took Place 27 June 1839. To Which is Prefixed a Short History of Barnwell Priory From its Foundation to the Present Time* by William White, the sub-librarian of Trinity College, Cambridge. Heffers publishing continues until 1975.

1896 Heffers moves into Cambridge city centre, opening a bookshop on the ground floor of 4 Petty Cury, leased from Emmanuel College and overseen by Ernest Heffer. The firm's reputation grows and the shop is gradually expanded, taking over all three floors; catalogues are produced proudly claiming 'The bookshop known all over the world'. The shop is later extended to number 3 and the upper floors of number 2.

1902 Heffers becomes a customer of the National Telephone Company and installs its first telephones at the Fitzroy Street and Petty Cury shops.

1903 Heffers acquires the freehold of 18/19 Sidney Street and opens the stationery shop. Overseen by Sidney Heffer and his sister, Kate, the shop, briefly called the 'Eastern Counties Educational Depot.' has a picture gallery, giving prominence to local artists and the topics of Cambridge and East Anglia.

1911 Heffers acquires the Black Bear Press in Hills Road, becoming Heffers printing works. The Eagle printing works, at one time in Hobson's Passage and already acquired by Heffers, is amalgamated with the Hills Road works.

1928 William Heffer dies and is succeeded as Company Chairman by his son, George who continues in the role until his death in 1947.

1930 The Sidney Street shop is rebuilt and the first art exhibition in the new gallery a year later is entitled, *Anthology of English Painting from 1900 to 1931*, featuring Augustus John. Sidney Heffer's son, John, who joined the firm in 1938, takes over the running of Sidney Street on his return from active service in 1946. John serves as company chairman from 1975 to 1984.

1931 Arthur Beak Heffer, elder son of Ernest and grandson of William, dies at the age of thirty-two. His focus at the firm was bookselling and publishing, leaving a gap which his younger brother, Reuben, fills.

1933 Ernest Heffer addresses apprentice booksellers in London, *Instructions to the Young Bookseller*. Ernest is company chairman for one year, from 1947 until his death in 1948.

1935 The printing works at 104 Hills Road are rebuilt.

1939 Heffers saves *The Cambridge Review* (*A Journal of University Life and Thought*) when its publisher, Fabb and Tyler, is forced to close. It continues for many years after the Heffers acquisition and, after 119 volumes in total, ceases publication in 1998.

1946 A major fire at the Petty Cury shop on the night of 12th November, rages for four hours, spreading to the Lion Hotel next door. Two firemen are injured and several thousand books, many valuable and some irreplaceable, are destroyed.

1952 Sidney Heffer publishes a short biography of his father, William. Sidney had become company chairman in 1948 and remains so until his death in 1959.

1955 Heffers acquires the Cambridge Express Printing Company.

1957 Heffers Penguin shop (the first in the country) opens at 51 Trumpington Street, Cambridge. The shop is closed in 1985. Heffers acquires R.I. Severs Ltd.

1959 Reuben Heffer becomes chairman of the three divisions (bookselling, stationery and printing) and remains so until his retirement in 1975, when he is succeeded by his cousin, John. Reuben dies in 1985.

1961 The firm is feeling adventurous and schedules a staff outing by air to Boulogne, France. Many had never flown before.

1964 Heffers Paperback shop opens at 13 Trinity Street, Cambridge, occupying the ground floor, sublet from the antiquarian booksellers, Deighton Bell. In 1988 the stock is transferred to the Paperback shop at 31 St Andrew's Street, Cambridge. Two printing subsidiaries are merged under the name of R.I. Severs and moved to new premises in King's Hedges Road. The rest follows in 1972 when this site is expanded and the Hills Road plant is sold.

1965 Heffers Penguin shop opens at 14 Pottergate, Norwich. The shop is closed by 1967.

1969 Heffers Children's Bookshop opens at 27 Trinity Street, Cambridge on St Valentines Day. The shop is relocated to 30 Trinity Street in 1979 and then closed in 2002.

1970 The main bookshop moves from Petty Cury to its present address, 20 Trinity Street, Cambridge. The interior is designed by architects, Austin-Smith:Lord, and the shop is formally opened by Lord Butler, Master of Trinity College.

1971 Heffers first charges undergraduate students for their copy of the Heffer Diary, setting the price at 10p. For a few subsequent years the diary is once again free to students but eventually the practice is viewed as not financially viable and it stops.

1972 Heffers Artists shop and Heffers Drawing Office Centre open in King Street. Later combined as Heffers Art & Graphic shop, it is sold in 2005. Heffers introduces the 'Heffer Selector', a blanket order service designed to automatically supply selected books to libraries. In the mid-1990s, a severe drop in UK library sales is experienced by all library suppliers as a result of budget cutbacks and re-organisation in public libraries.

1973 A new colour lithographic printing machine from Germany is installed at the King's Hedges print works.

1975 The Bookworm Club for young readers is launched. A paperback club for schools, this is a collaboration between Heffers, educational publisher E.J. Arnold & Son of Leeds, and four leading trade publishers. In 1986 the Early Worm Club is launched, for younger children. The clubs run until 1999, when they are sold.

1976 Heffers centenary is celebrated with a reception at Nevile's Court, Trinity College. W.P. Spalding's map shop at 3 Green Street is acquired (eventually renamed Heffers Map shop and is subsequently moved to Sidney Street shop).

1977 Heffers offices move to new premises at St Tibbs Row, Downing Street, Cambridge. Heffers purchases a £200,000 computer to handle its book ordering for British and overseas customers.

1978 Heffers Paperback shop opens at 31 St Andrew's Street. This is later renamed Heffers Plus and is now closed (the site is now occupied by the John Lewis department store).

1979 The Periodicals department, which had handled subscriptions to learned journals of all kinds, is closed.

1983 Heffers Grafton Centre shop opens (it is moved to larger premises at the Centre in 1996 and is closed in 2008). Stephen Heffer oversees the new shop. Stephen worked for the firm from 1971 to 1986 and dies in 1996. Heffers becomes the sole owner of the Bookworm Club. A Video and Computer Software Department is opened at Trinity Street. The book department at Sidney Street is closed.

1984 Nicholas Heffer becomes company chairman and remains so until the firm is sold to Blackwell's in 1999. Heffers starts accepting Access and Visa credit cards. The Sidney Street refurbishment is completed and now incorporates the Map shop. Heffers printers withdraws from hot-metal composition and from letterpress printing. An Aurelia four-colour press is installed.

1985 A major revamp of the Trinity Street shop is completed.

1987 The printing business is sold to a management buyout team headed by Richard Laming, who renames it Black Bear Press Ltd. Heffers acquires Deighton Bell, the antiquarian bookshop at 13 Trinity Street, Cambridge. In 1992 the ground floor is refitted to take Heffers' Art & Architecture department. The shop is closed after 1999. The offices move from St Tibbs Row to Rustat House, Clifton Road. In 1995 the firm buys the freehold. In 1999, after the Blackwell's takeover, Rustat House is sold.

1988 Heffers acquires the London-based Biography Bookshop and the business is transferred to Trinity Street, Cambridge. The Paperback shop in St Andrews Street, Cambridge is refurbished and almost doubles in size, incorporating an enlarged Video department, previously at Trinity Street.

1989 Heffers produces a catalogue to commemorate the French Revolution Bicentenary, 1989 in true Heffers fashion, with the strapline, 'Get it right at Heffers: a cut above the rest'. This is just one example of Heffers' stylish and notable catalogues.

1990 Heffers Sound opens next door to the main shop at number 19 Trinity Street, Cambridge. This is now absorbed back into the bookshop at 20 Trinity Street.

1991 The first *Bodies in the Bookshop* catalogue is published as part of an initiative overseen by Richard Reynolds, involving five authors. As a competition prize, the winner could produce the screen for one night only at a performance of *The Mousetrap*.

1993 Trinity Street is brought to a standstill in 1993 by a visit from Margaret Thatcher, to sign copies of her memoirs *The Downing Street Years*. Heffers hosts many celebrity signings and visits during the 1970s, '80s and '90s.

1995 'Heffers by Post', a mail order service, is launched with a selection of current books with some CDs, video, Filofax and stationery, distributed to customers all over the world.

1997 Heffers branch in Northampton opens and is closed in 1999. On 6th November Heffers website is launched, with 1.9 million titles on its database.

1999 Heffers is sold to Blackwell's of Oxford, a family that had had strong links with the Heffer family over three generations.

2000 The Sidney Street shop is closed.

INTRODUCTION

William Heffer, William Heffer,
Bowes and Bowes, Bowes and Bowes,
Galloway and Porter, Galloway and Porter,
Deighton Bell, Deighton Bell

This rhyme, sung to the tune of *Frère Jacques*, harks back to a golden age of bookselling in early- to mid-twentieth-century Cambridge, when the city was served by several excellent establishments, each with its own distinctive history and character. This book tells the story of just one; Heffers of Cambridge, founded by William Heffer in 1876. As a bookseller, Heffers enjoyed that golden age. And as a bookseller, Heffers was, and still is, 'known all over the world'. What may not be known worldwide, however, is that Heffers has also always been a stationer, and was once a prolific publisher, and a printer.

On 20th October 1933, Ernest Heffer (son of William) wrote to *The Times*, challenging the notion of Heffers bookshop as a 'craft emporium'.

EFFERINI CRAFTELLI
TO THE EDITOR OF THE TIMES

Sir, – It seems almost ungrateful to criticize such a delicious jeu d'esprit, *and we would not do it, except for one reference you make to Oxford. You say that Heffer's of Cambridge is a bookshop known even to Oxford men, and then go on to pack that bookshop with 'little crafts.' Mentally one conjures up visions of wool and of pewter, of seagrass stools and barbola, and the like, on intimate terms with and indeed almost dominating all that is best, and a great deal that is less than best, in the whole realm of books.*

Now, Sir, Cambridge by experience knows better; but Oxford, knowing chiefly by repute, might be led to have a wrong conception of what our bookshop really is. May we beg of you to correct this possible misconception before it spreads too deep for correction?

The Efferini Craftelli is carried on at our Sidney Street branch, whilst Heffer's books is in the Cury: and come there who will, they shall find neither frills nor furbelows: they shall hunt without success for wool and the silk and the straw that delight the heart of woman. The only craft "worked" there is the craft of books.

Yours faithfully,

E. W. HEFFER,

Director, W. Heffer and Sons, Limited,

3 and 4, Petty Cury, Cambridge,

Oct. 19.

Whilst, arguably, the impressions held by Oxford men, or what delights the heart of woman, may not concern us, it is a fact that the 'bookseller' and 'stationer' trades are from the same stable. Nicholas Chrimes, in his 2012 portrait of Cambridge, tells us that Cambridge University licensed sellers of books to work from 'fixed stations', initially in churches or outside their north and south walls. As one of the few stationary trades, the bookselling trade was considered superior to that of itinerant pedlars. The Latin word stationarius had been used to mean a trader with a fixed place of business, but booksellers secured this term for themselves (the 'e' in stationers was an eighteenth century derivation). [1] M. Oldfield, on the other hand, in his 1944 article on *Cambridge and its Stationers*, insists the derivation rests rather on the metaphysical translations, 'that which is established by custom' … than the literal rendering of a 'place of abode' or 'station'. [2] Either way, Heffers has been very much a fixed institution in Cambridge since its foundation in 1876.

In a similar fashion to E.W. Heffer's eloquent retort, I aim to convey something of the style and character of the Cambridge phenomenon that is Heffers. The stories revealed in this illustrated social history, kindly shared by past and present employees and by customers, will testify to the many sides of the firm.

Dr Julie E. Bounford
September 2016

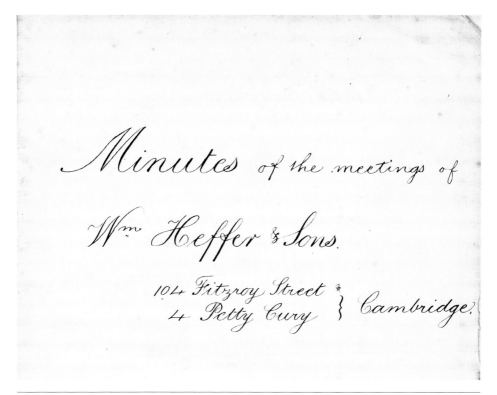

The first company Minute Book dated 1898.

1

"NO PARTICULAR BENT TOWARDS BOOKS"

William Heffer, son of Charles and Phoebe Heffer, was born in 1843 in the village of Exning, Suffolk, some twenty three miles from Cambridge. His father, an agricultural labourer, died in 1848, when William was very young. Described by Frederick Brittain [3] as an unlettered country man, it is true that in the beginning William had "no particular bent towards books". [4] His education was indeed limited and he began his working life in the neighbouring parish of Burwell, Cambridgeshire at the age of thirteen, driving a donkey and cart, delivering parcels to nearby villages.

At the age of seventeen William was living in Little Paxton, Huntingdonshire and working as one of two grooms to Sir Williamson Booth (descended from the Booth family, famous for distilling London gin). William may well have met Booth at the Newmarket racecourse, as both were fond of horses. Booth's obituary in the *Morning Post* states that he retired from the Turf as an owner of horses soon after 'Stampedo, the best he ever possessed', won the Northamptonshire Stakes in 1862. It is likely that William's services as a groom were no longer required after that time. According to Sidney Heffer, in his biography of his father, [5] William had a short spell in Yorkshire as an apprentice to a racing stable, before finding work by 1863 as a groom to Dennis Adams, surgeon, of 31 Sidney Street, Cambridge. The Yorkshire connection may have been made through his work for Booth who attended the Doncaster races, possibly with his grooms. If so, this would have been the furthest William ever travelled from the Cambridge area.

In 1863, Mary Crick, aged twenty-six, was working as cook to Mr Adams at his Sidney Street home and her elder sister Emma was the housekeeper there. William, it seems, began to show a romantic interest in Mary. Sidney Heffer wrote that Mary, 'a merry little woman', frequently exasperated William by her 'off-handedness', causing him many a heartache. William was also worried about money and how they might live on his pay. That failed to inhibit the romance and they were married on 28th May 1863 at All Saints' Church in Jewry, Cambridge. The following March, when William and Mary's first child, John Charles, was born, their address was 33 Park Street. [6] They were still there for the birth of Harry in 1865 but by the time Kate Adelaide was born in 1866, the family had moved to Burleigh Street. William's occupation was still that of groom in 1866, but two years on he had had an abrupt and unexpected career change. In October 1868, when George Herbert was born, his occupation was stated as 'publican' at an address in Burleigh Street. It seems that his concern about money had led William to take on additional or alternative work, which, at face value, clashed with his abstinence sympathies. Not impressed with the inebriated dinner guests that he had had to drive home when in Mr Adams's employment, William had turned to temperance; but this did not prevent him from taking on the better paid employment of running the Sir John Barleycorn public house, a long established hostelry at the Fitzroy Street end of Burleigh Street, on the east side of the road, behind the Eden Chapel. It is not known how long William was at this pub, but the following year, in October 1870, he was across the road at a new establishment, the Forester, at the junction of Burleigh Street, City Road and Fitzroy Street. He couldn't have been at the Forester for more than six months, however, as an Edward Cartwright was running it at the time of the 1871 census.

The Forester public house at the junction of Burleigh Street, City Road and Fitzroy Street in the 1890s.

The Reverend Edward Tucker Leeke, vicar of St Andrew the Less.
© National Portrait Gallery, London

By the spring of 1871, William was back in Park Street, once more working as a groom, possibly for Mr Adams again. At the time of the census, William and Mary were living at 10 Clement Court, [7] where their children Ernest William (1871), Lucy Mary (1873), Emma Louise (1874) and Frank (1876) were all born. (There was a William Heffer running the Wheat Sheaf public house in High Street, Chesterton during the time when 'our' William was back to being a groom – was this another William Heffer, or was 'our' William travelling all the way from Clement Place to man the Wheat Sheaf everyday? And there was another William Heffer, born 1838, who briefly ran the White Swan public house in Mill Road, Cambridge.)

William's rules as a pub landlord were, 'no brawling, no swearing, and no more drink to a man showing signs of sufficiency'. On 15th January 1876, the *Cambridge Independent Press* reported a rather amusing speech by William at a meeting of the Cambridge Church Temperance Association, when he related some scenes behind the bar during his time as a publican and gave some practical hints on the best method of curing a drunkard. The respect of the community he gained as a publication, despite not spending long in the trade, enabled him in 1876, five years after going back to being a groom, to take up the tenancy of a small shop and house at 104 Fitzroy Street. He was assisted financially by the vicar of St Andrew the Less, the Reverend Edward Tucker Leeke, who would have got to know William on his arrival in the parish in 1869, and who may well have been surprised to find a fellow teetotaller in charge of a public house.

In March 1876 an advert appeared in the *Cambridge Independent Press*:

THE FITZROY FANCY REPOSITORY,
104 Fitzroy-street, Cambridge.
To be disposed of, the above business, in consequence of a
death in the family, comprising Bookselling, Stationery, and Newsagency,
together with the Pictures and Picture frames, Trade &c – Apply as above.

Number 104 Fitzroy Street, near the corner of James Street, had been a bookshop for some years. In the late 1850s and early 1860s, an Emma Bowd, Bookseller, was there. From 1869 (when Miss Bowd married), a retailer called Thomas C. Fison ran it as a bookshop and stationers. Fison died young, in October 1872. His wife, Mary, managed to keep the shop going until her own death in January 1876, at the age of 28, orphaning their eight-year-old son. Sad though this is, without the Fisons dying young, there would perhaps have been no W. Heffer and Sons. In July 1876, William opened the doors of his shop for the first time. William and Mary's last child, Sidney, was born at Fitzroy Street in 1878.

In his tribute, given in the foreword to Sidney Heffer's biography of his father, Frederick Brittain regrets not ever having had the opportunity of speaking with William and reflects on the man's remarkable career; for he, 'was not an ordinary man'. Perhaps, as one would expect, Sidney Heffer begins his biography by saying William was, 'A man to be proud of, and to boast about, but no boaster; as strong in moral fibre as in physical strength; afraid of no one except his God; just but stern, with the full courage of his convictions.' Frank Collieson, at Heffers from 1962, described William as, "one of those absolutely straight and determined Victorian figures who feature in sepia photographs that we all know and he was very much of that era." He had a determination to get on, to better himself and do the best he could for his family.

William also played an active role as a representative of the business community, inspiring others to succeed. He sponsored prize-giving in schools across Cambridge. His prizes were for 'the neatest exercise book in the school' (Higher Grade School Park Street, 1883), 'the best and cleanest exercise book in the school' (St Luke's Schools, 1884), 'neatness' (St Luke's Boys' School, 1893), and 'the best set of

This photograph is one of three of a bust of William Heffer found in an envelope with 'Ralph Heffer' written upon it in Stephen Heffer's handwriting. Ralph (1893–1974), grandson of William, enjoyed working with his hands and could possibly have created the work. The location of the bust is not known, and it may have been destroyed.

notebooks' (Cambridge and County Girls' School, 1907). He also sponsored special prizes at the Cambridge School of Arts & Crafts. The 1906 Prize List included a special prize by Messrs Heffer and Sons for drawing the figure, ornament, or details from the cast. And in 1917 W. Heffer and Sons were amongst other notable firms and associations who donated to the prize fund for the Wounded Soldiers' Sports Day in aid of the 1st Eastern General Hospital Recreation Fund.

THE HEFFER FAMILY

William and Mary Heffer. On 23rd May 1923, in a feature marking the diamond wedding anniversary of William and Mary Heffer, the *Cambridge Chronicle* declares, 'There is romance, surely, in the story of Mr Heffer's business career'.

In 1923, William was still attending to the duties of the business at the age of eighty. Looking back on his achievement in building a successful family business, the word 'romance' conceivably captures something of the legend of William Heffer as the founder of such a well-known Cambridge institution; an institution that may no longer be in family ownership but still bears the family name.

Of William and Mary's nine children, seven became directors and five worked in the firm, which remained in the family for four generations from 1876 to 1999. This book is not about the Heffer family – it is about those who ran the firm and the people they worked with – Heffer family members and others. However, here are brief biographies of all William's children, and of those descendants who had a hand in running the company over 123 years. (Note that staff generally referred to members of the Heffer family as 'Mr' Reuben, 'Mr' Ernest etc. and the ladies as 'Miss', although this convention had mostly fallen out of use by the mid-1970s.)

Mary Crick (1836–1930)

Mary Crick, the future Mrs William Heffer, hailed from the village of Balsham, twelve miles south east of Cambridge, and was employed as cook at the home of Dennis Adams in Sidney Street, Cambridge where William worked as groom. A most capable cook and housekeeper, and a stickler for standards, all through her life Mary insisted on knowing everything that concerned the well-being of her family. In 1928, on the occasion of William's funeral, the Cambridge press observed that Mary possessed, 'as ideal wives should, the power to appreciate and the courage to criticise'. [8]

John Charles Heffer (1864–1935)

After a spell as a clerk on the railways and working for Matthew's, a well-known grocer in Cambridge, Charles, the Heffers' eldest son, emigrated to America at the age of twenty-one. During the First World War he was employed by the Shipbuilding corporation and then worked in the Ann Arbor offices in Manitowoc, Wisconsin until his retirement.

Harry Heffer (1865–1947)

Starting as an office boy at Cambridge department store Eaden Lilley, Harry, the second son of William and Mary, rose to become financial director. He also took an active interest in the financial affairs of Heffers, being of 'incalculable help in a hundred ways' (his early balance sheets described by Ernest as 'works of art and pages of mystery to most of us') [9] and played a prominent role in the National Savings Movement. Harry's son, Ralph Laurence Heffer, had a short spell at the firm.

Harry Heffer (from a 1947 press article).

Kate Adelaide Heffer (1867–1940)

The eldest daughter of William and Mary, Kate worked at the Fitzroy Street shop and founded the Sidney Street shop in 1903, with her brother Sidney. Described by Ernest as a 'splendid forceful dominating character', Kate was a moving spirit of the home and of the business.

George Herbert Heffer (1868–1947)

From school, George, the Heffer's third son, joined Barclays Bank at Ely, Cambridgeshire and later transferred to the Cambridge branch where he became Chief Clerk, retiring in 1928. In the same year he succeeded William as company Chairman, and was said to be a guiding spirit in the development of the business. His outside interests included acting as the treasurer of the Boys' Brigade and the Good Samaritan Society.

George Heffer.

Ernest William Heffer (1871–1948)

Ernest, fourth son of William and Mary, a 'sickly child' of a 'studious disposition', as an adult played a significant role in building up the University business after William announced his 25 per cent discount on all text books; a move in 1888 that caused a furore in the Cambridge book trade. Ernest attended the inaugural meeting of the Cambridge Chamber of Commerce in January 1917 and also served as President of the Antiquarian Booksellers Association. As his son, Reuben declared, Ernest, 'blew the stuff of books into the firm'.

In 1933 he gave an engaging lecture to London bookshop staff, entitled, *Instructions to the Young Bookseller*. He was company Chairman from 1947 to 1948. His obituary in *The Times* described him as, 'a bookseller in charge who knew something about the insides of books. If he found you dipping into a newly published book he might strongly recommend it, having read it himself the night before, or on the other hand, he might urge you not to buy such rubbish ... Both Cambridge and the book trade have lost a "character".'

Lucy Mary Heffer (1873–1951)

Lucy, second daughter of William and Mary, a 'Heffer man', worked at Heffers' Petty Cury shop on the bookselling side of the business in book-keeping and accounts. Bunty Heffer (wife of John – see below) remembers a sweet and gentle character: "I used to go in there often as a child to look at books and to see what was doing. I always read a lot. I remember being chased out by Aunt Lucy once – and given an apple."

Ernest Heffer.

Emma Louise Heffer (1874–1973)

Emma Louise, the Heffer's youngest daughter, known to everyone as 'Pom', [10] was a regular visitor to the Petty Cury and Sidney Street shops. She had a pet parrot, Joey, who always accompanied her. Bunty Heffer has fond memories of Aunty Pom: "She was gorgeous. So naughty and such a character." Bunty recalls that Pom would call in for coffee on her way back from church and the parrot had to have coffee too. Reflecting on the church service, Pom would say that she did not utter the responses, "as Joey might join in!"

Arthur Heffer (left) with Reuben and their sister Mary, who was not involved with the business.

Emma Heffer (Miss Pom) with Joey.

Frank Heffer.   Sidney Heffer.   Arthur Heffer.

Sheila Mann remembered Pom in her history of the Evelyn Hospital (formerly the Evelyn Nursing Home), where Pom spent her final years: 'New arrivals [babies] had to be taken to be ceremonially inspected by the inhabitant of Room 11, Miss Emma Heffer, formerly owner and matron of the Priory Nursing Home in Newmarket Road.' [11] Bunty tells a family story about the time when Pom, as a trainee nurse many years earlier, met Florence Nightingale who asked her, "who taught you to use your broom that way, dear?" to which she replied, "my mother".

Frank Heffer (1876–1933)

While still a child, Frank, second youngest son of William and Mary, had to have a leg amputated. His brother Ernest wrote, 'what he lost in the leg, he made up in animal spirits', and described him as 'having the face of a saint; but mischief was always in his vicinity'. Having studied Medicine at Sidney Sussex College, Cambridge, Frank was brought into the business in 1900 with an expectation that he would learn French and German at the firm's expense. He became managing director of the firm's printing works, after the Black Bear Press (Dixon's Printing Works Ltd) was purchased in 1911.

Sidney Heffer (1878–1959)

Following a brief spell in the Post Office, Sidney, the Heffers' youngest son, worked in the family's first shop in Fitzroy Street and in 1903 co-founded the Stationery shop in Sidney Street, with his sister Kate. He was Chairman of the company from 1948 to 1959. Sidney wrote and published a biography of his father in 1952, copies of which were given to Heffers employees at the time. In the Preface he states: 'As no records of my father were kept by any members of his family, I have had to depend solely upon memory. The writing of this biography has consequently been no easy task, yet none the less a pleasant one.'

Arthur Beak Heffer (1899–1931)

Arthur, elder son of Ernest and grandson of William, caught a chill on a Wednesday and on the following Sunday, 1st November 1931, died from pneumonia, aged thirty-two. Arthur had spent ten years in the firm, following his graduation in Modern Languages at Queen's, Oxford, which he attended after recovering from injuries sustained on the Western Front in October 1918 as a member of the 8th Battalion of the Queen's (West Surrey) Regiment.

Described as an 'exceptionally keen' member of the English Folk Dance Society, Arthur was a popular and well-known figure in Cambridge. The immediate mourners at the church of Little St Mary's, Cambridge, were joined by representatives of the staff of Heffers and of the University (the Vice-Chancellor), the Old Persean Society, the Associated Booksellers of Great Britain and Ireland, the Borough Library, the Publishers' Representatives Association, Cambridge Booksellers and the English Folk Dance Society. Arthur's focus at the firm was bookselling and publishing; his death left a gap which his younger brother, Reuben, subsequently filled.

Reuben George Heffer (1908–85)

Reuben, younger son of Ernest and grandson of William, was educated at the Perse School, Cambridge, where he acquired an interest in modern languages, which he read at Corpus Christi College, Cambridge. He also read economics. Having trained at the London School of Printing, he joined the firm's bookselling side after the untimely death of his brother, Arthur. In the Second World War he joined the RAF, serving in flight control and as a squadron leader. He took charge of the bookshop in Petty Cury in 1948 and was Chairman of the company from 1959 to 1975. He was on the council of the Booksellers Association, of the 1948 Book Trade Committee, of the Society of Bookmen, and of the Sette of Odd Volumes. [12] John Welch, appointed by Reuben as the first general manager in 1964, described him as a man of considerable charm; unfailingly generous of his time and quiet advice: 'Honest and caring, he was above all a liberal man. Though holding firm views, he never inflicted them on anyone. His great talent, giving him abiding pleasure, was to encourage success in those younger than himself.' [13]

Reuben was largely responsible for the continued existence of *The Cambridge Review* [14] from 1939 and his other activities included serving as a magistrate for twenty-seven years, and with the Marriage Guidance Council, the Trustee Savings Bank, and the Cambridge Preservation Society. The Open University awarded him an honorary MA degree in 1979. Frank Collieson, in *Remembering Reuben*, wrote that within the book trade, while eschewing office, Reuben was undoubtedly influential, his authority being genuinely modest and understated. Of Reuben he declared: 'It was a joy to watch him open a book. No spine-cracking for Reuben: the book, whatever its format, would sit easily in his left hand as if measured for it: while the fastidious fingers of his right would turn the pages slowly and without injury *from the top*.' [15]

Reuben Heffer.

24

Charles W.S. Heffer (1920–95)

Educated at the Perse School and in Switzerland, Charles, son of Frank and grandson of William, returned to England at the beginning of the Second World War and joined the RAF. A director of Heffers from 1953, Charles oversaw the printing division from 1939 until the site at Hills Road was sold in 1973 and the business transferred to King's Hedges Road. He was also a director and vice-chairman of Cambridge United Football Club.

John Noel Miles Heffer (1919–2005)

Son of Sidney and grandson of William, John was educated at the Leys School, Cambridge. He joined the firm in 1938. On the outbreak of war in 1939, he gained a commission in the RAF and served in the Middle East and India. In 1944 he married Margaret Elliott Moore (known to everyone as Bunty), the daughter of Ralph E. Moore, of George Stace ladies outfitters in Petty Cury. On his return from active service in 1946, John was responsible for overseeing the Sidney Street shop and was appointed as a director of the company in 1949. He served as company Chairman from 1975 to 1984.

In a 1979 interview with the *Cambridgeshire, Huntingdon & Peterborough Life*, he said, 'I try not to be remote either from staff or from customers. Anyone can get in touch with me at most times, and I encourage others of the management to adopt the same principle.' [16] The article noted that he was anything but remote and seemed to have the secret of being in several places at once. He was a commissioner of taxes, a director of the Royal Albert Old People's Almshouses, and a member of the Committee of 104 Air Training Squadron, RAF Cambridge. On John's retirement, Nicholas Heffer, in his 1994 annual letter to shareholders, stated he would be missed by the board, particularly for his determination and sense of humour.

John and Margaret (Bunty) Heffer.

Nicholas Heffer (b. 1937)

Elder son of Reuben and great-grandson of William, Nicholas was educated at the Leys School, Cambridge and Corpus Christi, Cambridge where he read Mathematics and Economics. He subsequently trained in London as a chartered accountant and, after qualifying, spent three years working in Toronto. He joined Heffers in 1965 when he was appointed company secretary. In 1969 he became a director and in 1984 Chairman of Heffers. He remained with the firm until it was sold to Blackwell's of Oxford in 1999, as there were no other members of the family wanting to join the company. He was a director and later Chairman of Book Tokens Ltd, still an essential support to the national book trade. In Cambridge he was Chairman of the Cambridge Building Society and a director of the Cambridge Water Company.

William Heffer (b. 1940)

The younger son of Reuben and great-grandson of William, he trained at the London School of Printing and subsequently worked in the firm at Severs printers (acquired by Heffers in 1957), until he left in 1968 to run his own antiques business in King Street, Cambridge.

Stephen Heffer.

Stephen John Heffer (1948–96)

Son of John and great-grandson of William, Stephen worked with the firm for fifteen years from 1971. He assisted the managing director, John Welch, on the bookselling and publishing side and played an instrumental role setting up the Children's Bookshop and the Bookworm Club. He also made regular visits abroad both in Europe and America, retaining very useful personal contacts with librarians overseas. His travels were noted regularly in the staff newsletter, *Trinity Street News*. He also managed the Grafton Centre shop when it first opened in 1983. An artist, Stephen left the firm in 1986 to train as a mature student at the Camberwell School of Arts and at Winchester. He worked as an artist in Barcelona, London and Norfolk and he died in London in 1996. An exhibition of his paintings was held at the Sidney Street Gallery in 1998, providing, as described in the brochure, a unique opportunity for friends and visitors to view the 'breadth of his vision'.

2

BOOKSELLER AND STATIONER

FITZROY STREET: TOYS, TOBACCO AND TELEGRAMS

William Heffer's original shop at 104 Fitzroy Street was probably rented from a landlord called George Johnson and opened in July 1876. Between 1876 and the mid-1880s, William built up a burgeoning stationery and bookselling business at number 104. Initially, the stock was very mixed and included many low-cost items such as needles and cotton, envelopes, labels and notepaper. However, space was restricted and the shop floor urgently needed to be expanded. Next door at number 103 (the numbers in Fitzroy Street ran sequentially along each side) was Walter G. Bonnett, 'Picture Dealer, Tobacconist & Toy Dealer'. In 1887 Bonnett went into receivership. Seizing his chance, William acquired the stock and premises and began trading from number 103 as well as 104. Ernest, then aged sixteen, was immediately put in charge of the additional premises and hated it, describing the episode as a 'pitiful pettifogging affair'. The two shops were separated by an archway, leading to a yard at the rear. William replaced the gateway with a window and converted it to shop or storage space – this was number 103a.

SANTA CLAUS IS COMING.

SPECIAL AGENT IN CAMBRIDGE: W. HEFFER.

JUST ARRIVED,

A very Large Assortment of Goods suitable for Presents
FOR YOUNG AND OLD.

In the STATIONERY DEPARTMENT

He offers a well-assorted Stock of PHOTO & SCRAP ALBUMS, STORY BOOKS, BIBLES, PRAYER & HYMN BOOKS, LETTER WALLETS. CARD CASES, PURSES, &c., &c.,

Also CHRISTMAS & NEW YEAR CARDS of the Newest Designs.

In the FANCY DEPARTMENT

He has an Endless Variety of TOYS & GAMES of all descriptions. HORSES & CARTS, PERAMBULATORS, NOAH'S ARKS, VASES, VIEW GOODS, WALKING STICKS, &c. JAPANESE GOODS, also a beautiful assortment of WHITE WOOD GOODS for Painting.

A Handsome Show of DOLLS of all sizes and prices, DOLLS' HOUSES, FURNITURE and TEA SETS.

Special Discount to all Purchasers in this Department.

Please Note the Address:

W. HEFFER,

BOOKSELLER & STATIONER,

THE POST OFFICE, 103, 103A, & 104, FITZROY ST., CAMBRIDGE

1889 advertisement in the *Cambridge Chronicle and University Journal.*

Trade directories at this time list William Heffer at number 103 under the heading 'Fancy Repositories' – in other words, toys and novelty goods. Initially, William also continued selling tobacco, as Bonnett had, although Sidney notes that it was with little enthusiasm as it attracted the 'wrong kind of customer'. We know from a newspaper report of a twelve-year-old boy caught shoplifting a briar pipe from 'William Heffer, tobacconist, 103 Fitzroy Street' (it was Ernest who apprehended him) that William was still selling tobacco as late as February 1889. Heffers the Tobacconist may not have lasted much beyond this date, but William carried on selling 'fancy goods' in one shop, while next door at 104 he continued to build up the stationery and bookselling business. Christmas time was especially busy, with box adverts placed in the local press (1889 and 1891) advertising calendars and cards for sale, as well as an 'endless variety' of toys, games, perambulators, vases, walking sticks, 'Japanese goods', 'white wood goods' for painting, dolls, dolls' houses and tea sets from the 'Fancy Department'.

104 Fitzroy Street in 1876.

To supplement a meagre income in the early years, William worked as a waiter in one of the college halls in the evenings (enabling him to buy cheap food from the kitchen). He also worked as a Proctor's 'Bulldog', a constable who occasionally carried ancient insignia at public events and patrolled the streets after dusk to check if junior members of the University were wearing their gowns. Traditionally, Bulldogs patrolled in pairs, one being chosen for his sprinting abilities and one for long distance stamina. We do not know if William had sprinting abilities, but he certainly had stamina – throughout his life. He also kept an allotment (next to Hawkins' Bakery on Midsummer Common) and soled and heeled his own children's boots to save money. After his retirement and up until shortly before he died, William took a daily walk of around three miles, calling on all his business premises.

The shop opened at eight o'clock in the morning and closed at eight in the evening, except for Saturdays when it closed as late as ten (as we will see, Heffers were to participate in the early-closing movement). Around the time William acquired number 103, he had been persuaded by the General Post Office of the need for a sub-post office in the area, and so he opened one, employing a full-time assistant to run it. In both the 1891 and the 1901 census William added the Post Office occupation to that of stationer and bookseller (he called himself 'Postmaster' in the 1901 census, although technically he was a sub-Postmaster). The post office brought hundreds of new customers into the shop, 'not all of whom were desirable' according to Sidney, but they did nevertheless bring business (Fitzroy Street was not the most salubrious of areas at that time). William also became a newsagent for the Cambridge press and undertook his own paper delivery rounds, as did his children.

The range of stock at Fitzroy Street expanded to include, newspapers and periodicals, educational, reward and story books, bibles, prayer and hymn books: 'We traded as Stationers and Newsagents, and gradually secured a merited reputation of Scholastic and Educational Stationery and Materials.' Second hand books were also stocked at Fitzroy Street from 1898. William always said, 'It's the depth of stock that matters. If you are going to stock note books, you must have fifty types.'

Described as 'Our Birthplace' in a 1909 booklet about the business, [17] the freehold of 104 Fitzroy Street was eventually bought by William in 1899 (he bid £1,100 for it – £123,000 at today's value) and later leased to

Fitzroy Street in early 1900s. The shop was located opposite the Eden Chapel which can be seen at the far end on the right.

Messrs W. & R. Fletcher Ltd. [18] It remained in the firm's ownership until the early 1920s (described much later by Ernest as having become by then 'a rather dingy shop in a rather time worn environment'). Next door, number 103 was retained as a sub-post office into the twentieth century. 'W. Heffer & Sons, Ltd., stationers, printers and newsagents' was also advertised as a 'Telegraph, Money Order and Post Office' in the 1913 trade directory ('Telegrams are dispatched from this office, not delivered').

1925 promotion for Anchor Boxes and Puzzles.

Number 103 was run by Ellen Hyde, Post Office Clerk, who had been engaged by the firm in 1903, along with an assistant, Miss A.B. Stanley. By 1916 Miss Hyde had left to be Postmistress at Great Shelford and by this time Fitzroy Street's days were numbered. It is listed under the Heffer name for the last time in the 1918 telephone directory, bringing to a close forty years of Heffers in Fitzroy Street. For thirty years the Heffer family lived above the shop at number 104, but in 1903 they moved to 7 Mortimer Road, a large, eleven-room house overlooking Parker's Piece – equidistant from Fitzroy Street and Petty Cury.

THE FIRST DEALS

The 1880s was a decade of tremendous growth for W. Heffer and Sons, starting with hymn-book sales to a captive audience and ending with the firm's first publication. By the 1890s William Heffer had added 'Bookseller' to his occupation of 'Stationer' and, as we shall see later, he was already a publisher. His first major success at bookselling was a sale-or-return deal on the 1877 hymn collection, *Sacred Songs and Solos*, by the American revivalists Ira David Sankey and Dwight Lyman Moody, widely known as *The Sankey and Moody Hymn Book*.

On their second UK mission, in 1881, Sankey and Moody visited Cambridge and preached at the Guildhall. William sold the hymn-book at the venue each evening before the meeting began. The audiences built up through the week and the Sunday night meeting attracted nearly 2,000 University men. As Sidney declared, it was a gold mine. Heffers continued to sell the publication for many years to come and copies were aptly stored at the Sidney Street shop, which had a Church Supplies department (although the supplies did not include communion wine).

As a member of the Cambridge Sunday School Association, in 1881 William's apostolic connections provided another business breakthrough when he turned his mind to the supply of Sunday School prizes. Ernest tells a tale of the time he – Ernest – recommended Marryat's *Japhet in Search of a Father*, the story of a foundling in search of his father, as a Sunday School prize to a vicar who threw it back at him after having read it. The 1909 booklet on the history of the firm promotes the Sidney Street stock of books, 'especially and carefully selected as being suitable for Sunday School and Day School Prizes'. Sequestering trade from the London suppliers by selling the books at his Fitzroy Street shop, William's scholastic custom grew as he began to supply elementary schools in Cambridge and surrounding villages (he walked many miles, taking samples to schools around that part of Cambridgeshire). William also began selling materials for home education and there was a thriving Children's book department at Fitzroy Street. The educational supply side of the business was promoted with slogans such as 'Every description of Educational Material and Apparatus supplied at London prices' and 'The only house where you can see all Kindergarten games and materials'.

The Sidney Street shop in 1903.

By the turn of the century, the stationery, bookselling and post office business at numbers 103, 103a and 104 included what he called the Eastern Counties Educational Depot. Despite being out of town (Cambridge was much smaller at that time), the Fitzroy Street outlet became a magnet for teachers. William also had stalls at the teachers' conferences held in the Cambridge Corn Exchange in the town centre. When he first opened the Sidney Street premises in 1903, the banner heralded the line of business, although the scholastic supplies side dried up sometime after the 1902 Education Act when William's tender as a supplier to the newly formed Education Committee was not selected.

Another profitable line early on was the supply of Stone's Filing Boxes to academics and students at their Cambridge colleges. Initially, calling on University customers was a daunting prospect. Sidney wrote that William's heart was frequently in his mouth, as he wondered what kind of reception awaited him from this or that don; but he was respected, never calling without having something of interest to show. What did attract a great deal of interest, and much controversy, was the discount that William offered on university textbooks.

DISCOUNT WARS

For two centuries or more, Cambridge stationers had indulged in price-cutting, much to the chagrin of their London counterparts. Years of under-selling had bitterly divided the book trade and in 1890 publisher Frederick Macmillan wrote to *The Bookseller* [19] proposing a 'net book' system, whereby books were sold by retailers at a price fixed by publishers. In describing the origins of what became the Net Book Agreement, which ran from 1900 to 1997, McKitterick, in his history of the Cambridge University Press, acknowledges the considerable hostility that had developed between Heffers and the established academic booksellers in the town; a hostility concealed by the Syndics' agreement to allow William to obtain university text books from the London warehouse on the same terms as other Cambridge booksellers. [20]

It wasn't the terms to secure the books that caused the outrage; it was the 25 per cent discount that William, the outsider (from out of town), gave to his growing army of satisfied friends and customers. By this audacious action in 1888, William had broken the London booksellers' monopoly of the textbook trade. The 1909 booklet about the firm declared that a 'new era in bookselling' had been inaugurated. It was also the year that Heffers became a limited company (the firm's first Annual Meeting was recorded as taking place in July 1898 and the share capital cited as £1,587 10s 3d – around £176,000 at today's value).

William was never afraid to sell discounted books despite protestation from other booksellers, and seized any opportunity that came his way. For example, in the early years at his Petty Cury shop, he had the chance to pick up the remaindered stock of a large quarto volume, *The Interleaved Parallel New Testament*. William sold the volume at 6 shillings to Cambridge dons and their pupils, a considerable discount on the full price. In 1902 William held a meeting to discuss the 'advisability' of a proposal by other booksellers to make the 25 per cent discount a seven-day principle, or a principle allowed for the whole term. The conclusion was minuted as, 'we should follow our own rules as before'. A letter was then sent to rival bookseller Robert Bowes esq., at Trinity Street, stating the following:

> **Are You Aware ? ? ?**
> THAT
> The only House in Cambridge
> Where you can see all
> **Kindergarten Games and Materials**
> IS
> **W. HEFFER & SONS,**
> THE DISCOUNT BOOKSELLERS,
> 103, 103a, and 104, FITZROY ST.
> **THOUSANDS OF STORY & PICTURE BOOKS FOR ALL AGES.**
> Christmas Cards and Calendars in great variety.
> Bibles, Prayer Books, Hymn Books, Photo, Scrap, Stamp and Post-card Albums.
> A LARGE ASSORTMENT OF GAMES FOR YOUNG AND OLD.
> Everything Sold at best value and at Lowest Discount Prices.
> BOOKS of every Description can be obtained at our Petty-cury Establishment.
> **W. HEFFER & SONS,**
> FITZROY STREET & PETTY CURY,
> TELEPHONE 0347.

We have very thoroughly considered the proposed change in our own discount methods, and regret to inform you that our decision is against the proposed. In arriving at this decision we have been prompted by no spirit of arbitrariness or want of friendly feelings but the question at issue, is for us, beset with great difficulties, and would also lead practically to the disorganisation of our trading.

The Discount Bookseller, 1902 in the *Cambridge Independent Press and University Herald.*

We should be most happy to consider any other question which the Society might bring before us with a view to bringing about friendly relationships hitherto not existing between us.

In reply, Bowes, who had been liaising with other members of the book trade on this issue, declared that his own desire has been for friendly relations, a desire shared by others, and that joint action would be best for all. However, he asks, 'how can that be brought about

APRIL, 1924 *The* No. 1

RECORDER

The Silent Salesman of New Books reduced in Price. All absolutely New Copies

Banner of the first edition of *The Recorder.*

when practically you have determined that your policy shall continue to be one of isolated action?' Undaunted, William carried on his trade.

In 1924 William issued *The Recorder*, a catalogue of 'remainders', Heffers' latest book bargains. The second edition of *The Recorder* in May, provided an explanation of 'remainder':

'Over 10,000 volumes were published during the year 1923, and as most Publishers stated, they are fortunate if 10% of their books turn out a good investment, it will readily be seen that unless Publishers periodically reduced their stocks, the accumulation would make the question of warehousing an impossible one to solve. The idea that because a book is "Remaindered" it can have no literary value, has long since been disproved. Many of our greatest and some of our modern books have once been Remaindered. To have a Remainder is no stigma, it is but an experience.'

The Recorder boldly announced:

ALL BOOKS GUARANTEED ABSOLUTELY NEW
Latest Book Bargains
A WONDERFUL BARGAIN
NOW REDUCED IN PRICE

There developed over time a distinction between 'net' and 'non-net' books and, in some quarters, a distaste for discounted and 'non-net' books. Claire Brown (*née* Johnston), a bookseller who set up Heffers' Children's Bookshop in 1968/69, recalls that the Sidney Street shop dealt mostly with 'non-net' books and text books: "If someone had done an order for several books from our shop and also wanted a couple of non-net, we'd lower ourselves to getting them from Sidney Street."

Frank Collieson, at Heffers from 1962, recalled the discounting side of the business: "We were a great remainder dealer then. Give them the old one, two, three. You went to a publisher and if he'd got a stack of books you'd offer a pound a copy. And then you'd retail it at two pounds to the trade and eventually it would go out to the customer at three pounds."

The Private Libraries Association, in its quarterly journal, applauded the opportunity for customers to acquire discounted books in October 1964:

'It is possible to get slightly damaged copies of Oxford University Press books, and if you are in luck this is a very useful way of acquiring some of those lovely reference books, and more conventional items that have been rejected as below standard-perhaps a minute water-stain on the boards, or a torn or folded page.'

Heffers officially pulled out of the remainder business in 1972. It was stated that the prices of remainders were not the bargains they once were and it was difficult to compete with paperbacks and publishers' own reduced price offers, 'as book prices rise, so do the prices of the remainders; with the result that remainders today are not always the apparent bargains they once were.' Richard Reynolds, a bookseller with over thirty years' experience at Heffers (and, in 2016, still with the firm), recalls the time when managing director John Welch strongly objected to a window display of discounted gardening books at the Trinity Street shop.

Clive Cornell, a bookseller who joined Heffers in 1958 and spent his whole career at the firm, reflects on the irony of Heffers' defence of the Net Book Agreement when it was under threat in the mid-1990s. When the Agreement did finally collapse, Nicholas Heffer, in his 1996 annual letter to shareholders, acknowledged the demise and declared that the intense flurry of discounting that followed made little impact on Heffers and apparently did not increase the market overall. Heffers' policy at the time was to carry out carefully targeted price promotions.

EARLY CLOSING

Judy Wilson, in her fascinating history of Matthew's grocers of 20 Trinity Street (Heffers took the premises in 1970 – *see Chapter 5*), noted the long hours that staff worked in retail. [21] By 1871 a local agreement was reached in Cambridge that many shops would shut early one afternoon a week in the summer months instead of the normal time of eight o'clock in the evening.

In 1892, William Heffer was an active member of the Committee of the Cambridge Early Closing Association, a committee that, according to the *Cambridge Independent Press*, comprised 'the best known, most influential and most enthusiastic men in the town'. [22] Sidney went so far as to declare William to be the instigator of half-day closing in Cambridge. William had realised that not everyone was cast in the same mould as himself, that for others 'relaxation was as necessary as food'. The Committee's objective was to obtain a two o'clock closing during the vacation and a five o'clock closing in University term time, on a permanent basis.

Public support was vital and the Cambridge Early Closing Association local branch held regular social events to raise awareness of their campaign. For example, in January 1892 they organised a penny popular concert at the Guildhall, attracting a large and enthusiastic audience. Amongst the several performers was one Sidney Heffer, a former chorister, who sang, *The Gallant Salamander*. William, as a committee member, seconded the Chairman's remarks and vote of thanks. Many traders had initially promised their support for the campaign but the support fell away and it was not until 1912 – when the Shops Act (repealed in 1994) made it obligatory for shops to shut at one o'clock, one day a week, for a staff half-day – that the campaign was finally won. In Cambridge, this day was Thursday. William was also instrumental in bringing sub-post offices into the movement, helping to ensure that they too benefitted from the change.

Notice in the *Cambridge Independent Press and University Herald*, 1892.

The Petty Cury bookshop at No. 4. A note on the reverse of the original photograph identifies the gentleman as a Mr Bullock.

3

PETTY CURY – A DEDICATED BOOKSHOP

When, in the early 1890s, other booksellers started offering a similar discount to William, he decided it was time to open a branch in the town, to 'meet the threat on its own ground'. In 1896 he took over the lease of 4 Petty Cury from a chemist, Dennis Greenwood. The building was owned by Emmanuel College. This was the same year that Gustave David (known to everyone simply as 'David') set up his famous Cambridge marketplace bookstall.

Lease of the Petty Cury premises at No.4 with the signatures of Dennis Greenwood and William Heffer.

This year, also, William took on employees: Frederick Anstee as an apprentice, and a fully trained bookselling assistant, F.J. Sebley. Unlike Frederick Anstee, not needing to learn the trade (having been a bookseller's assistant since 1881, and previously employed at the Deighton Bell bookshop), F.J. Sebley was, according to the Heffer family, 'in every sense a bookworm'. Before his arrival, 'there were only new books on the shelves, but with his knowledge and interest second-hand books were stocked'. A renowned collector of first editions, he remained with Heffers for forty years. On his retirement from the firm in 1936, the Cambridge press acknowledged Mr Sebley as a 'real book lover, if ever there was one'. Arthur Heffer wrote:

> 'Mr Sebley is now retiring with a pension, to enjoy for a long time, as we would hope, that greatest of all possible joys, the companionship of his own books. What greater treat can there be for a bookseller, who for the largest stretch of his life, has spent himself in recommending books to others, than to be able leisurely to enjoy the books he has gathered round himself, promising that some day he will read them?'

F J Sebley pictured (*centre*) in the Petty Cury shop.

Frederick Brittain entertains us with a tale about Sebley from his 1947 biography of renowned Cambridge academic and writer, Arthur Quiller Couch ('Q'):

'One of the earliest functions to take place in my dining room' was a lunch given by Q and some other senior members of the College in honour of Mr F. J. Sebley, on his retirement after forty years' service with Messrs Heffer, the Cambridge booksellers … After the lunch the Master, Arthur Gray, rose to propose the health of the guest of honour. He knew both Mr Heffer and Mr Sebley very well but was apt to be absent-minded. Accordingly, throwing (as he always did) great emphasis on every third or fourth word, he said: "It gives us great pleasure, gentlemen, to have with us to-day our good friend, Mr Heffer." (Here Q plucked him by the sleeves and spoke to him in stage whispers) "What's that, Q? Not Mr Heffer? Very well then. As I was saying, it gives us great please to be here to-day to do honour to our good friend, Mr Heffer." (More sleeve plucking.) "What did you say, Q? Not Mr Heffer? Quite so. How stupid of me! Definitely not Mr Heffer."'

1930s Dictograph machine from Heffers.

The first significant development at Heffers in the twentieth century was the installation of a telephone system, as recorded in the Minute Book in September 1902: 'After a long discussion as to whether the business would be benefitted by being connected with the National Telephone Company, it was decided to try the telephone for one year.' 0347 was the main number for Petty Cury and two extensions were provided: 0347a for 'Fitzroy Street, booksellers' and 0347b for just 'Fitzroy Street' (i.e. the post office). (In 1911 these separate 0347 numbers were replaced with one number for all branches, 862.)

Initially, in 1896, only the ground floor at number 4 Petty Cury was available to Heffers, as the others were sublet to a lodging-house keeper. At that time the 'Curyites' (so-called by colleagues at the main shop) were regarded as an appendage to Fitzroy Street. As the firm's reputation grew during the 1900s, the shop expanded to take over all four floors. It was divided into several departments, all crammed with stock, as described in the 1909 booklet:

> 'Visitors to this, our Book Shop, constantly remark to us: "How do you find your Books?" "How do you know what you have got?" The questions are not unwarranted, for, though the exterior of the shop is small, the interior – consisting of four floors each 40 feet in depth – is the reverse, and with every available space shelved and crowded with Books: with Books in portentous stacks invading the floors, the questions are very pertinent.'

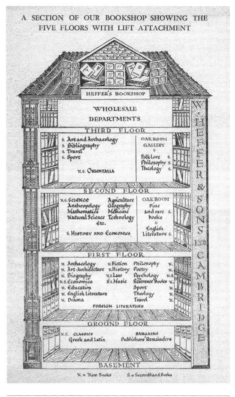

Layout of the Petty Cury shop from the Heffer Calendar of 1937/38.

Philip Ward, in the *Cambridgeshire Broadsheet* marking Heffers' centenary in 1976, wrote, 'No 4 had all the defects of its age: the invoice girls worked in an attic, connected only by a tiny lift with the packers in the dark, Dickensian basement.' Even in the 1960s, there were eleven women crammed into the top office and occasionally the lift would get stuck between floors.

A major change in the firm came in 1928, when William Heffer, still company Chairman, died at home on 9th August, in his eighty-fifth year. George replaced him as Chairman. Shortly afterwards, Heffers acquired number 3 Petty Cury, doubling the shop's size. In 1929 the *Cambridge News* described it as a wonderful new shop, a book-lover's paradise:

Working in the top office in the 1960s.

'In the basement are "remainders" at reduced prices while the ground floor is devoted to the latest publications and an extensive foreign literature section. A wide range of second-hand volumes occupies most of the first floor where connoisseurs of original editions will find much to interest them at prices from £5 to £250. On the second floor are oriental, foreign travel and fine art books while higher still are Heffers' own publications, many of local interest.'

Ten years later, in 1939, Heffers took over the upper floors of number 2 and by 1964 the layout was slightly different, as described by Jean Sanderson in the Private Libraries Association's quarterly journal of October 1964:

'It looks quite ordinary from the street outside, but come through the front shop that was once a chemists, and up the gracious stairs into the Oak room, handsome and galleried, for the better quality second-hand and antiquarian books, and, to your left, the Science Department. Above this is the Oriental Department. Each department keeps records of its customers' interests and special requirements, and many catalogues are issued … descend the back stairs, which are not so humble as they sound, into the Foreign Department, and perhaps go down into the basement where the representative rather than comprehensive Children's section is found, the domestic arts and the Classics tucked away at the far end.'

Many employees remember Petty Cury as a more intimate shop than the later Trinity Street premises, with "nice wooden verandas that really suited the books". The Second-hand and Antiquarian department in the 'Oak Room' had a veranda built in 1939, and bookseller Tiny Copping would sit and go through *The Clique* [23] every week to check demand and what they could supply. Eve Stafford, a shorthand typist, remembers having a desk on the shop floor at Petty Cury. It felt, to Eve, that she was a part of the team and it was good to have day-to-day contact with customers. The Petty Cury shop smelled of books and polish and had bow windows of

The ground floor of the Petty Cury shop, occupying numbers 3 and 4.

The interior of the shop in the 1940s, the veranda just visible in the upper picture.

Interior of the Petty Cury shop in the 1960s.

leaded glass, affording good viewing from the street. In the mid-1950s bookseller Robert Hill had the job of opening and closing the outside bookcases of cheap second-hand books located in the side passage. (Signet Classics, particularly editions of Shakespeare, were sold from these bookcases in the 1960s.) This passage gave access to a trade entrance and a bicycle shed.

Marion Davenport, who worked at Heffers and met her husband, Dudley, there, says: "Before I started there, my friend and I used to go down town but we never went in Heffers because we always felt it was too posh. It gave that appearance. Although we liked books. We went in Bowes."

Heffers reputation as being 'a bit posh' was given a boost in the late 1960s when Prince Charles, soon to be invested as the Prince of Wales, became a student at Trinity College. His arrival in October 1967, when he was greeted by the Master, Lord Butler, attracted excited press coverage. As a freshman he studied Archaeology and Physical and Social Anthropology, switching to History in his second year, before leaving for the University College of Wales in April 1969. In 2016, His Royal Highness acknowledges that he was indeed a customer of Heffers during his eighteen months at Cambridge. Most of his 'shopping', however, was done by his tutor, Glyn Daniel who, with his wife, Ruth, were virtually daily customers at Heffers.

THE UNPACKING AND PACKING DEPARTMENT

Books coming into Petty Cury were delivered via two external doors in the side passage that opened onto a lift that came up from the basement. The books were dropped onto the lift and sent down for unpacking. Clive Cornell recalls that every morning the word would be, "has Suttons been yet?" Suttons was the delivery firm. In the 1950s it was possible to get books delivered in two to three days if they came via the giant London wholesaler Simpkin Marshall, otherwise, it could take two to three weeks. The Packing department (which did both the unpacking and packing) was located in the basement. Robert Hill would occasionally help to unpack books and says it would take the best part of an hour to unwrap everything. It was a very busy department with three full-time gentlemen and a lady who came in everyday to do the franking for the outgoing deliveries that were then taken to the Magdalene Street Post Office by Felix Askem. Felix also cleaned the leaded shop-front windows, swept the side passage and did odd jobs.

The Packing department.

Staff, with Felix Askem standing second from right.

William Heffer, great-grandson of the firm's founder, has childhood memories of Petty Cury. Although he didn't venture down the stairs into the basement very often – that was seen as alien territory. He remembers Reuben talking about the tinsmiths sealing up tea chests with a soldering iron, packed with books that were destined for the Far East.

The printing works with the Standard Vanguard van.

Heffers used Royal Mail and other distributors but also had their own delivery service using a Bullnose Morris van. When Queen Elizabeth (later, the Queen Mother) came to the Royal Show in Cambridge in 1951, the company invested in a brand new Standard Vanguard van; presumably to make a good impression. By 1987/88 the firm had disposed of nearly all its vehicles, deciding instead to lease vehicles under a contract hire scheme. By then, the firm's own garage facilities had already closed.

FIRE, FIRE!

On 25th April 1939, Heffers had a narrow escape. Early that morning the Central Cinema in Hobson Street, which backed onto the Sidney Street shop, was burnt to a shell. Luckily though for Heffers there was no damage to their shop.

Staff kept a regular fire watch at the Petty Cury shop throughout the Second World War, although the log book is a far from exciting read. Probably the most thrilling thing to happen during that time was Denis Matthews' 1941 report: 'Went upstairs to make a hot drink noting at the same time that everything was in order … Came down again and consumed some real HAM sandwiches! (Is it true there's a war on?).'

Although Cambridge was subjected to bombing raids, the Petty Cury shop survived the war undamaged as did most of central Cambridge. However, long after any need for a fire watch, on the night of 12th November 1946 there was a serious fire on the premises. It raged for four hours, spreading to the Lion Hotel next door, and seven National Fire Service units attended the scene. Bunty Heffer remembers how frightening it was when John received a call at two o'clock in the morning. Two firemen were injured and several thousand books, many valuable and some irreplaceable, were destroyed. A series of scientific books, ready for despatch to the

News photograph showing Audrey Wright (*rear left*) and colleagues sorting through fire-damaged books.

Library of Congress in Washington D.C., was destroyed. The total damage was valued at £20,000 for stocks and fittings £5,000 for the building (£778,450 and £195,00 at today's value). [24] Audrey Coleman (*née* Wright) remembers the aftermath:

> "We didn't know anything 'til we got to work and there'd been this awful fire. Miss King said we'd better first go back for a little while because the Police and everyone were there. We went to her mother's house in Clarendon Street and then we came back and had to help clear up. All of us put turbans on our heads. There was all the smoke and an awful lot of damage. We had tarpaulins up and we had our national cash machines transferred to the basement. All the books were charred. It was horrible."

Peter Coleman, employed by the Electricity Board at the time, worked on the repairs: "They didn't close for long. It was no more than two or three days before they were going again. It was a bit chaotic. Customers were around and you had to make the place safe." Peter recalls, "We used to smoke and no one said you mustn't but Mr Ernest would come round and ask, 'how many have you had today, my boy?'" In his 1933 address to apprentice booksellers (they were known as shop assistants at the time), Ernest stipulated that none of the assistants' fingers showed evidence of having been tinted a yellow hue, 'not designed by nature'. He clearly took a keen interest in such matters.

The FIRE at HEFFER'S

Customers may be assured that the recent fire at our premises will cause little or no curtailment of our service. Our records are intact; postal business will continue as usual; stocks are quickly being replaced. We are confident of being able to meet all requirements of the Christmas trade.

HEFFER'S BOOKSHOP

W. Heffer & Sons, Ltd., Cambridge.

A notice was placed in *The Times*, 21st November 1946, assuring customers 'that the recent fire at our premises will cause little or no curtailment of our service…'.

Audrey also remembers that it all seemed to come into place again quite quickly. Not all the damaged books were successfully removed, however. Over a decade later, Clive Cornell observed charred books on the shelves when he started work at Petty Cury as a shop assistant in 1958, and Frank Collieson saw the scorch marks still there in 1962.

In January 1947, at the Cambridge Assizes, Kenneth Edward Holmes of Anlaby, Yorkshire, an ex-RAF wireless operator and air gunner, was found guilty but insane on two charges of setting fire to Heffers and the Lion Hotel in Petty Cury. He was also convicted of stealing property to the value of £42 2s 10d (£1,640 at today's value), including books from Heffers. Holmes was ordered to be detained as a criminal lunatic 'until the King's pleasure be known'.

Ernest wrote to the press, expressing his appreciation for the response of Cambridge people to the incident:

Goodwill Came Out of the Fire
KINDNESS OF CAMBRIDGE PEOPLE

It is with pleasure that we publish the following letter from E. W. Heffer of Messrs. W. Heffer and Sons Ltd :–

Dear Mr Editor, –If you would experience the full depth or height of human goodness, just indulge in the luxury, mess, waste and horror of a fire. It is only then that you know what kindness really means. We have been inundated with offers of help, of sympathy – and much else besides, and it cheered us in a very dark hour.

The N.F.S. were magnificent – and incidentally, what a lot of good-looking people there are in the world. In the old days, in all probability such a fire would have meant complete destruction, but this was very quickly localised, and although a terrible amount of damage has been done, a great deal has been saved, and that is due to the N.F.S. They have spread protective sheets and save a great deal from the burning and the wet.

Very soon a whole legion of willing people appeared. First, the insurance fold and they were magnificent. Then came bricklayers, plumbers, electricians and a host of others beside. We had a rudimentary telephone system installed within a few hours and so the talk could go on.

It is almost life starting life again. We have been in the Cury for 50 years, and this is the first major tragedy that we have had, but in the end we are quite sure that goodwill came out of the fire. It is not like beginning again. There are masses of scattered threads about and we shall weave them into a fabric which shall be worthy, not only of Heffers but we hope, of Cambridge, because after all, books do mean something to Cambridge. Whoever was responsible for the fire worked more than he knew – the less said of him or them, the better.

We shall have to ask the world to be patient with us and forbearing. All our ledger-posting and accounting machines, electrical equipment and so on, have been hopelessly burned and we are almost naked – but unashamed.

Our staff has been splendid. The ladies turned themselves into charladies and the men worked like navvies and all because of the fire.

This is not an advertisement, Mr Editor – you may not perhaps publish it – but I should like you to know our reaction as a firm and how grateful we are to all concerned.

It is impossible to acknowledge letters and telegrams at present (though we shall hope to be able to do so) because in the meantime we are trying to carry on.– yours sincerely,

E. W. HEFFER, W. Heffer and Sons, Ltd.

Another good thing to come out of the fire was Audrey and Peter's union. They met during the clean-up operation and subsequently married.

LEARNING THE TRADE

In the early years, apprenticeships were generally advertised on the basis of a one-month trial followed by the first year services free, the second year a small sum for pocket money and the third year to be considered. Not exactly generous terms and conditions from today's perspective. Some apprentices turned out to be dishonest and had to be removed. On those occasions a letter may be sent to the parents to inform them of any financial loss to the firm. It is noted in the first Minute Book that one such apprentice, Nightingale, taken on in June 1900 as Clerk at 2 shillings per week, was deemed in 1902 as not 'fitted for a bookseller'. The firm advised his father and the following year he was 'discharged … through being dishonest'. But of course, there were many who went on to have a successful bookselling career. Ernest writes: 'It would be impossible to detail the numerous errand boys, apprentice boys and assistants who entered our employment but mention may here be made of a few who coming to us in almost the beginnings of

Booksellers and assistants in 1937 on the stairs at Petty Cury. The photograph was taken by Ernest.

really vital things have cast in their lot with us and stayed the course.' In the early twentieth century, members of the Heffer family and employees were rewarded with occasional bonuses. For example, in 1904 Ernest and Kate received a bonus of £50 each and Miss Hyde, assistant

Frederick Anstee at his desk. Frank
Stoakley stands to his left.

Ernest Heffer.

Winifred Anstee with her manager,
Frank Stoakley.

at Fitzroy Street, a bonus of £10. Employees were also given wage rises, usually 2 shillings a week and sometimes a financial contribution or 'present' for their holiday. (£1 in the early 1900s would be worth approximately £110 at today's value; 2 shillings would be about £11).

Frederick Anstee and F.J. Sebley were the first employees at Heffers, at least on record. Since then of course hundreds of people have worked for the firm and indeed, there have been periods when Heffers employed well over 500 people at any one time across the bookselling, stationery and printing divisions. Heffers regularly recruited young people straight from school, encouraging them to take on responsibility early on.

This is how a few of them got started and how they fared. We will hear more from some of them throughout this book.

Frederick Anstee, at Heffers from 1896 to 1944, one of those named by Ernest, was recruited as a boy. Sidney described how it happened in his biography of William:

> 'Gradually better goods were added to the stock, and the increase in the business necessitated employing an errand boy. One lad was anything but a bright specimen – practically uneducated and from a miserable home. It has already been stated that William was unlettered. Realising how this had handicapped him, he tried to help the lad by insisting that he should write in a copy book and work out simple sums each night, bringing the results to his employer the next morning. The boy profited by this strange tuition, so much so that he eventually became head assistant in the science department at Petty Cury – no mean achievement.'

No mean achievement indeed. Frederick died suddenly at the age of sixty whilst still in service. Ernest Heffer, his manager for many years, was deeply affected by his death, as expressed in this letter to Frederick's widow, in June 1944:

Dear Mrs Anstee,
This is one of the most painful letters I have ever had to write. Your husband has been with me for forty-seven years, and during that time he has never failed me for a moment; he was faithful to the minutest part of things.

I have never known him late; he was scarcely ever away for illness; I have never seen him bad-tempered nor flustered, often when things were almost over-pressing. When I came through in the morning with the letter, I knew that he would be at his desk, calm and imperturbable; and now he is no more. Believe me, I regard it as a great personal loss; and the loss will be accentuated as time goes on. Nothing can obliterate a contact of forty-seven years.

My every sympathy goes out to you and to your family, and please let me tell you this; that if at any time I can help you, I shall only be too delighted to do so, and I hope you will not hesitate to approach me.

Yours sincerely,

E. W. Heffer

Director

Obituaries were published in *The Bookseller* – 'He was known, appreciated and respected by a great number of eminent scientists throughout the world' – and in *The Clique*:

'His department was that of Mathematics and Physics, Botany and allied subjects. From youth up, and as manager of this department, by his energy and intelligence he safely proved his merit, bringing about in his department alone a world-wide connection ... There are very few specialising in this country in those subjects of which he was a master and his firm will have difficulty in replacing him.'

Frederick's youngest daughter, Winifred (Win), joined Heffers in 1947 to work in the Science Department and stayed until 1973. His eldest daughter, Lilian Agnes, had worked at Sidney Street from the age of fifteen until she married in 1939. And his grandson, Bryan Anstee, spent his whole working life at the printing works. The Heffers clearly thought very highly of Frederick and his family as shown by this note from Lucy to Frederick's widow in 1947, just after Win joined the firm:

Dear Mrs Anstee,
I send you my Christmas wishes and small gift. I do hope you and your family will spend a happy season. I must tell you how happy we are to have your daughter with us at Petty Cury. I am quite sure Mr Anstee would be very pleased if he could see her here in his department.

Yours very sincerely,

Lucy M. Heffer

Triss Driver, Frederick's granddaughter, is rightly proud of her family's association with the firm and indeed, views Heffers as "our" family firm. No doubt Heffers will have engendered a similar sense of loyalty in a number of Cambridge families.

Frank Stoakley, who had worked under Frederick Anstee for over twenty years, replaced him as the head assistant of Science. He also had a distinguished sixty-year career at Heffers. Frank, named by Sue Bradley in her 2008 oral history of the book trade [25] as a bookseller who built and ran a science department of international repute, referred to his former manager as a fatherly man: "He didn't down you because you wanted to know something; he wanted to help." Frederick Anstee was a vast improvement on Frank's first manager at Heffers in the Oak Room. That manager, who had come from Blackwell's in Oxford, would fall asleep at his desk in the afternoons. Frank was instructed to drop a pile of books as a warning if there was any sign of Ernest coming. He had to do it so often that Ernest complained about the clumsy boy who was always dropping books. On his retirement in 1980, the *Cambridge Evening News* applauded Frank Stoakley's encyclopaedic knowledge, saying that even after Heffers installed a computer to handle all the buying and selling, the staff still found they needed him for his expert knowledge.

Heffers often recruited young people straight from school, although Frank Stoakley, who joined the firm in 1920, had had a fortnight at Deighton Bell before his manager arranged for him to attend an interview with Ernest at Heffers, along with nine other candidates. Ernest set them sums and an essay, and asked a few geographical and general knowledge questions.

Frank Stoakley stated in his own recollections that Heffers had first employed female bookselling assistants during the Second World War. In January 1917, the firm had placed the following advertisement in the *Cambridge Daily News*:

> OWING to depletion of staff incidental upon military demands, Messrs. W. HEFFER AND SONS, LTD., have VACANCIES for Packer and Stockkeeper, Experienced Lady Clerk (Type-writing), Experienced Lady Assistant (Stationery), Bookbinders (Men and Women), Printer's Reader, Compositors and Machine Minders, Bookseller's Assistant. All male applicants must be ineligible for the Army.—Apply, in first instance, by letter, to the Secretary, W. HEFFER AND SONS, LTD., Cambridge.

Recruitment drive during the First World War.

However, in November 1918 the firm placed an advertisement in the same newspaper: 'WANTED, well-educated BOY and GIRL for Bookselling Department – Apply, W. Heffer and Sons Ltd, 4 Petty Cury, Cambridge.'

Joan Clark (*née* Stubbings), shorthand typist at Sidney Street, was not quite fifteen years old when she started work there in 1941. Gerald Criddle, an artist based at Sidney Street from 1955, who worked on promotions, displays and greetings cards, moved to Heffers from Cambridge department store, Joshua Taylor. Gerald had worked there with a colleague who moved on to Heffers but then took a position elsewhere and recommended Gerald as his replacement. Although young and inexperienced, Gerald had a two-week handover before being left relatively unsupervised in his new role.

Recruited by Reuben in 1955 at the age of fifteen, Ann Kidman (*née* Warren) attended her job interview wearing bobby socks and accompanied by her mother who had given her special permission to have her hair cut short. Many started their time at the firm as Saturday girls or boys, plus holiday work and a full-time position on leaving school or sixth form. Children's author, Pippa Goodhart (*née* Jennings) worked at Heffers as a teenager in the mid-1970s and managed to earn enough money to buy her first cassette tape player. Later on, after training as an infant school teacher, she was appointed by John Welch to work in the Children's Bookshop and was there for five years, ending up as shop manager. Three years after having worked at Blackwell's Children's Bookshop in Oxford (Heffers was not the first to open a children's bookshop), Claire Brown met John Welch at Christchurch Preparatory School over a cricket tea and was invited for an interview in Cambridge. He then recruited her to set up the Heffers Children's Bookshop in 1968.

Hugh Davenport (known as Dudley) began his three-year apprenticeship at Heffers straight from boarding school in 1950. Dudley's aunt knew Mr Littlechild, a Petty Cury manager, who gave him an interview and started him on 12s 6d a week (£20 at today's value). Shop assistants were supposed to work their way through the bookshop, from the top floor, starting with Mr Sharp in the Oriental department. Dudley didn't actually get beyond Science and dealt with a wide range of scientific subjects including botany, zoology and medicine. He recalls how he learned the trade:

> "I originally started by carrying the books from the basement where they were unpacked. I did the orders and got to know the books that way. I didn't have an exam or anything. You just had to learn it. You dealt with the whole thing, customers, account holders, cash. The departments all looked after their own books."

Dudley left Heffers to work at Galloway & Porter in 1967, where he stayed for a further thirty-one years.

At school, Clive Cornell learned from his careers master that Heffers were looking for someone to join their Foreign department. Interviewed by Reuben, Clive had to do some quick thinking when asked what his father did for a living. Believing there was less chance of losing the position to some another candidate whose father may be a college lecturer, Clive said his father was a farmer rather than a farm worker, which was the reality. His tactic paid off and he started as a shop assistant at Petty Cury on leaving school in 1958. Like Dudley, Clive was involved with the mail orders as well as dealing with customers in the shop. He learned very early on that if you had a complaint to deal with, whether it be in the shop or more often, with a mail order customer, a defensive position got you nowhere. However, if you went back with a humble apology and an offer to replace the book, you would have a customer for life.

Clive also helped to produce book lists and catalogues. On one occasion very early on, he had the job of pricing some rather expensive books from France and he wrote the price in the book with a biro (a permanent marking ball-point pen). When Mr Boasten, his manager, spotted this, he hit Clive on both sides of his head saying, "You don't use bloody biro, Mister!" Clive never did it again. Being in the Foreign department, Clive needed to build his language skills. He'd done German and French at school and at Heffers he used the 'Teach Yourself' books to learn the Cyrillic alphabet so he could tell the difference between Chekov and Tolstoy and get them in the right order on the shelves. Reflecting on his language and linguistics specialism, Clive feels he opted for the easy side of bookselling: "General books are damn difficult to sell. If

The Petty Cury shop.

you're a Medieval historian, the man who really knows what the market for his book is the man who wrote it. It's much easier to target potential buyers."

Of course, not all started straight from school. Having heard about the possibility of a job via a friend, Eve Stafford was recruited in 1949 by Reuben for a temporary part-time job over the Christmas period. At the time of her appointment, Reuben told her he wanted to be sure that she would not be offended when it came to the time when, after Christmas, that the firm would say "thank you for your services and goodbye". That time, however, never came and Eve remained there until 1970, even though she was never given a contract of employment.

Rosemarie Hill (*née* Eicher) had trained as a bookseller at home in Bern, Switzerland, and joined Heffers in 1955 when still a student with a view to improving her English. Arriving in Cambridge very late one February night, Rosemarie made her way to the lodgings secured for her by the firm. The next morning when she turned up at Petty Cury, Reuben wasn't there and they didn't know what to do with her. So they sent her home again to unpack. When she returned to Petty Cury, Rosemarie was introduced to everybody and was told: "You must meet Robert. He likes foreigners. He'll take you to the International Club." Robert Hill did indeed like Rosemarie and they ended up getting married. Robert himself went from Heffers to do a degree at the University and then on to work for Frank Bell at Bell's School of Languages in Cambridge. He remembers the school as having a similar culture to Heffers. This may not be surprising as Reuben and Frank Bell were great friends and Reuben was a trustee of the school.

Frank Collieson, joining Heffers in 1962, worked closely with Clive Cornell. Initially at Heffers Printers, Frank went on to the publishing side and after the move from Petty Cury to Trinity Street took on responsibility for design and publicity, whilst Clive was responsible for sales. Frank, who wrote everything by hand in brown ink, recalled:

"I did it my way. There was always something being published or printed. I wanted it right. What's the point of spending hundreds of pounds and not getting it right?... If I pick up a book with an error, I'm undermined by it. I don't want to look at it again."

Frank's style became, in essence, Heffers' style at a time when bookselling was very different to how it is today.

In 1962, Susan Green (*née* Gilbert) walked through the door of the Sidney Street shop and asked for a job:

"I got off my school bus in my uniform. We hadn't had much of a career talk at school. I didn't really know what I wanted to do. I walked into Heffers and asked if they had any vacancies. I was told to wait for a few moments please. Then I was ushered into this office and met Mr Court who was the Director of Sidney Street. He asked me a few questions. I was leaving school on the Friday and I started on the following Monday."

When Susan started, she went straight into the office on the ground floor and was, she thinks, given a lot of responsibility whilst still a girl. At 8.15 each morning, she collected the money bags which had come up from the safe in the basement on a pulley lift. All the departments took their bags from her, and at the end of the day she took the bags back and put them away. Susan also cashed up any account payments made the previous day. She left Heffers briefly to work for an insurance agent but decided to return, joining the staff at Petty Cury in 1966. It was the same sort of work, but for Susan the atmosphere was more laid back than Sidney Street. She recalls that on her twenty-first birthday, Reuben invited her to choose a book and put it on his account. She chose an Agatha Christie novel, which Reuben inscribed.

When Stephen Perry first started his job at Sidney Street in 1967, he had to learn how to address the customers. At the time, Norman Biggs, the manager, had his office on the ground floor by the stairs to the basement with a hatch to the main floor. Upon hearing Stephen answer the telephone, he opened the hatch and said, "Stephen, when you answer the telephone, would you just use your surname, otherwise they'll think you're a lady. It's only the ladies who say Miss or Mrs". The ladies who worked in the Sales Ledger and Invoicing offices at Petty Cury remember that they were never called by their first names.

Suzanne Jones (*née* Leonard) also joined the firm at a young age, in 1973. Her first manager, Rod Pavasars (a Latvian bookseller who had joined Heffers in 1968) declared at the outset, "if you can't use a duster, you're no use to me!" She recalls she had "a brilliant time". "At the age of seventeen I was thrown into this rather rarefied literary world. It was wonderful. It gave me opportunities I wouldn't have had anywhere else. I had an absolute blast for thirty-four years."

In 1985, *Trinity Street News* (the in-house newsletter) voiced the firm's intention that all staff, particularly young people in their first job, should have every opportunity to move from department to department so that they gain as wide an experience as possible so they may be considered for promotion. The newsletter stated it 'will help everyone to understand what Heffers Booksellers is about and therefore find the work here more interesting'.

Richard Reynolds started at Heffers in 1981. Now internationally renowned for his expertise in crime fiction (he chaired the 2016 CWA Goldsboro Gold Dagger Judges Panel), Richard recalls his own recruitment at Heffers after a spell of working in a bookshop in Manchester. Richard had mugged up on all aspects of bookselling, including the Penguin list, before his interview. However, manager John Cheshire, who interviewed him, didn't ask about books at all. They talked instead about classical music, an interest he discovered they both shared. Richard was offered a job looking after the sports books. He then moved on to travel and biography but now specialises in crime. "You need people like Richard Reynolds," says Suzanne Jones:

"Richard is running a niche bookshop within a bookshop, purely through his knowledge and expertise – and the fact that he's who he is. Which is why people go back to him. If I lived in Cambridge I would get my books from Richard just because it would be a pleasure to go in and discuss books with him.

At one time everybody at Heffers was a ferocious reader. You would always find someone who could give you advice, someone on the customer's wavelength."

In 1972 David Wilkerson was offered a job at Heffers – before receiving his O-level examination results, which he thinks was just as well. "It was all I wanted to do: go and work at Heffers. I was an avid reader and it was the ideal job." David earned £8.50 a week as a trainee sales assistant/bookseller (£108 at today's value).

Years later, Amy Wilkerson, David's daughter, spent her Saturdays and school holidays from the ages of sixteen to twenty-one also working at Heffers. "Heffers stands for something. It's always about your passion. Heffers helped me develop how to express my passion for books, how to encourage readers. It was a really good training ground." Amy gained a lot of knowledge from working in the bookshop and understands the expectations that customers have of booksellers. She is now working for Penguin Random House, still sharing her passion for children's books.

Robert Webb also joined Heffers straight from school, in 1975. It was a temporary summer job, while he reconsidered A-levels and the big question of 'What To Do Next'. His father, John Webb, already ran the History department at Trinity Street. Robert felt at home surrounded by books and it was nice to be able to work alongside his father. John had started with the firm in 1947, after a stint at King's College Library, running things while the librarian and assistant librarian had been away on war service. (Incidentally, Robert's grandfather had also been a bookseller, in the 1910s, before he opened his own Cambridge bookshop in 1920. Webb & Brown, at 73 Bridge Street, became a casualty of the Great Slump of the late '20s and early '30s.)

Robert's salary in 1976 was £20 per week (£151 at today's value), a large proportion of which was spent at Andy's Records, a stall on Cambridge market – a favourite lunchtime haunt. He stayed with the firm for longer than planned, moving to the Science department and Orders Handling department, before leaving for London in 1979 and a job at Dillons bookshop.

John Skelton was at Trinity Street from 1973 to 1976. He had remained in Cambridge after completing his degree, and trained to be a teacher, although ultimately deciding against that. The advertised role was as a junior bookseller in the Social Science department and he was interviewed by bookseller Malcolm Campbell, who offered him the job at £17 per week. He had worked as a bus conductor for six months before applying for the post at Heffers and had been earning £27 per week plus overtime payments. However, having managed to save some money, he was willing to take a drop in pay in return for an interesting job. After starting at Heffers, bookseller Robert Machesney asked to see him and offered him £18 per week to work in the Literature department. As his degree was in English (and for the extra £1 per week), he joined Literature. John says: "In some ways Heffers was old-fashioned, but it had a relatively young senior management team who were successfully expanding its local and international business and giving opportunities to young booksellers like me to regenerate shop departments and kick-start their own careers." He went on to become managing director of the Open University Press.

In 1974 the firm recreated the position of departmental manager, with the aim of encouraging staff to take on more responsibility. These managers worked closely with general management in the solving of day-to-day problems in the shop and had specific responsibilities for the staff, sales and stock in their own departments.

Liz Davies was offered a job at Heffers in 1981, after attending a dinner party at her husband's college where she had met John Welch. She started in the English and Foreign Literature department and discovered she was the only member of the team without a degree, and the only 'part-timer' because she was doing slightly shorter hours and no Saturdays. She recalls, most of her colleagues were over-qualified to work in a 'shop' but did it gladly because Heffers, as an institution, was, "the hub of the universe for graduates wanting to get into publishing and other literary careers".

Having decided to move to the Cambridge area in 1986, Ronald Hall (also known as Andy), called in unannounced at Trinity Street and asked to see John Welch, with whom he had previously worked in London. Ronald was fluent in several languages and asked John to let him know if Heffers

The Trinity Street shop in 1970.

might need translation work at any time, or to recommend him to anyone local for this purpose. John invited him to lunch, and to his surprise, offered him a job as a bookseller.

Lisa Newman completed her A-levels in the summer of 1988 and didn't know what she wanted to do for a living. A vacancy for a full-time assistant was advertised in the *Cambridge Evening News* during that summer and it was a case of, 'right place, right time'. Following her interview, she was offered the job with a starting annual salary of £4,550 plus overtime (£7,475 at today's value). From quite early on in the job, Lisa was selecting and buying new stock from sales representatives. She had responsibility for looking after publications from Hodder & Stoughton, and Grafton Books:

> "Looking back, I think it was quite incredible that I was trusted to do this so new to the job and lacking any real experience. I remember in my first meeting with one of the reps asking the question, 'how will I know what quantity of books to order', as it seemed quite daunting. How would I know what was a potential bestseller? It wasn't long before I got a feel for it and began to enjoy seeing all of the new titles yet to be published, instead of feeling terrified in case I got it wrong!"

Lisa considered herself lucky that neither of the representatives she saw on a regular basis tried to take advantage of dealing with a newbie. Lisa also considers she was given a lot of responsibility early on, and at a young age. She would occasionally help out at the Heffers Grafton Centre bookshop, which made a change though was at times challenging when she was trying to quickly find where anything was kept.

Julian Sedgwick was recruited to Heffers in 1991. Now an author, he was then fresh out of Cambridge University and at a loss as to what to do next. Seeing an advertisement in the Trinity Street window, 'Oriental Dept Bookseller wanted', he decided to apply (his first aborted degree at Cambridge had been Oriental Studies). After a brief functional interview with Personnel and a longer chat with bookseller Michele Thomas, Julian was offered the job and shown the stock-card boxes and microfiche *Books in Print* (the UK publishing database). Within the week his manager had gone on holiday and he was buying new titles from publishers' representatives. "I hadn't really a clue what I was doing but felt I'd found a home for the time being." For the first four years Julian worked in the Oriental and African department in the basement, before taking over running Classics when that department manager, Ian Catchpole, retired.

Becky Proctor came to Heffers as a bookseller, having previously worked at Dillons bookshop in Cambridge in 1992, and noticed immediately that Heffers had a far greater depth of stock than Dillons. To arrive in Heffers felt like a step up for Becky: "We just had amazing stock." Within a very short period of time, Becky would be meeting the publisher representatives. "We had autonomy over what we ordered ... if you see a book that's interesting ... you know what's going to be popular and what fits in with what you've got."

After graduating with a degree in Politics in the early 1990s, Marcus Sedgwick (now an author), was invited by his brother Julian, to come to Cambridge, rent a room from him, and see whether he too could get a job at Heffers. There were two jobs going at the time, one in the Politics department and one at the Children's Bookshop. As Julian already worked in the department adjoining Politics, the firm decided that Marcus should go to the Children's Bookshop. This was where – and how – his writing career started. Marcus says:

> "It was a wonderful place to work, though I had a worrying introduction to the job. On my third day I was aware of a mother with two rather wayward toddlers, who spent a couple of hours (without exaggeration) 'browsing' (i.e. reading for free) the picture books. We'd all remarked on this, but suddenly, the next second, they were gone. Fearing a touch of shoplifting had occurred, we investigated the picture book department and discovered three picture books smeared with, well ... let's just say one of the toddlers had been wandering around the shop in a nappy ... For some reason (new boy?) I was the one dispatched to consign the books (wrapped in one of those indestructible Heffers plastic bags) concerned to the waste bin in Trinity Street. Those bags really were tough – we once saw one on the news on a bulletin from war-torn Beirut."

Marcus then feared all weeks might be like that first one, but fortunately it never happened again. Instead he learned a great deal about children's books, made lots of friends who he still has to this day, and worked alongside a group of people many of whom were also destined to become authors and illustrators – including Julian, his brother.

The Children's Bookshop in 1979.

4

SIDNEY STREET – PENS, PICTURES AND PRAYER BOOKS

"We are at war with Sidney Street."

Heffers Booksellers' saying

Heffers resolved to secure their Sidney Street premises (numbers 18 and 19) in March 1903. The city centre location, which previously had been John Swan's furniture business, was unoccupied and the firm moved in just two months later. Unlike Petty Cury, Heffers acquired the freehold to Sidney Street and, initially, the upper part of number 19 was leased to a Mrs Roff at the rent of £90 a year (£10,000 at today's value). Kate and Sidney Heffer oversaw the management of the Sidney Street shop, in 1903 engaging R.S. Digby as their first assistant.

Frederick Denham, formerly of Haymarket Booksellers in London (and who had originally proposed a Heffers branch in Hitchin in 1903 – *see 'Branching out', below*), was engaged by the firm to set up a 'Unique Bookshop' within the Sidney Street premises, under an agreement whereby he would receive a salary and also draw a commission based on profits. Also, Sidney Street would receive 75 per cent of the profit on all books that had been sent from Petty Cury to Sidney Street. Denham did not remain in his position for long, however. It was noted in the first Heffers Minute Book in May 1904, that he had ceased to be an employee on being, 'convicted on his bankruptcy'. Furthermore, in September the firm resolved to write to Denham in America regarding money owing. Where exactly Denham was at this time is unclear, as the records show that in April 1904 he had been sentenced at the Central Criminal Court (the Old Bailey), London to nine months' imprisonment, after being convicted of obtaining a Second Folio Shakespeare by false pretences, and of disposing of it, 'otherwise than in the ordinary way of his trade' within four months of his bankruptcy. [26]

To set up the shop, many fixtures and fittings from Fitzroy Street were transferred to Sidney Street. A notice was placed in the local

The Sidney Street shop prior to the 1929–31 rebuild.

If in a look round the main shop at 19, Sidney Street you should not find just what you require, we enumerate here a few of our stock items :

Artist's Materials of every description, Albums, At Home Cards and Indicators.

Blotting Pads, Book Cases, Blackboards, Bridge Sets, Boxed Stationery, Balances.

Cabinets, Compasses, Crayons, Chalks, Cash Boxes, Card Games, Cash Books.

Diaries, Date Blocks, Drawing Materials, Deed Boxes, Duplicators, Dance Cards.

Envelopes, Empire Typewriter, Easels, Etching Boards and Papers, Embossing.

Fountain Pens, Foolscaps, Folios, Files, Filing Appliances, Fancy Goods, Flexible Curves.

Gum, Geometrical Instruments, Games, Graph Copiers, Gazetteers.

Hardtmuth's Pencils, Hieratica Note, Household Requisites.

Ideal Fountain Pen, Inks, Inkbottles, Instantaneous Binders.

Jam Covers, Japanese Serviettes, Journals, Jig Saws.

Knives, Kohinor Pencils, Key Labels, Kitchen Paper, Kalamazoo Ledgers.

Leather Goods, Ledgers, Letter-files, Letter Clips, Letter Trays, Letter Balances.

Manifold Books, Memo Tablets, Menu Cards, Mathematical Instruments, Microscopes.

Neocyclostyles, Note Paper (immense variety), Newscutting Albums, Novels, Natural History Books.

Official Envelopes, Office Furniture, Onoto Pens, Order Books, Oil Paints.

Portfolios, Purses, Progressive Games, Poker Patience Playing Cards, Paints, Puzzles.

Quill Pens, Quill Nibs, Quinto Games.

Revolving Book Shelves, Rulers, Rent Books, Race Games, Reading Glasses, Rubbers.

Story Books, School Bags, Safety Fountain Pens, School Sundries, Stylos, Swan Pens, Stamp Albums, Sealing Wax, Stencil Papers.

Typewriters and Materials, Tourists Cases, T Squares, Tablets, Tissue Papers.

University Stationery, Union Files, Unspillable Inkwells, Umbrella Rings.

Visitors' Books, Vertical Filing Cabinets, Visiting Cards, Vulcanised Penholders.

Waterman and Waverley Fountain Pens, Whatman Papers, Writing Cases, Watches.

Your enquiries esteemed. Your orders promptly executed.

Zealous principals and assistants entirely at your service.

We hold the sole Agency in Cambridge for the undermentioned :

Kalamazoo Loose-Leaf Ledgers, Ledger Sheets and Binders.

Aston and Mander's Mathematical and Engineering Instruments.

The Stolzenberg and Stanley Files.

The " Libraco " Co.'s Card Index and Vertical Filing Cabinets.

The " Refereader " Book Rest and Reading Stand.

In 1909 the firm promoted a comprehensive range of stock on offer at the shop in an A to Z listing.

press to alert customers. Sidney Heffer notes that in 1952, a counter from Fitzroy Street was still in use at Sidney Street – a tangible link with the company's humble origins.

In 1909, the firm held a sale of pictures and stocked thousands of prints and reproductions of many masterpieces. An exhibition of nearly 6,000 pictures, including 'Medici Prints' and works by local artists, coincided with a display at the Petty Cury shop of bookbinding. Heffers converted a part of the Sidney Street premises into an art or 'picture' gallery and began to hold regular art exhibitions which very quickly established a 'no mean reputation'. From the beginning, the firm gave prominence to local artists and the topic of Cambridge and East Anglia. The 1909 booklet states: 'Cambridge, with its Historic buildings and its wonderful "Backs" and up-river scenes, possesses a charm of its own which invariably appeals to the visitor and the inhabitant. Hundreds of artists have found its beauties and portrayed them with pencil, etching tool, and brush.'

There can be no doubt as to the opinion of the local press, demonstrated by a review in the *Cambridge Daily News* of 19th May 1920 of Mr Debos's 'Exhibition of Water Colours':

> 'Without exception the exhibitions [at the Sidney Street gallery] so far have been chiefly remarkable for the fact that they represent actual art. Futurism, Cubism, Post Impressionism, and other forms of moral anarchy have been rigidly barred, and the exhibitions have in consequence won the respect and patronage of level-headed

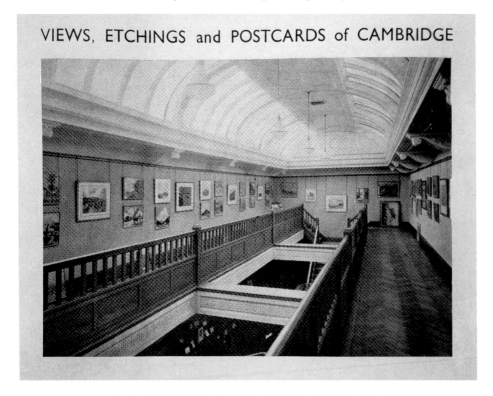

'Mr Heffer's new gallery'.

men to whom art born of the beautiful appeals. Whilst the artist is described as an Impressionist, his art is stated to be "sane, clear cut and true to life", unlike that of the misguided, whose distorted horrors left us with acute eyestrain.'

Heffers also had a link with Agnews of Bond Street, London, who now and again would produce a small exhibition for Sidney Street. After the rebuilding of Sidney Street, an exhibition featuring Augustus John entitled, *Anthology of English Painting from 1900 to 1931*, was preluded at 'Mr Heffer's new gallery' in 1931, before making its way to the French Gallery in Bond Street, as reported in *The Spectator* in December 1931. The pictures were selected by Mr Gerald Kelly RA who, apart from having what *The Spectator* described as a 'blind spot' in his preference for the 'insipid and over-representational' work of Alan Beeton, did well to choose not only John but other notables such as Walter Sickert, Duncan Grant, Gwen John and Stanley Spencer.

Norman Biggs joined Heffers in 1954, after graduating from university, and having worked for a similar firm in Bristol. He became director of the stationery division. He recalls that the gallery had a lot of autonomy and that they showed local artists who brought their families and friends. Mrs Cope who worked at the cash desk on the ground floor in 1981, would often walk around the art gallery during her lunch break. She says, "everything was such top quality and the atmosphere was so personal. Such a nice place to be."

The gallery was also used for other types of exhibition. In 1985 it hosted a Waterman Pens exhibition, officially opened by the president and director general of Waterman Pens, Francine Gomez, dubbed the 'Iron Maiden' of French industry. As reported in the Cambridge press, the exhibition featured six showcases covering one hundred years and the development of Waterman Pens since its early days in the United States. Many of the exhibits belonged to Heffers; pens made of white and yellow gold, of Vulcanite and Bakelite, and silver. Incidentally, the brand was used by George Orwell for writing *Nineteen Eighty-Four*, James Joyce for *Finnegan's Wake* and by also Admiral Byrd on some of his Antarctic expeditions. Another unusual exhibition that year, even for Heffers, featured a collection of second-hand Japanese Kimonos, brought to Cambridge by antique dealer Roger Strange.

Over the decades there were many locations and departments, all with a certain degree of autonomy. Norman Biggs sums up the organisation in this way:

> "It was a very interesting firm, we did so many different things, there were so many facets to the business ... What was so nice about Heffers was that it was very family oriented, it was friendly and not too disciplined. There were rules but it wasn't a highly structured organisation. There were quite a lot of people in it who were, in a way, running their own businesses under the Heffer umbrella. They could do the buying and selling and they didn't have to worry about all the other things, the accounts and so on."

Many thrived on running their own domains. Some didn't. One assistant general manager, who joined the firm in the late 1960s from the Gas Board, despite getting on well, decided to leave after twelve months because he couldn't stand not being able to know the detail of every department. The response from Heffers who were sorry to see him leave was, of course you won't know the detail; nobody does!

The rebuilding of the Sidney Street shop, previously mentioned, started during the Great Slump when most of the country was suffering an economic downturn. It took three years and during this time the business was temporarily relocated to St Andrews Street. The new shop was given a Georgian frontage, with columns of grey polished granite and the upper part faced with red Flemish bricks and Weldon stone dressings to the windows. The art gallery, with its barrel-shaped ceiling, was located on the third floor.

After the Second World War, Sidney Street started sending out their own representative, mainly to the Cambridge colleges, and they successfully secured more business. The shop became well known for many things, in particular church supplies, pens, artistic window displays, greetings cards and personalised stationery. Sarah Burton, who worked there briefly before it was closed in 2000, depicts the shop as a "tower". A most apt description for a store whose several floors were stacked with many and varied riches. So much so that Norman Biggs would jokingly say to the booksellers, "it's all right for you; you only sell one product. At the stationers we have ten different businesses doing completely different things!"

Sidney Street shop decorated to celebrate the 1937 Coronation of King George VI and Queen Elizabeth.

The Church Supplies department at Sidney Street was, as Norman puts it, "distinctive", and had many regular customers. They sold bibles, prayer books, popular theology, rosaries, crucifixes, palm crosses and so on. Norman recalls:

> "The difficulty always with it was getting the right person to run it. You needed somebody who knew the world of the church but who also had a head for business. And sometimes the two didn't go together. When the New English Bible came out there were queues of customers into the department." [27]

Another well-known Sidney Street department sold pens. Reginald 'Nobby' Clarke was a pen mechanic for sixty-one years, starting at the firm in 1914 and retiring in 1975. Following on in the Pen department was Louis Janus, at Heffers for thirty-eight years before retiring in 1996. Both men enjoyed meeting customers from all walks of life, including many celebrated ones – Nobel Prize-winning scientists and Lord Runcie, the former Archbishop of Canterbury, amongst them. When Nobby began his long career at the age of fourteen the upper floors of the Sidney Street shop were still let to the landlady who ran the lodging house. On his appointment as an apprentice (he was introduced to Heffers via Clare College Choir), Nobby was paid 2s 6d a week (£13 at today's value). He served directly under William Heffer for the first three or four years and remembered him with respect and affection. Also notably working in the Pen department for many years as an assistant, was Miss Star, fondly known as 'Twink' by her colleagues (from the nursery rhyme *Twinkle, Twinkle, Little Star*).

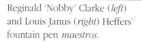

Reginald 'Nobby' Clarke (*left*) and Louis Janus (*right*) Heffers' fountain pen *maestros*.

Over the years, fountain pen technology advanced extensively and both Nobby and Louis frequently attended pen mechanic courses in order to keep up to date. In the early days, most pens had to be filled using a pipette, until a self-filling version was invented. Heffers kept a comprehensive stock of old pen parts, including old pens no longer manufactured, although the majority of repairs involved the nib, the most expensive element. Some fountain pens were very valuable and on two occasions, in 1960 and 1967, the department was subjected to major thefts of stock worth over £500 (£8,400 at today's value). The response of the firm was to declare, 'The theft will not affect our business at all … We will simply order more pens.'

Geoffrey Smallwood, a loyal fountain pen customer who moved to the Cambridge area in 1970, remembers "Mr Louis" as quiet person, very informed, always very helpful and wanting to see you happily satisfied:

> "It was his knowledge and skill, interpreting what you wanted, he was very helpful. He was also interested in local history and after his retirement Mr Louis walked around Cambridge looking upwards, because he was interested in buildings. So often people look at buildings at ground level only and do not appreciate their heritage from looking up and seeing what has *not* been altered."

Claire Brown, bookseller, relied upon Louis: "He was the only person who could repair my pens. He wasn't affected about them, never saying 'this should be in a museum'. He would say, 'this should work for a bit longer now'." Norman Biggs recalls Pens as "our star department" and, in particular, Nobby who, according to Norman, was one of the people who made Heffers what it was. Dudley and Marion Davenport used to see him strolling about Cambridge in a bright blazer with a straw boater. Bunty Heffer recalls him as "Mr Inky Fingers" and remembers the lovely ladies on the pen counter. Richard Heffer, son of Bunty and John, recalls that for generations of children it was a big occasion when you were old enough to write with a fountain pen: "You were taken along to Heffers to try some out."

Stephen and Veronica Perry (*née* How), at Sidney Street from the late 1960s, recall Nobby popping out the side door, exclaiming he was "just going to see the vicar", or "just going to see the doctor" as he headed for the Prince of Wales public house. Another long-serving Sidney Street staff member, artist Gerald Criddle, who worked there from 1955 to 1970, before leaving to set up his own art gallery in King's Parade, also remembers this. Gerald's artistic talents were employed in putting together many inventive and award-winning Sidney Street window displays.

Prize winning Palace Diary display, 1958 and (*right*)
Gerald Criddle receiving one of his awards.

Gerald recalls the building itself, "there was a
quality about it, you nestled into it".

Over the years Gerald earned a total of
£998 in prize money for the firm. Often, he
would go up to London to the presentations.
On one occasion he was presented with a
cheque by the publisher Sir George Harrap,
made out to him personally and not to Heffers.
Sir George insisted that Gerald should have the
money as he had done the work. However,
Heffers directors did not view it that way and
insisted the money be set aside for purchasing
window display materials.

*Mr. G. H. Criddle, of Heffer's, winner of the 'Palace
Diary' Window Display Competition, receiving his
cheque for £50 from Miss Eileen Allen, editor of
'Woman's Own', at the party given by Harrap's last
week.*

Gerald was also involved with greetings cards and calendars. For many years, Heffers had
stocked a wide range of cards from suppliers such as J. Arthur Dixon and Valentines. Publisher
Gordon Fraser brought art to the masses via his distinctive greetings cards. He had attended St

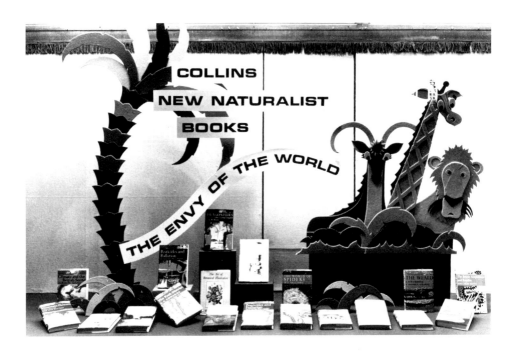

Gerald Criddle's entry for Collins 1968 New Naturalist window display competition (*top*), and his Proctor and Bulldogs paper sculptures, 1963.

Johns, Cambridge, and founded the Minority Press whilst living in the city. Through this Cambridge connection, Heffers knew him well. The firm printed Fraser's early publications and were appointed his sole distributors. In the 1950s and '60s the industry was beginning to change with greetings cards from US companies imported by publishers such as Hallmark and Hanson White.

Gerald recalls answering his phone one day to John Heffer, who wanted to see him immediately in the boardroom. Whenever John wanted to show someone something, he would slip it into a large notepad and fling it across the table. If the person on the receiving end side-stepped in order to avoid a collision, John would exclaim, "butter fingers!" On this occasion, Gerald caught the pad and inside were two Hanson White greetings cards, known as 'slim-jims', with black and white illustrations. One depicted a vicar at a sale saying, "oh Miss Smith, what a lovely pear you've got!", to a very glamorous female holding up some fruit. The other also featured a vicar, this time standing behind a stall which held a large vegetable marrow and a lady saying, "my goodness, vicar, you have got a big one!" Gerald thought they were funny. However, John did not and exclaimed, "they are disgusting. This is Heffers, not W.H. Smith. What is Mrs Webb thinking about?" He asked Gerald to speak to Mrs Webb, the buyer responsible for cards. On doing so, he discovered that whilst being pleased with the new stock of up-to-date designs, Mrs Webb had no clue about the innuendos.

Every Christmas, Sidney Street stocked hundreds of different cards and calendars. By 1960 'turnover' calendars were very popular following the development of spiral and 'Wire-O' bindings. Supplies of superior quality calendars were obtained from Denmark and Germany. At one time Gerald dealt with 140 companies supplying Christmas orders. Calendars and cards were not only sold through the shop but could also be mailed on behalf of customers to recipients worldwide.

Sidney Street also had, for many years, a thriving Social Stationery department, with a huge range of cards, note papers, die stamp and printed materials that could be customised. In the 1950s, the Cambridge colleges would commission Christmas cards with college crests, hand-tied with the college coloured ribbons. These were very popular. Norman Biggs recalls when things began to change. Once people started to produce their own letters on their computers, you could see great changes on the horizon: "The IT revolution was the most significant thing. Almost every department in some measure, apart from the gallery and artists' materials, was affected."

There was a lot of activity in the basement at Sidney Street; a typewriting repair service existed for around fifty years before it was eventually moved to King Street, when the firm acquired the Cambridge Express Printing Company in 1955. There was a schoolbook contract business, also moved to King Street; and a picture framing service. (Joan Clark, at Sidney Street from 1941 to 1949, remembers a cutting machine in the basement – operated

One of many office supply products carrying the Heffer brand name.

by a gentleman who had part of a finger missing.) She also remembers being sent out by the formidable Mrs Snell (described as a pillar of the business) to join a queue, not knowing what she was queuing for. During the Second World War a queue meant there must be something worth having and so whatever it was, you joined it. On one occasion it turned out to be jellies. (Rationing didn't only occur in the 1940s and '50s. During the three-day week in the 1970s there was a nationwide shortage of toilet rolls. While such a product would not normally be found on the Sidney Street A–Z, a supply was secured and eager customers queued for their ration.)

Norman Biggs recalls some of the early stationery devices such as Heffers' first line in calculators; an entirely mechanical, German device, shaped like a small Swiss roll, with rotating rings, a handle to crank out the calculations, and a bell to warn operators when they were subtracting.

In 1976, Heffers acquired the business of map distributor W.P. Spalding, of 3 Green Street. Spaldings had been the official Cambridge agents for the Ordnance Survey and the operation later became a department of Sidney Street. The Map department manager at that time, described as being "aggressively nice", was very territorial about his department and did not like anyone else to serve his customers. Most fitting.

David Wilkerson, who had a spell at Sidney Street in 1981 as manager of the Book department, remembers the shop as having a very different atmosphere to Trinity Street, where he also worked. He describes it as, "a very gentle shop, nice people and run very properly". Joan Clark remembers how kind people were to each other. According to Mrs Clark this kindness even extended beyond the shop premises. Her memory of watching the policeman directing the traffic on the junction with Market Street right outside seems fitting – she says she felt looked after.

Suzanne Jones spent three months working at Sidney Street in 1983, before going into a management position at Trinity Street: "It was a much more an 'Are you being served?' environment. It worked for them

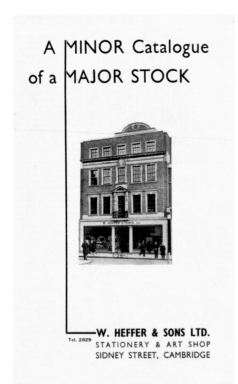

A MINOR Catalogue
of a MAJOR STOCK

W. HEFFER & SONS LTD.
Tel. 2829 STATIONERY & ART SHOP
SIDNEY STREET, CAMBRIDGE

An early catalogue for the Sidney Street shop (*left*). A still (*above*) from the film *City in the Sixties: Cambridge* showing a policeman on traffic duty outside Heffers. © ITV Anglia, courtesy of East Anglian Film Archive (University of East Anglia).

perfectly well." (Suzanne is referring to a 1970s and '80s British TV comedy about a department store, written by Croft and Lloyd.)

Sidney Street underwent a number of refurbishments over the years. In the 1930s there were two staircases. At some point a bridge was built between them and the middle area filled in to create more floor space. Stephen Perry, a floor manager, recalls the time in the early 1970s when the solid oak fittings were replaced with polished pine, and the lift shaft being boxed in. The result was felt by some employees to be rather gloomy.

In 1984 there were more changes. It was decided that the Sidney Street Book department was no longer justified, particularly following the opening of the new shop in the Grafton Centre. Norman Biggs wrote in the staff newsletter in April 1983: 'it would now be right for the Stationery Division to withdraw from general bookselling ... Bibles and Prayer Books which have always been a Sidney Street speciality will be stocked at 20 Trinity Street.' The aim was to develop the sales of home computers and video games, combined with office equipment. The substantial works, which took three to four years to complete, included repairs to the roof, cleaning the front of the building, increasing the floor area of the upper gallery, refitting and equipping the Map department with a new IMTEC 6000 plan and printer, and refitting the Commercial Stationery and Office Equipment departments.

By 1988, according to the firm's directors, Sidney Street sales were buoyant and ahead of target. By the mid- to late-1990s the firm was again reviewing the profile of Sidney Street and further refurbishment was undertaken. In 2000, soon after the Blackwell's takeover, the shop premises were sold.

The Sidney Street shop in 1984.

heffers:

drawing of Trinity Street
by Sandra Pearson

heffers:

a famous bookshop
now at a new address

20 TRINITY STREET
CAMBRIDGE
ENGLAND CB2 3NG

This is the headquarters of a group of bookshops and
services in Cambridge with customers all over the world.
Our service—described in detail overleaf—extends to
libraries, institutions, schools and private bookbuyers
everywhere.

5

TRINITY STREET –
'UNIVERSITY AND GENERAL'

'We must pay the fullest attention to shop customers.'

Trinity Street News, 1972

In 1962, the press reported that Emmanuel College was planning to sell the site occupied by Heffers bookshop in Petty Cury to City Centre Properties (owned by Jack Cotton and Charles Clore). The developers had already purchased the Lion Hotel next door. The 1950 Holford Report had originally proposed the redevelopment of the area. In 1958, the City and County Councils had reached agreement on a way forward, but in 1959 a planning enquiry concluded that the case for increased shopping in the city centre had not been made and the planning application was turned down.

However, by 1962 the University was proposing that the Lion Yard area be redeveloped for civic purposes, including a central library and arts centre. City Centre Properties undertook to see that Heffers would be rehoused on a suitable site 'within the immediate area of their present shop' as the lease on the Petty Cury shop still had a decade or so to run. In 1964, Heffers were approached by Trinity College, who were planning to build a large undergraduate hostel at number 20 Trinity Street, opposite their main gate. [28] The offer of a long lease on the ground floor and basement areas was accepted, and over five years of planning began. Heffers appointed their own architects, Austin-Smith:Lord, to collaborate with the University architects for the overall scheme.

The historic Georgian façade at number 20 was retained as far as possible above ground level. A contemporary *Design Journal* editorial review described the wide shop-front in bronze and plate glass as providing a 'simple and elegant showcase onto the street'. [29] Internally, everything was altered in a radical new concept in bookshop design. Roughly twice the size of the Petty Cury shop, Trinity Street's 20,000 square feet total floor space was divided between shop floor (11,000), offices (5,000), and ancillary services and storage (4,000). The latter included space for central handling, invoicing and packing – at the time, more than two-thirds of Heffers' trade came from postal deliveries, and half was in exports. The general manager, John Welch, had told the press when the shop-fitting commenced that, in Petty Cury, "we have invoice girls in the attic and packers in the basement". [30] The new layout would clearly be an improvement. Unlike Petty Cury, Trinity Street was to have a conference room, air conditioning and carpeting throughout the sales areas.

Once the building work was completed, the movement of stock from Petty Cury to Trinity Street could commence. This, in September 1970, was a major operation, carried out by the removal firm Bullens ("Bullen to move a Heffer!" quipped one employee). It took six and a half days, night and day, to transfer more than 80,000 books. Frank

News photo of the queue outside Petty Cury in 1970.

Collieson remembered a poignant moment when Reuben Heffer stood on the roof of Petty Cury, watching the move from above. Clive Cornell remembers that he, Clive, had to stay overnight at the Trinity Street premises during the move because of a threatened flood.

Trinity Street finally opened its doors to customers on 19th September 1970. Postcards were published and distributed, announcing Heffers' 'University & General Bookshop'.

A week later, the firm held a book sale at Petty Cury, before closing its doors there for the very last time after seventy-four years. Thousands of old and damaged books were reduced to between sixpence and £25 in the sale. Hundreds of people gathered outside and were allowed into the shop in shifts. The *Cambridge Evening News* reported that, 'nearly 400 people were waiting when Heffers opened the door to the shop and offered the accumulated but unwanted stock left over from their long stay in Petty Cury.' [31] If the overall feeling amongst staff and customers was one of excitement at the move, Robert Hill also recalls that some were clearly subdued and stood about the Petty Cury shop during the sale, hardly anyone speaking.

The adjustable shelving at Trinity Street covered 95 per cent of the walls and totalled two and a half miles in length. This accommodated academic and general books, new and second-hand, in specialised departments. These included History & Economics, Oriental, Philosophy & Theology and Social Sciences (all in the basement), General & Reference, English & Foreign Literature and Arts (on the ground floor) and Science & Medicine (around the upper gallery). There was a large and welcoming Information Desk at the front of the shop, generally staffed by two people. The Children's department had already moved into its own shop, across the road, a year earlier (*see p.81*). Each department had been allocated a reference letter – 'Z' was for History, 'C' was Science, 'A' was for General, etc. – and staff generally referred to the departments by this letter. The letter was also, together with the month and year, pencilled in the flyleaf of every book before it was shelved for sale.

Reuben welcomed the relocation, stating at the time: 'Since the war, Petty Cury has gone

A department listing for customers at Trinity Street.

The new shop, "like an ocean liner".

very much downhill. It's not the milieu it was ... I'm glad we moved. Petty Cury [the shop] became almost unworkable in the end. It was so Dickensian.' The first year at the new shop saw cash sales on average almost double those at Petty Cury (and, five months after the move, the firm, along with the rest of the country, also adjusted to decimalisation). Reuben also, perhaps through modesty, commented: 'Don't let anyone say this is a luxurious new store. We have carpet because it's the cheapest thing to have ... The bookcases are inexpensive and there's hardly any walls.'

With the move came a total rebranding of Heffers' retail look (*see p.128 on advertising*), outside and in. The bronze facia at Trinity Street was adorned not with the previously used 'W. Heffer & Sons Ltd', but simply 'heffers', in a contemporary, all-lower-case font. New bags (and now also plastic carriers) and bookmarks were designed in the new 'house colours' of deep blue with green roundels, replacing the grey-striped paper bags that had been used at Petty Cury. The Children's shop had their own colour theme of orange and red.

The new look for Heffers.

The overall appearance of both new shop and brand was bold and eye-catching in 1970, and is still instantly recognisable as Heffers today. The shop was widely hailed in the book trade as a stunning achievement in design and a huge improvement in bookselling conditions after Petty Cury. Invited to formally open the new premises, Lord Butler, Master of Trinity College, expressed his reaction to the shop in his opening address. He described the design as ingenious and attractive, combining great spaciousness with a, "superabundance of cosy private nooks where book lovers can tuck themselves away for hours on end perusing their favourite volumes". When Alison Blair-Underwood (*née* Rimmer) first walked into Trinity Street in 1974, to her it felt vast, "like an ocean liner" – by chance mirroring press descriptions of the Wolfson Building of Trinity College (the student hostel behind the Trinity Street shop) as a 'liner stranded in dry dock'. As Suzanne Jones says: "Trinity Street was a radical, timeless design and still looks great even now." The optimism at this time is reflected in a private note written by John Welch to Frank Collieson, kindly shared by Frank's daughter, Jenny,

> *Since the varied talents of the General Managers were first assembled early last year, I have watched with great confidence the emergence of a fine team ... I look forward, as a member of that team, to great things ahead for you and for us all, in the many happy years I hope we shall work together for Heffers and for the tradition which we have together done something to generate and, I believe, enhance.*
>
> John Welch to Frank Collieson, 17th September 1970

Despite the generally positive reception amongst staff and customers, the new premises at Trinity Street did not suit everyone. Claire Brown, who had also worked at Blackwell's in Oxford, was particularly sorry to swap Petty Cury's polished oak for carpets and chrome:

> "It was a great pity that Heffers didn't adopt the sensible Blackwell's policy, which was, and is, to keep it looking exactly as it did in the nineteenth century. Heffers, when it left Petty Cury, in the passionate urge to be new and up to date, did what happened to Joshua Taylor [another Cambridge retail institution]. The actual physical shop is your shop window. What Cambridge and Oxford had to sell was the past. The fact that there is a modern business going on is beside the point ... They did lose a lot when they left the Petty Cury."

For Eve Stafford (typist from 1949 to 1970), the move meant very different working conditions. The typists, around fifteen of them, were put into the basement, away from the shop floor and out of view. At first, their desks were arranged in rows, but they rearranged them into a semi-circle. Typists were no longer connected to a specific department but worked as a pool, and they now had no contact with the customers on the shop floor.

The Book Handling department was also in the basement, with a delivery bay accessed from the rear of the building, via Sidney Street. However, it was business as usual, at least for unpacking and packing. Bookseller Julian Sedgwick recalls a package of books arriving at Trinity Street from a Koranic institute in Pakistan, sewn up in goatskin. He also recalls being asked to pack a large order into two-kilo bundles, so they could be distributed evenly on the donkeys that would carry them over a pass in Afghanistan.

The new arrangements throughout the shop were regularly reviewed and adapted. In 1973, the staff newsletter, *Trinity Street News*, declared that the division between 'academic' and 'popular' was no longer relevant, since all parts of the shop were arranged by subject and catered for the whole spectrum of books in those subjects. The only variation was large glass-top display cases on the mezzanine level, which exhibited publications from all departments and antique books going as far back as 1520. The aim was to 'recover the "centre table" principle that we had at Petty Cury where people came in just to look at "new books" – whatever the subject.'

Over the years the Trinity Street shop itself has undergone various alterations. In the early 1980s, structural work was carried out to increase the selling space downstairs. The Music department was expanded to offer music scores and sheet music, and a Video and Computer Software department was introduced in 1982, providing both VHS and Betamax tapes for sale, or rental at a charge of £2 per day (£7 at today's value). Video

1988 catalogue cover for Heffers' video department.

titles ranged from *Delia Smith in the Kitchen* to *An American Werewolf in London*. John Welch quoted in *The Bookseller* and *Publishing News* in 1982 said: "Like TV, video is not an enemy of the book but complementary: customers find a connection and an affinity between the two … This is not an experiment but a commitment for Heffers. We believe that books and video go together, for we are retailers of knowledge and communication – that is our business." The Video department was designed by Austin-Smith:Lord at a cost of around £8,000. The stock cost £10,000 (£27,700 and 34,630 at today's value). It was moved to the Paperback shop (later renamed Heffers Plus) in St Andrews Street in 1988.

Following the first rent review, satisfactorily negotiated for the end of March 1984, the firm decided it was an appropriate time to consider major changes in the design of the ground floor at Trinity Street. Trading profit had been affected by the rent increase but the mood was still optimistic in the light of the increases in business since 1970. In 1985 the busy front area was entirely redesigned and smaller changes made elsewhere. The result was a greater circulation area for customers (by eliminating an existing bottleneck) and a new enlarged Information Desk, which from 1986 was no longer a cash desk. The total cost of these alterations was around £100,000 (£273,658 at today's value). During these alterations the shop remained open and occasional customer comments were reported, such as, "pity you didn't think of all this when you first moved in!" and "what are you doing to *my* shop!?"

After the Blackwell's takeover in 1999, the offices and boardroom were converted into shop-floor space and the Cambridge press reported that the bookshop was set to lose its 'view of [the] Garden of Eden', Whewells Court, a part of Trinity College grounds which the former

The Trinity Street shop interior, 'a radical, timeless design'.

Chairman's office overlooked. The shop, however, still retained an excellent reputation, as described in Sylvia Christie's 2010 *Varsity* magazine review, in which she declared that Heffers 'effortlessly bridges the gap between the commercial and the specialist, has a second-hand section worth a browse and incredibly helpful staff, so it's hard to find fault'.

TRINITY STREET NEWS

The official staff newsletter, for some time variously named *Heffers Bookselling News*, *Trinity Street News*, *The Magazine* and *New Shop News*, was generally known as TSN, but sometimes referred to as the 'high-brow journal', *Trinity Street Nause*. During the 1970s and into the '80s, the official edition was penned by John Welch. Unofficial versions, intermittently produced and circulated by anonymous members of staff over the years, were titled *Trinity Street Bad News*, *Trinity Street Blues*, *Heiferdust* and *Hefferlumps*.

An advertisement in *Heiferdust*, produced to mark the 103rd anniversary of Heffers:

BOWES? DILLONS? GALLOWAY & PORTER?
GET YOUR BOOKS FROM WHERE YOU OUGHTA

heffers: *Bookselling News*

heffers: TRINITY STREET NEWS

Established 3rd July 1970

heifers : TRINITY STREET BLUES.

 heiferdust:

WHY SETTLE FOR LESS?

SPECIAL ISSUE : We are very excited by this very special issue, produced to celeb-103rd anniversary of William Heffers first shop in Cambridge. Although ... not fall until July this year, we just happen to have some ... telling us just the other day in the Senior ... on this occas-

hefferlumps:

Nuggets of Wisdom from the Bowels of Trinity Street

Banners from 'official' (*top two*) and unofficial versions of the staff newsletter.

THIS BOOK
COMES FROM

HEFFERS

THE BOOKSHOP
THAT IS
KNOWN ALL
OVER THE
WORLD

PETTY CURY
CAMBRIDGE

THIS BOOK
COMES FROM
HEFFER'S

THE BOOKSHOP
THAT IS
KNOWN ALL
OVER THE
WORLD

PETTY CURY
CAMBRIDGE
ENGLAND

THIS · BOOK · COMES · FROM
HEFFER'S BOOK SHOP
The Bookshop that is known all over the World.
Petty Cury
CAMBRIDGE
ENGLAND

THIS · BOOK · COMES · FROM
HEFFER'S BOOK SHOP
The Bookshop that is known all over the World.
Petty Cury
CAMBRIDGE
ENGLAND

This book
comes from
Heffer's
Bookshop

The Bookshop
that is known
all over the
world

Petty Cury
CAMBRIDGE
England

This book
comes from
Heffer's
Bookshop

The Bookshop
that is known
all over the
world

Petty Cury
CAMBRIDGE
England

This book
comes from
Heffer's
Bookshop

The Bookshop
that is known
all over the
world

Petty Cury
CAMBRIDGE
England

This book
comes from
Heffer's
Bookshop

The Bookshop
that is known
all over the
world

Petty Cury
CAMBRIDGE
England

This book
comes from
Heffer's
Bookshop

The Bookshop
that is known
all over the
world

Petty Cury
CAMBRIDGE
England

This Book comes from **HEFFER'S** Bookshop ❧ The Bookshop that is known all over the World ❧ Petty Cury CAMBRIDGE England

This Book comes from **HEFFER'S** Bookshop ❧ The Bookshop that is known all over the World ❧ Petty Cury CAMBRIDGE England

Doubtless your ideal Bookshop is one where you can get any book at any time, New or Second-hand, English or Foreign. We do not claim to have arrived at such perfection, but it is our ideal.

Please send for our Free Lists of New and Second-hand Books, mentioning the subjects in which you are interested.

W. HEFFER & SONS LIMITED
3 and 4 Petty Cury Cambridge, Eng.
Tel. 4262
Cables: 'Heffer Cambridge'

THIS BOOK COMES FROM

Heffers

PENGUIN BOOKSHOP

51 Trumpington Street Cambridge

Other shops of W. Heffer & Sons Ltd.
STATIONERY SHOP *Sidney Street*
BOOKSHOP *Petty Cury*

This book comes from

Heffers
Paperback Shop

Trinity Street Cambridge Telephone 61815

For all British American and European paperbacks

Over the years, Heffers has distributed millions of bookmarks with their books. Besides the obvious primary function of marking place in a book, they clearly had the secondary function of reminding the reader from where books could be obtained, with the same useful expanatory text printed on the reverse of many of the designs (*see centre above*). Before the Second World War, they also had a third function. Being printed on stout thin board, they were a useful device for slitting any untrimmed pages in a book. However, the stout card was considered too expensive in the post-war years. Whatever the quality of the board, the bookmarks, with their attractive and eye-catching designs, became very popular with customers and are now considered to be collectors items, especially those commememortaing special events (*see the centenary bookmark on page 159*).

Heffers decided to commission a special bookmark for their Penguin shop in 1957, along with bags and boxes. Created by the publisher, the initial design had to be revised in order to remove the apostrophe from 'Heffers' and insert the word, 'Cambridge'. By this time, Heffers had opted to eliminate the apostrophe as part of their identity (at least one early example pre-empted this decision). The reverse of the Penguin bookmark was left blank so that the reader could use it for note taking. Despite an initial print run of thirty thousand in early 1958, Reuben had to order fifty thousand more later that same year, stating, 'We seem to be using about fourteen hundred or so of these very successful bookmarks per week, so that by now they are probably littered all over the world as they fall out of the books.' (*memo from Reuben to Herbert Newman at the printing works, 23rd April 1958*).

Portrait of Reuben Heffer by John Ward, 1975.

6

BRANCHING OUT

In 1903 William Heffer considered a proposal from Frederick Denham to establish a bookshop in Hitchin, Hertfordshire (approximately 30 miles from Cambridge). This would have been the first 'branch' shop. In the end, it did not go ahead as the premises required extensive alterations and would have been too costly. (This was perhaps for the best, as things with Frederick Denham proved problematical as can be seen in the chapter on the Sidney Street shop.) Other Heffers branches followed, however, but it was to be fifty years before the first of these opened its doors (Sidney Street excepted as this was not considered a 'branch'). At one time there were as many as ten Heffers shops in Cambridge, known in the firm as the 'outside shops'. Over the years, two branches were also opened beyond Cambridge but with little success. Following years of innovation, expansion, relocation and contraction, under Blackwell's the business was settled into one site, Trinity Street, where it now remains.

THE PENGUIN BOOKSHOP

> *'It was not until we started a shop devoted entirely to Penguins (including, of course, all the related birds!) that I fully appreciated the overall pattern of the series, and was able to see arranged in a methodical way the whole of the remarkable range of a thousand or so titles.'*

Reuben Heffer, writing as 'The Bookseller' in *Penguins Progress 1935–1960*

The first 'outside' shop was Heffers Penguin Bookshop, opened in 1957 at 51 Trumpington Street, Cambridge (on the corner with Pembroke Street), and leased from Pembroke College. Besides being the first for Heffers, it was also the first bookshop in the UK dedicated to Penguin and its associated paperback brands (Heffer's own publications relating to Cambridge were also sold at this shop, as stipulated by the agreement between Heffers and Penguin). It was also something of a coup for Heffers in the Cambridge bookselling trade. The premises had been used as a storeroom since the closure of Hall's bookshop just before the Second World War ('J. Hall and Son, Booksellers Ltd', started by Willam Crabb Hall in 1861) and it appears that Galloway & Porter had already registered strong interest in the premises with owners, Pembroke College. In August 1956, on hearing about Heffers' plans for the shop, George Porter wrote to Penguin expressing his dismay,

> *This probably you will consider strange that I should write to you on this matter, but we have been waiting for some years for the shop which has just been taken*

Illustration from *Penguins Progress*.

in Trumpington Street and apparently this is more or less through a bookseller for Penguin books, and I consider that the service we have rendered in regard to your publications should have warranted you getting in touch with us, but of course we can take this into consideration later as we are also limited for space and naturally it will mean that some action will come about with us in regard to the space which we now allocate to Penguin books – I realise that our losing these premises is no fault of any individual though we have been in touch with Pembroke College reminding them of our letters in regard to having the property whenever it was likely to be let.

In 1957, Heffers placed a notice in the book trade press formally announcing that the new shop, to be known as 'Heffer's Penguin Bookshop', uses the name Penguin with the permission of Penguin Books Limited and that the publishers, 'have no proprietary or other interest what so ever in this bookshop, or in the trade or business thereof'.

Designed by Peter Bicknell, the shop was hailed by the *Cambridge Daily News* as an innovation and an 'Attractive New Nest for Penguins'. [32] Reuben declared in a letter to booksellers AB Sandberg Bokhandel in Stockholm, that the architects, 'have found great satisfaction in adapting what had been a very dirty warehouse for so many years to the special purpose of stocking and displaying the Penguin range'. After the shop was opened, in July 1957, Penguin brought Richard and Toby Blackwell to Cambridge to view it. The building works cost £1,961 (£44,260 at today's value). Pembroke College contributed to the cost of building a partition between the bookshop and

The new Penguin shop on the corner of Pembroke Street and Trumpington Street. Premises now occupied by an extended Fitzbillies.© Penguin Books.

Fitzbillies next door. Heffers were anticipating sales of 600 books per week, with an estimated annual turnover of £4,160 (£93,894 at today's value) and an annual profit before tax of £276 (£6,230 at today's value), not allowing for the extra Penguin discount (as part of the arrangement, Heffers had a 'private' deal with the publisher for an additional 2.5 per cent extra discount on all books purchased from them).

Postcard promoting Heffers' new venture.

Robert Hill, during his time at Petty Cury in the 1950s, had been responsible for the Penguin 'stack' on the ground floor at Petty Cury, displayed close to the cash desk. Robert was then put in charge of the new shop for the first six weeks (before leaving Heffers for a job in London). Robert thought the shop a "splendid thing". Gerald Criddle, on the other hand, recalls that the book trade at the time found the idea of a shop dedicated to one publisher ridiculous. Whatever the view, the shop's very existence exemplified the enterprising spirit of William, the firm's founder, who would undoubtedly have given it his seal of approval. Reuben's son, William (great-grandson of the founder), whilst a student at the London School of Printing in the 1960s, would occasionally work at the

The 1958 Penguin Books catalogue.

Penguin Bookshop in the holidays, standing in for a "Penguin girl". His brother Nicholas also worked there during his holidays.

Over the years Reuben, had built such a good relationship with Penguin Books that he was invited to be a contributor to publication *Penguin's Progress 1935–1960*, a celebration of the publisher's Silver Jubilee, issued in 1960. He was in good company; other contributors 'from the outside' were Compton Mackenzie, Michael Grant, Elliott Viney and Richard Hoggart. In 1975, Trinity Street hosted an exhibition on their mezzanine level to mark Penguin's 40th anniversary.

Nineteen-sixty was also the 30th anniversary of the death of author D.H. Lawrence, and, to mark the occasion, Penguin Books decided to publish seven of his titles, including the unexpurgated edition of *Lady Chatterley's Lover*. Charged under the Obscene Publications Act of 1959 for doing so, the publisher was put on trial at the Old Bailey, represented by Michael Rubinstein, 'the book trade's lawyer' and defended by Gerald Gardiner QC. On 2nd November 1960, Penguin was acquitted when the jury passed a 'not guilty' verdict. In the end, Reuben, who had been listed as a possible witness, was not one of the thirty-five called.

Penguin went on to sell three million copies of *Lady Chatterley* over the next three months and Heffers contributed to those sales. Prepared for a favourable verdict, the invoice office at Petty Cury had already typed invoices, so they were ready to go out with the orders as soon as the trial was over. Dudley Davenport recalls the big rush for copies at Petty Cury, "the place was packed out". Naturally, the recently-opened Penguin shop was hectic too. In his published memoirs, Michael Black, an editor at Cambridge University Press at the time, recalls looking from his office down into the street on publication day:

> 'Heffer's Penguin Bookshop was directly opposite my window, and on that morning there was a very long queue. There still used to be errand-boys in those days, and more than one had taken time off to join the queue and was standing there with his bike. I reflected mildly on the literary tastes and interests of errand-boys – but I suspect they weren't any different from other people's.' [33]

There may well have been a Heffers board meeting to discuss the question of stocking the book, although clearly by the time of the trial the firm was in favour. As William says today of his father, Reuben, "I'm sure he would have been perfectly happy to stock it". And as Norman Biggs reflects: "The view taken was that you couldn't censure, and certainly not in a place like Cambridge."

Sidney Street took a different approach, however. Gerald Criddle recalls it was deemed that the sales would be managed by Mr Hobson, the store's book buyer. Customers were to be shown the cover and then the book placed in a plain bag. After it had been on sale for a few weeks, Miss Dudley-Hay, in the Church Supplies department, had a customer enquire after the book. Her most emphatic response, heard by everyone right across the floor, was a loud cry to Mr Hobson, "this gentleman wishes to purchase a copy of *Lady Chatterley's Lover*, will you attend to it?!" (Incidentally, Heffers office girls at Petty Cury had been told they were not to concern themselves with the content of the book. This may have been irresistible for some but they recall that they were more intrigued by books on forensic medicine with their graphic illustrations – occasionally giving themselves nightmares.)

The Penguin shop was refurbished in 1971 but in May 1985 it was closed. The reasons given for the closure were the shop's isolation from the city's main shopping areas and the lack of parking facilities close by. By that time, of course, paperbacks were stocked in all bookshops and elsewhere; a very different scene to 1957.

THE CHILDREN'S BOOKSHOP

'There's much more to life in the Children's Bookshop than simply reading the picture books, and emerging from the Staff Room dressed as Peter Rabbit from time to time.'

Lindsay Fraser, Children's Bookshop manager, 1991

Heffers had always stocked and sold children's books, and although it is not clear when they first introduced a devoted children's book department, as mentioned earlier, it was thriving at the Fitzroy Street shop. In the early years of the twentieth century, perhaps this would have been a natural destination for the newly-recruited female staff. Reporting on the death in 1977 of Mrs Dorothy Moore (*née* Ely), the eighty-five-year-old widow of the well-known Cambridge philosopher Professor G.E. Moore, *The Times* noted that she 'had a passionate interest in children's literature, and when younger had run a pioneering children's book section in a Cambridge bookshop every Christmas'. [34] Perhaps this was Heffers. If so, whether the department's existence was purely seasonal or for how many Christmases it was run by Mrs Moore, is unknown. By the 1950s a Children's department was well established in the basement of Petty Cury.

The *Cambridge Evening News* signalled the opening of the first Children's Bookshop at 27 Trinity Street, on 14th February 1969, by quoting John Welch: "We shall cover every field there is – from the earliest picture books for the youngest children to what I call bridging books taking children into adult reading."

The new shop had almost four times the book capacity of the Children's department at the Petty Cury shop. In charge were Miss Claire Johnston (manager), Miss Kirsten Christensen (an experienced bookseller from Denmark) and Miss Katia Sagovksy. At this time there was only a handful of specialist children's bookshops in the UK. Clive Brown, Claire's fiancé at the time, wrote to his parents about the new shop in February 1969:

Interior of the Children's Bookshop with its popular distorting mirror.
© Historic England Archive

Although I have been myself almost living with the shop over the past few weeks, I have only just realised how good and successful the whole concept is. Claire's main idea was that it should be a shop for children, where they would feel at home, and could sit and browse and read as they wanted. Things have been unobtrusively scaled down to children's size, and one feels about fifteen feet tall without quite knowing why.

Illustration from the flyer for the Children's Bookshop 21st birthday celebrations in 1990.

The children loved the décor, the distorting mirror (bookseller, Janet Tinling's idea) and the dungeon. Ten years later, in 1979, a larger Children's Bookshop was opened at 30 Trinity Street, replacing the original shop. This had an extra 700 square feet on the ground floor and 250 square feet in the basement. Architects Austin-Smith:Lord designed the enlarged shop. Stephen Heffer was heavily involved in the setting up of this bookshop.

Claire recalls they had a great deal of autonomy, which seemed to continue throughout the years. Pippa Goodhart, who incidentally went on to become a successful children's author, managed the shop much later, in the 1980s, and recalls also having a free hand in what was stocked and in organising events. The calendar included frequent visits from publishers, authors and illustrators. Jean Clarke, (a Heffers bookseller for thirty-four years – and known as 'Jean the Bean') recalls collecting the stock from the main Trinity Street shop and wheeling it in a barrow across the road, and Pippa would make the return walk with the takings in a paper bag at the end of the day.

In 1990 the shop celebrated its 21st birthday with a fortnight of special events culminating in the Mad Heffers Tea-party hosted by Master Tom Kitten.

Writing in *Bookselling News* in 1991, Children's Bookshop manager, Lindsay Fraser says:

'New books, other than those by Roald Dahl, are very unlikely to be bestsellers. Children's books rarely receive much review coverage. They earn their reputations by being read and subsequent word of mouth more than anything else. Those that are likely to survive to entertain future generations will grow in sales volume year by year.'

Amy Wilkerson, who worked at the Children's department in the Grafton Centre bookshop, recalls that book reviews written by children were prominently displayed there. As Amy says, "it's important that children see their opinion matters. They must also have time to spend in bookshops, to sit and go through books."

Isabella Mead shares a special memory of the shop when, in 1994, aged eleven years, she won a poetry competition with a poem entitled *The Carnival of Books*. The competition was a part of the Cambridgeshire Children's Book Festival, an event that Heffers regularly supported. The awards ceremony was held at the Children's shop, where Isabella's poem had been framed and displayed. Author June Counsel presented the awards. Isabella won a £25 book token and £100 worth of books from Heffers for her school, Mayfield Primary in Cambridge. Isabella went on to a career teaching literature, as a secondary English teacher in East London, a teacher trainer in Rwanda, and in education departments at the Roald Dahl Museum and Story Centre, and at the Story Museum in Oxford. "The award ceremony remains my proudest moment. I still look at the letter when I need a bit of self-belief. Thank you, Heffer's Children's Bookshop!"

Cambridge artist and illustrator, Naomi Davies, also had a proud moment when, as a child, she won a Heffers handwriting competition in the late 1980s. She was awarded a calligraphy set.

The logo used for the poetry competition in 1994.

In 2002 Blackwell's announced the closure of the Children's Bookshop, stating that the plan was to move the shop so it can become, 'a shop within a shop' at the Grafton Centre branch. As we see below, the Grafton Centre shop itself closed in 2008, and in 2010 Blackwell's opened a dedicated Children's 'bookshop' within the Trinity Street shop.

PAPERBACKS

Heffers' Paperback shop at 13 Trinity Street, on the corner of Green Street, first opened in 1964 and was an immediate success. It was a modest, ground-floor-only space, sublet from Deighton Bell's antiquarian bookshop next door, and had a reputation for being slightly 'alternative', as was the trend with small independent bookshops at the time. For ten years the shop opened late until eight o'clock every weeknight. It was refurbished in 1971.

From 1977, Stephen Heffer was the director with responsibility for all 'outside' shops: the Paperback shop, the Penguin Bookshop and the Children's Bookshop. In 1978 another Paperback shop was added to the list, at 31 St Andrew's Street, beneath Heffers' new Book and Orders Handling Offices in St Tibbs Row (*see p.127*). John Welch declared: 'I do not think a better designed or more attractive paperback shop exists.'

In January 1988, after Heffers had acquired Deighton Bell (see below), the original Trinity Street Paperback shop was closed and the stock transferred to St Andrew's Street, which had been refurbished at a total cost of £145,000 (£368,000 at today's value) to a design by Austin-Smith:Lord and almost doubled in size to 3,000 square feet. This was now a large and very handsome shop incorporating an enlarged Video department, which had previously been in the main bookshop in Trinity Street. By 1991, Heffers Video had around 1,200 titles and 1,960 active members renting from the video library. Lisa Newman worked there from 1988 to 1991: "I remember every year having to pull together a huge order of videos for the British Antarctic Survey, which would be shipped out to them to watch in their research stations. Occasionally Stephen Hawking and his children would come in to the shop to rent videos." 31 St Andrew's Street was later rebranded as Heffers Plus. However, in the 2000s, the building was demolished to make way for the new John Lewis department store.

The Paperback and Video shop, 31 St Andrew's Street.

HEFFERS SOUND

Heffers started selling classical records at 20 Trinity Street in the 1980s. After the removal of the Video department in 1988, the Music department was expanded and became Heffers Sound, relocating in October 1990 to 19 Trinity Street, it specialised in classical and jazz. Mark Jones worked at Heffers Sound from 2001 to 2005:

"I'd been a fan of Heffers Sound since my teens, when I'd rifle the racks in search of records I'd heard on Radio 3 and stare up at shelves heaving with Wagner box-sets I couldn't afford. I also loved the aroma of the shop. Impossible to describe, it was utterly distinctive, in a pleasing way. I can still summon it up in my memory – an aroma I associate with lazy afternoons spent bunking off sixth-form to go in search of fabulous music."

One year, on the last Saturday before Christmas, whilst putting a refund through for a Russian student, Mark accidentally swiped her debit card before first entering the amount to be refunded. Automatically, the till instantly refunded the first four digits of her card number. On the busiest and most profitable day of the entire year, Mark had given away £4,567. His manager was very understanding and the money was

Advertising slogan devised by Frank Collieson.

returned after a week or so (the student had to ask her bank to refund the refund). The cash register was reprogrammed to prevent a similar error from ever happening again.

Business was clearly taken very seriously in this branch, to the extent that 'industrial espionage' was occasionally undertaken by staff members: Sarah Burton, at Heffers Sound for seven years from 2000, was once sent over to the local Borders bookshop to assess their classical music department and report back. Blackwell's have since absorbed the Music department back into the main Trinity Street shop.

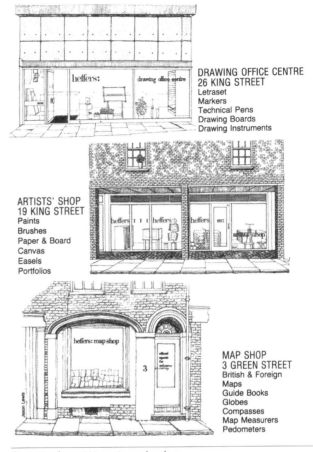

DRAWING OFFICE CENTRE
26 KING STREET
Letraset
Markers
Technical Pens
Drawing Boards
Drawing Instruments

ARTISTS' SHOP
19 KING STREET
Paints
Brushes
Paper & Board
Canvas
Easels
Portfolios

MAP SHOP
3 GREEN STREET
British & Foreign
Maps
Guide Books
Globes
Compasses
Map Measurers
Pedometers

Illustration from 1980s stationery brochure.

MAPS

Heffers Map shop at 3 Green Street was bought from W.P. Spalding in 1976, and the branch was rebranded as a Heffers branch, before being relocated to the third floor of Sidney Street in 1983. Heffers were official Ordnance Survey agents. There was later a Heffers Map shop at 61 Clifton Road in Cambridge. Currently maps are sold at the Trinity Street shop.

ART & GRAPHICS

Heffers Artists Shop at 21 King Street and the Drawing Office Centre across the road at number 26 were opened in 1972. In 1989 they were combined to form a single Art & Graphics shop and on 11th July the *Cambridge Evening News* announced, 'Shuffle of shops leaves Heffers a King Street run'. The shop was sold by Blackwell's in 2005, although artists materials are still sold at Trinity Street.

THE GRAFTON CENTRE

In October 1983, Heffers opened their largest outside shop in Cambridge at the Grafton Centre (part of the Kite redevelopment – so-called because of the Kite-like shape of the development area). The shop was overseen by Stephen Heffer and Fiona Waters, and initially managed by Suzanne Jones. *Trinity Street News* announced in 1983: 'It will be a

The Grafton Centre shop.   Stephen Heffer and Suzanne Jones greet Her Majesty.

general bookshop in the fullest sense of the word'. The intention was to stock nothing but books. At the time, the shop boasted a larger floorspace than any of the other outside shops – at 1,500 square feet.

The *Cambridge Evening News* noted on 10th August how close the new location was to where the firm began, declaring, 'Heffers go back in going forward'. Indeed, the new store was just a few yards from the site of the original Fitzroy Street shop. Four of the six staff came from existing Heffers stores and the other two were school-leavers. When formally opening the Grafton Centre in May 1984, Her Majesty Queen Elizabeth went into Heffers where she met Stephen Heffer and Suzanne Jones.

In 1991, *Heffers Bookselling News* reflected on the shop's purpose: 'We opened this bookshop to pre-empt any other bookseller opening in the Centre and to extend our offering of stock, styles, service and staff to what is essentially a different set of customers. We had a particular eye also on the proximity of Anglia Higher Education College.'

The shop manager at this time, Judith Taylor, wrote: 'Being sited in a residential area of the city, we cater very much for the local population – families, local schools and colleges, local businesses, their employees and, at weekends, "out-of-towners" on a shopping expedition.'

The opening of the Grafton Centre shop had prompted the closure of the Book department at Sidney Street, as part of the major changes that took place in the firm in 1984. In 1996 Heffers moved the shop to larger premises within the Grafton Centre shop, saying that it had been too small to attract enough customers. The new shop had approximately three times the selling space, at about 4,500 square feet. This branch survived longer than the other outside shops, finally closing in 2008.

ANTIQUARIAN

Heffers had a Second-hand book department up to 1974 when, due to lack of space, the stock was sold to Deighton Bell, an antiquarian bookseller older even than Heffers (in Trinity Street since 1794). From 1974, all departments were individually responsible for second-hand sales where appropriate, and Heffers retained a search service for out-of-print books via *The Clique* magazine. In April 1987, the *Cambridge Evening News* reported John Welch as saying:

"When I came to Heffers in 1964 my first achievement was to lease part of their ground floor to set up Heffers Paperback shop ... When we closed our own secondhand department [in 1974], we sold the stock to Deighton Bell and since then our relationship has been very good, recommending customers and referring orders and vice versa."

In 1987 the relationship became even closer when Deighton Bell was acquired by Heffers to become the firm's dedicated second-hand and antiquarian bookshop. The shop-front was remodelled and the ground-floor partitions between it and the Paperback shop were removed. However, according to J.R. Topham, in his 1998 history of Cambridge publishing and bookselling, with the high cost of renting the property, there was a commercial imperative to make more intensive use of the premises so in 1992 the ground floor was refitted to take Heffers' Art & Architecture department. However, like most of the other outside shops, this was closed following the takeover by Blackwell's.

BEYOND CAMBRIDGE

The original proposal for a shop in Hitchin (*see p. 77*) may have come to nothing, but there were two other ventures outside Cambridge that did, however, go ahead; in Norwich and Northampton. Heffers opened a Penguin Bookshop at 14 Pottergate, Norwich in 1965 (perhaps detecting an emerging academic market with the inauguration of the University of East Anglia in the city two years previously). It was a short-lived experiment, an attempt to repeat the success of the Cambridge Penguin shop but was closed by 1967. An equally short-lived Heffers branch in Northampton opened around 1997/98, but was closed following Heffers' sale to Blackwell's in 1999.

One of Heffers' tactical acquisitions was the business of the Biography Bookshop in London's Covent Garden, bought in 1988. This stock was transferred to the main Trinity Street shop. Quoted in the *Cambridge Evening News* in January 1988, John Welch stated: "I have always felt that the Biography Bookshop was a splendid example of specialisation in the world of book-selling ... Biography is a vital bridge between academic and general books." Bookseller Richard Reynolds remembers the acquisition and believes the firm made it in order to access the Biography Bookshop's customer list. Richard had the task of fitting all the stock in:

"Literature had to 'budge up' and make room. We ended up with twenty-four big drops [bookcases] of biography and within a year cut it down to twelve ... We were getting calls from all over the world for the biography section. We also had complaints, including one about Marilyn Monroe being shelved next to Lord Mountbatten. Some seemed to think we were dumbing down."

Resolving the stock amalgamation taught Richard a great deal about researching stock.

This book comes from

Heffers
Penguin Bookshop

14 Pottergate
Norwich NOR68G
Telephone 20898

EVERY TITLE IN PRINT IN STOCK

COMMERCIAL STATIONERY AND OFFICE FURNITURE

A Drawing Office Supplies department was originally established at Sidney Street and moved to the Drawing Office Centre in King Street in 1972. The business continued to expand at the new location and some parts were subsequently transferred to premises in Malcolm Place, Cambridge, where a showroom, a small warehouse and buying and order offices were established, the Drawing Office Centre itself remaining close-by in King Street. The expanded operation included office furniture besides drawing office equipment. After further expansion in the early 1980s, the commercial stationery operation was moved to a new showroom of some 6,000 square feet. This was sited opposite Heffers printing works in Kilmaine Close, in the King's Hedges area of Cambridge.

In late 1989, Heffers took on the lease of a larger showroom (9,000 square feet) at Cambridge Business Park, on the other side of Milton Road from the Science Park, and the Kilmaine Close showroom was closed. On 24th January 1990, the *Cambridge Evening News* hailed this new facility as a one-stop shop, the first of its kind, a business supermarket. The new operation was officially opened by former ICI Chairman, Sir John Harvey-Jones MBE (who, incidentally, as an author, did book signings at Trinity Street from time to time).

Although not in the city centre, the opening of a Staples stationery superstore, at Mitcham's Corner, had an impact on commercial stationery sales in the main Sidney Street shop. During 1991/92, shop sales were down 5 per cent and commercial stationery down by 14 per cent. Profit was still down in 1993/94, despite the new Staples store not having a significant effect on the direct and contract sales of the Kilmaine Close showroom. The economic recession across the UK was a contributing factor. After very protracted negotiations over tenancies at the Cambridge Business Park showroom, the decision was taken to move out of the site entirely. Eventually, the Office Furniture and Large Scale Mapping departments were moved from the Business Centre to spare accommodation on the first floor at Rustat House (*see p.140*).

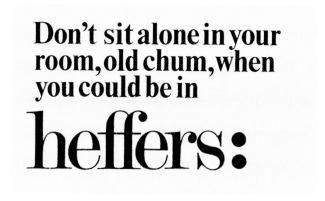

Advertising slogan devised by Frank Collieson.

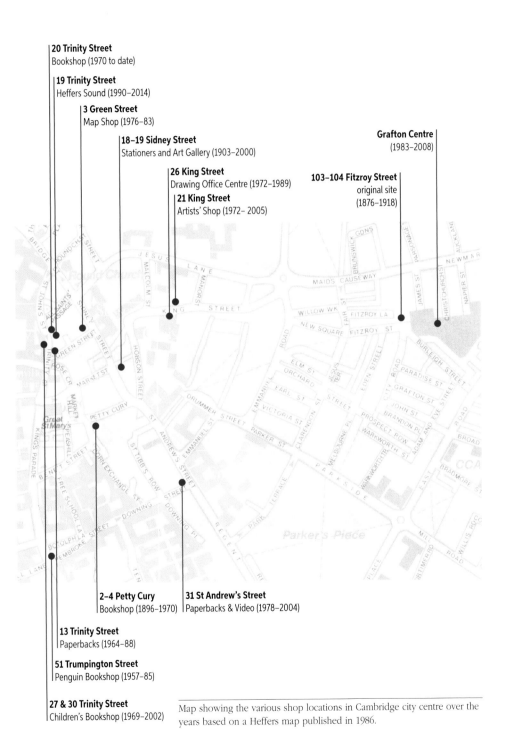

20 Trinity Street
Bookshop (1970 to date)

19 Trinity Street
Heffers Sound (1990–2014)

3 Green Street
Map Shop (1976–83)

18–19 Sidney Street
Stationers and Art Gallery (1903–2000)

Grafton Centre
(1983–2008)

26 King Street
Drawing Office Centre (1972–1989)

21 King Street
Artists' Shop (1972– 2005)

103–104 Fitzroy Street
original site
(1876–1918)

2–4 Petty Cury
Bookshop (1896–1970)

31 St Andrew's Street
Paperbacks & Video (1978–2004)

13 Trinity Street
Paperbacks (1964–88)

51 Trumpington Street
Penguin Bookshop (1957–85)

27 & 30 Trinity Street
Children's Bookshop (1969–2002)

Map showing the various shop locations in Cambridge city centre over the years based on a Heffers map published in 1986.

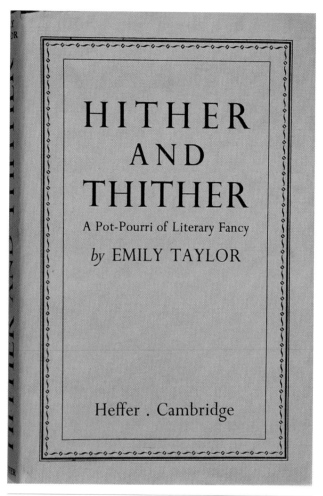

HITHER
AND
THITHER

A Pot-Pourri of Literary Fancy

by EMILY TAYLOR

Heffer . Cambridge

"Infinite riches in a little room" – In this small book a variety of subjects, all significant, and of very near and human interest, is treated with the charm which is bred of sympathy and with purpose born of passion. It is the underlying feeling which gives quality and character to the book. The interest never flags, and the style is clear and natural, so that the reader can, with the author, subdue under his yoke vast stores of knowledge gathered in many fields and penetrate to the heart of the matter.

Flap copy from this 1938 edition of a Heffer publication, priced at 4s 6d net. Topics covered include *Absence of Mind*, *Cheese*, *Attics* and *Bridges*.

7

PUBLISHER AND PRINTER

CREATING HEFFERS CLASSICS

For much of the twentieth century, Heffers was not just a celebrated bookseller and stationer, but also a publisher and printer. In fact, the first publication to bear the name on its title page – 'Cambridge: W. Heffer, Fitzroy Street' – was issued in 1889. It was a small blue cloth-bound book of some fifty-five pages, by the sub-librarian of Trinity College, one William White, with the snappy title, *A Jubilee Memorial of the Consecration of Christ Church, Cambridge: Which Took Place 27 June 1839. To Which is Prefixed a Short History of Barnwell Priory From its Foundation to the Present Time.* As Heffers was then solely a retailer, it was printed by Metcalfe & Sons of Cambridge.

Why William decided to publish the book is unknown (perhaps White was a friend or a valued customer). From this inauspicious beginning, all went quiet for a few years until he launched his publishing list proper in 1900, with *Lyra Fumosa*, a short volume of 'college canticles' by the Welsh physicist and educator Ernest Howard Griffiths, selling for 3 shillings (the cost of publishing and the profits were divided equally between author and publisher). A brief notice announcing the publication appeared in *The Times*.

Heffers first described itself as a publisher in advertisements in the very early 1900s. The list grew with the firm's expansion into printing. By the start of the Second World War, the firm was issuing upwards of forty titles a year on a wide range of subjects. Most, if not all, presumably manufactured at Heffers own printing facility. Distribution to the book trade was initially via the London

wholesaler Simpkin Marshall – until an incendiary bomb destroyed their premises in December 1940 (Heffers had used the firm for the carriage of their goods, on and off, since 1898). They also used Suttons.

Chris Jakes, Librarian in charge of the Cambridgeshire Collection until his retirement in 2016, says "a lot of Heffers volumes were of local interest. If you wanted a book published about Cambridge, having it published by Heffers added that local connection and little bit of kudos to your publication." A charming little book of sonnets by Maude C. Sidgwick, priced at 1s 6d, published by Heffers in 1919 as part of a series, was described in the *Cambridge Daily News* as, 'full of the large sunlight of spiritual things' and 'altogether a sane healthy little volume'. The general and ethical subjects of the sonnets ranged from 'Destruction', 'Food' and 'Entanglements' to 'Vision', 'Inspiration' and 'Perfection'. [35] A guide map of the borough of Cambridge published by Heffers in 1920 (also priced at 1s 6d) was described as 'one of the most useful publications I have seen for quite a considerable time' in the *Cambridge Daily News*. [36]

By the 1950s the Heffers list comprised monographs, essays, texts and pamphlets on everything from topography, drama and natural history to theology, mathematics and biochemistry, as well as local guidebooks, private publications and contemplations on current affairs. As Frank Collieson acknowledged, this was a period during which similar bookshops throughout the UK, notably John Smith in Glasgow, James Thin in Edinburgh and Blackwell's in Oxford were all moving into publishing: "It's incredible now to think of it but I'm so glad they did." Alison Blair-Underwood agrees: "They were avant-garde. There was no rhyme or reason to the publishing and it was really interesting if you have an eclectic mind."

Heffers publishing was wound down in the 1960s and ceased altogether in 1975, leaving behind a list of largely forgotten titles. Nevertheless, some had sold well, such as Arthur B. Gray's historical miscellany *Cambridge Revisited*, still in print in the 1970s; the botanist J.C. Willis's perennially updated *Tube-Bus Guide to London*, with maps drawn by his daughter Margaret (third edition, 1932); and Arnold Whitaker's *Concise Anatomy of the Foot* (1931), which had strode into its fifth edition by 1936.

A few Heffer originals have become genre classics, including *The Insect Man*, a 1936 biography of entomologist Jean-Henri Casimir Fabre by Eleanor Doorly (later reissued by Puffin), and *The Stoneground Ghost-Tales* (1912) by E.G. Swain, a colleague and contemporary of the supernatural-story master, M.R. James. Two more classics are the *Apted Book of Country Dances* (1931) by William S. Porter, and *Maggot Pie: A Book of New Country Dances* (1932), collected by William Porter and Marjorie Heffer. Both ran to several editions and had a special place in the Heffer family's affections. Ernest's eldest son, Arthur Beak Heffer, had been a leading light in the Cambridge Morris dance circle. It was Arthur's widow, Marjorie, who co-authored *Maggot Pie*, a book of new dances to old tunes, in his memory.

The firm took a great interest in publications on the topic of phonetics and as early as 1914 published *English Humour in Phonetic Transcript* by G. Noel-Armfield. This offering was part of the 'Heffer's Phonetic Series', published without orthographic transcript (no cheating allowed). In the same series (and again without orthographic transcript), we have *Poetry for Repetition*, by C.M. Rice MA.

Much later, in 1946, Heffers published, *A Phonetic Reader for Foreign Learners of English*, by E. Leonard Tibbitts BA, British Council Linguistics Officer

These two extracts from *English Humour in Phonetic Transcript* are perhaps not easy to decipher but are timeless classics.

1.

ˈhiz ˈfəːst ˈpeiʃ(ə)nt.

ə ˈdɔktəz ˈlitl ˈsʌn wəz ˈplei(i)ŋ wið ə jʌŋ ˈfrend in ðə ˈsəːdʒ(ə)ri, (h)wen ˈsʌdnli ðə bɔiz ˈoup(ə)nd ə ˈkʌbəd in (h)witʃ ð(ɛ)ə wəz ə ˈskelit(ə)n, ˈmʌtʃ tə ðə ˈhɔrə(r) əv ðə ˈvizitə. (h)wen ðə ˈlætə(r) əd¹ riˈkʌvəd səˈfiʃ(ə)ntli frəm ðə ˈʃɔk tə ˈstænd ði əˈnaunsmənt, ðə ˈdɔktəz sʌn iksˈpleind ðət (h)iz ˈfɑːðə wəz iksˈtriːmli ˈpraud əv ðæt ˈskelit(ə)n.

"ˈiz (h)iˈ," ɑːskt ðə ˈlæd, "ˈ(h)wai?"

"ai ˈdoun(t) ˈnou²," wəz ði ˈɑːnsə, "bʌt, ai ˈθiŋk it wəz (h)iz ˈfəːst ˈpeiʃ(ə)nt."

6.

ˈ(h)wɔt dəz ˈdʒɔˈmeikə¹ˈ ˈmiːn?

ˈmeni ˈpiːpl mei (h)əv ˈnoutist ðət in ˈveri ˈræpid ənd ˈsʌm(h)wɔt ˈkɛəlis ˈspiːtʃ ðə ˈwəːdz ˈd(uː) ˈjuˈ ən(d) ˈˈdid juˈ ə(r) ˈɔˈf(t)n prəˈnaunst² ˈdʒə.ˈ ðis ˈslipʃəd prə-nʌnsiˈeiʃ(ə)n ˈsʌmtaimz liːdz tə ˈmisʌndəˈstændiŋ. ðə ˈfəlouiŋ ˈʃɔːt kɔnvəˈseiʃ(ə)n biˈtwiːn tuː ˈhʌzbən(d)z³ əˈfɔːdz ən əˈmjuːziŋ igˈzɑːmpl əv ˈsʌtʃ ˈmisʌndəˈstændiŋ.

ˈfəːst ˈhʌzbənd : "mai ˈwaif s ˈgɔˈn tə ðə ˈwest ˈindiz."

ˈsek(ə)nd ˈhʌzbənd : "dʒɔˈmeikə?"

ˈfəːst ˈhʌzbənd : "ˈnou,—ʃiˈ ˈwent biˈkɔˈz ʃiˈ ˈwɔntid tə ˈgou."

(reprinted 1950 and 1955). The somewhat comedic fables in this publication include 'The way to make coffee', 'Miss Farmer loses her nearest and dearest', 'Rupert behaves well' and 'A slip of the tongue'. Daniel Jones MA, Dr Phil., writes in his Preface: 'He has written all the texts himself, and has been at pains to ensure that the narratives are in an easy and natural style such as would normally be used by Southern English speakers.' Presumably any

At *Saynte Benedict's Churche* we did put yᵉ ſyde auter upon wheeles & did ſelle it, yᵗ it myght be once more an ice cream Barrowe. And over yᵉ ſaide Barrowe, in yᵉ voyde panell wᶜʰ did crye oute for an inſcription, we did write theſe ſeemlie wordes: 𝕾𝖎𝖘𝖙𝖊 𝕰𝖒𝖕𝖙𝖔𝖗. We burned yᵉ Valance yᵗ made yᵉ high auter appere like yᵉ bedde of goode Queene Victoria, & for yᵉ reſte did ſtraitlie require yᵉ churche to be orderede agayne as it was in yᵉ ſecond yere of Maſter Davey, whenne it was without trifling gaudes & was exceedinge goode. Item, we brake downe .i. Children's Corner.

And whenne we hadde made an ende of our Viſitatione of Cambridge, we haſted awaye withe all ſpeede leſt we ſhᵈ ſuffere a Miſchief.

PRINTED BY W. HEFFER & SONS LTD., CAMBRIDGE

Two paragraphs from Brittain and Manning's whimsical pamphlet.

Northern accent, or indeed any other English regional brogue, was deemed too difficult for foreigners to comprehend. A companion volume, *English Conversations*, by N.C. Scott, was also published by Heffers.

While the phonetics publications are perfectly serious in their intent, there were occasional volumes that definitely aimed to amuse. *Babylon Bruis'd and Mount Moriah Mended* by F. Brittain & Bernard Manning, Fellows of Jesus College, first appeared in 1940 and has been reprinted a number of times. This twelve-page pamphlet is a parody of William Dowsing's journal. Dowsing, a sixteenth-century Puritan iconoclast, visited some 250 parish churches in Cambridgeshire and Suffolk, breaking up icons, pictures, crosses, crucifixes and so on, in late 1643 and in 1644. He also visited all the Cambridge University colleges with the same intent.

Not all Heffers publications sold in great numbers. A biography of the code-breaker Alan Turing by his mother, Sara Turing, was published in 1959, five years after Turing's death: a brave move on the part of Heffers. Despite receiving good reviews, according to the author in 1967, scarcely 300 of the 500-copy print run were sold. It has since been reissued, but these days a first edition is one

Alan M. Turing

by SARA TURING

HEFFER · CAMBRIDGE

First edition of *Alan M. Turing* by his mother, Sara Turing, published by Heffers in 1959.

of the more collectable – and expensive – Heffer publications. The *Times Literary Supplement* of February1960 reviewed the book, stating what is especially valuable is the anecdotal material showing how one type of mathematician is made.

Heffers were not always so courageous in their publishing and printing decisions. According to the *Cambridge Independent Press*, in April 1916, the firm 'very properly refused' to print a bill announcing an open-air meeting on Parker's Piece, arranged by the Independent Labour Party with guest speaker, Miss Sylvia Pankhurst, 'whose views on the war have made her even more notorious than her antics as a suffragette'. Although in their 1909 booklet on the firm, Heffers included in their list of questions they attempt to answer with their informed literature, 'Where can I get particulars for or against a debate on "Women's Suffrage"?', perhaps a 'Stop the War' meeting was a step too far.

Several publications on the Heffers list were cast into the bargain bin, never to reappear. Intriguing titles like *The Problem of the Future Life* (1925), *Whatsoever Things are Lovely ... Think on these Things* (1927), *Mathematical Snack Bar* (1936), *The Delights of Dictatorship* (1938), *Finland in Summer* (1938), *The Taylors of Ongar* (1938) and *Prayers for a One-Year-Old* (1927) were all remaindered in the 1940s. The stock of another, *The Two Coins: An English Girl's Thoughts on Modern Morals* (1931) by E.D. Hutchinson, was returned to the author's agent in 1932.

CONTENDERS FOR THE ODDEST TITLE

Those who work in the book trade, and others, may know about the annual *Bookseller*/Diagram Prize for the *Oddest Title of the Year* (of a book), instigated by Diagram Group director, Trevor Bounford, at the Frankfurt Book Fair in 1978. Amongst the neglected Heffers treatises on, for example, the history of education in Iceland, works on the artificial insemination of cattle, and the syntax of attican Greek, are several other curious or bizarre titles that would have been worthy contenders for the prize, remembered here:

> *The Physiology of the Human Labyrinth* (1910) by S. Scott.
> *Through a College Keyhole* (1911) by AGC (aka August Gabler Christoph, 1767–1839).
> *Elizabethan Drama and its Mad Folk: The Harness Prize Essay for 1913* (1914) by Edgar Allison Peers.
> *Bits of Things* (1914), poems by 'Five Girton Students' (who were, it seems, Monica M. Curtis, Rosalind G. Smith, Sigrid L.S. Pearson, Margaret I. Postgate and Kathleen M. Coates).
> *Divorce as it Might Be* (1915) by E.S.P. Haynes.
> *Control: An Address to School-masters, and to All who Work, or are About to Work, with Boys* (1916) by E.A. Fenn.

Some odd sounding titles are worthy of further explanation.

> *An Introduction to String Figures: An Amusement for Everybody* (1920) by W.W. Rouse Ball.

Based on a lecture given at the Royal Institution, London, by the author, a Fellow of Trinity College and a Cambridge town councillor, the making of string figures is described as a game common among primitive people, a hobby that is fascinating to most and readily mastered. A review in the *Cambridge Daily News* on 30th October 1920 suggests that Mr Rouse Ball might consider the advisability of instructing his fellow town councillors in the art: 'It might help them to pass the time during exceptionally dull debates, and it would add to the harmony of the proceedings.' For his lecture and publication, W.W. Rouse Ball drew on Kathleen Haddon's 1912 publication *Cat's Cradles from Many Lands* (Longmans, Green & Co). It sold well and Heffers published a second edition in 1921, followed by a third.

Dover Publications republished it in 1971, as *Fun with String Figures* by W.W. Rouse Ball and Walter William Ball. However, Heffers' interest in string did not end in 1921: from 1934 they published several editions of *String Games for Beginners,* by Kathleen Haddon.

Haddon, an anthropologist, extolls the benefits of string games as one of the best possible ways of making friends with 'natives', citing her own experience of arriving alone at a village up the Fly river in Papua where no white woman had been before. Remembering her string, she began to make some cat's cradles and immediately the natives crowded round delighted to see her new figures and eager to show her theirs. As she says, 'string can tie up friendships just as securely as it ties up Christmas parcels'. The title was included in the 1968–69 catalogue of Heffers publications with this recommendation: 'It's exactly the thing for any parent with any car-sick child, with any child who's got mumps, measles chicken-pox or anything else. [Broadcaster] Cliff Michelmore's enthusiastic review on the radio of this old Heffer publication sparked off a tremendous demand for it.'

(*Above*) promotion for *String Figures* on a Heffers bookmark, and (*below*) 1958 edition of Haddon's *String Games.*

> *Sketches from a Library Window* (1922) by B. Anderton.
> *The Oral Method* (1922) by H.E. Palmer.
> *Cupid's Auction* (1923) by E. Hamilton Moore.

> *65 Don'ts for Church Organists* (1921) by John Newton.

This book of instruction must have sold well as it was revised in 1922 and was followed by *Don'ts for Choirmasters* (1924), *Don'ts for Choirmen* (1925) and *Don'ts for Choirboys* (1926). Frank Collieson acknowledged that it was possible between the wars to publish minor works and sometimes people paid to have them published; works that people bought, works that people reviewed. The 'Don'ts' would have been written by a practical organist or choirmaster and contained good advice such as, 'don't keep the boys late on practice nights. Nine o'clock is too late. All mothers will tell you that'.

> *And in the Tomb Were Found …* (1923) by Terence Grey.

Dramatic reconstructions of early Egypt in verse, which, according to a review in *The Spectator,* had 'a sensuous charm in their decoration, but the body of the book is rather boneless'.

Some Truths About Opium (1923) by Herbert Allen Giles.

Frank Collieson commented: "It may be considered subversive today but this was by the professor of Chinese in the University of Cambridge. An historical and literary study of opium. Towards the end you get a warning note that indulgence in opium is moreover supposed to blunt the moral feelings of those who indulge. 'If your servant smokes opium, dismiss him with as little compunction as you would a drunken coachman.'"

Chaos in China: A Rhapsody (1924) by Prof. H.A. Giles.
Prehistoric Man and the Cambridge Gravels (1926) by Rev. F. Smith.
Essays – Mainly Rejected (1926) by E. Binney.
Christ's Hospital from a Boy's Point of View (1928) by W.M. Digues La Touche.
Table Tennis To-Day (1924) by Ivor Montagu.
Stars and their Uses (1925) by E.B. Leggett. (A second edition was printed privately for the author in a run of 500; twelve were kept for sale by Heffers.)
Egypt and the Isle of Wight (1928) by J. Rendel Harris, is a series of essays from this biblical scholar on subjects such as mustard, barley, the Gold Coast and 'a new Stonehenge'.
The Fringes of Her Gown (1928) by A. Laurie-Walker. (The author paid all the production costs.)
Slowly Forward: 366 Points for Oarsmen, Coxswains and Coaches, from the Writings of Steve Fairbairn. This was followed in 1934 by Fairbairn's *Chats on Rowing*.
My Quota (1931) by J.E. Swallow.
Paper Aeroplanes: A Book of Essays (1931) by H.G.G. Herklots.

The Science of Shaving, published anonymously (1931). This publication, written in the style of Chaucer, quotes 'The Merchant's Tale':

'he kisseth hire ful ofte;
With thikke brustles of his berd unsofte'
(Lines 611–612)

And contains the footnote: 'I've had evidence that where a woman and a rubber shaving brush abide under the same roof, the former is apt to misappropriate the latter for facial massage.' Frank Collieson described this as a marvellous work, a form of belle-lettres. "I suspect that the author who wrote under a nom de plume paid for it … It would have been printed in the small editions and it would have been noticed in those days in the many undergraduate papers like *The Cambridge Review*. Quite impossible today to do it."

Economics is a Serious Subject (1932) by Joan Robinson.
How Many Children Had Lady Macbeth? (1933) by L.C. Knights.
Plagiarism: An Essay on Good and Bad Borrowing (1933) by W.A. Edwards.
Camps for Men (1933) by Michael Sims-Williams.
Life Saving Made Easy: A New and Original Method (1934) by H.C. Hopkinson.
It Might Have Happened: A Sketch of the Later Career of Rupert Lister Audenard,

First Earl of Slype, KG, PC, Twice Prime Minister of Great Britain (1934) by R. Egerton Startwout.
The Schoolboy: A Study of His Nutrition, Physical Development and Health (1935) by G.E. Friend.
New Yet Old (1935) by Denzil Laborde.
The Pronunciation of Twi (1939) by Ida C Ward. This was later followed by two titles in 1951 from Jack Berry: *The Pronunciation of Ewe* and *The Pronunciation of Ga.*
Shakespeare's Son-in-Law, John Hall (1939) by Arthur Gray.
Road Accidents in War-Time (1941) by H.M. Vernon.
Shakespeare on Aliens Learning English (1942) by David Daube.
To What End is the Dawn? (1942) by F/Lt CR Sanderson.
The House Cow: How to Buy and Look After Her (1949) by Stuart & Pamela Johnston.

The 1968–69 catalogue of Heffers titles included *East Anglian Studies*, edited by Lionel M. Munby, with this recommendation:

'The time for publishing such a collection is opportune. Eastern England is a region unduly neglected by government agencies and by planners. It is a rapidly growing area with a varied character of its own. Its geography and history, the factors which explain a modern community, need to be better known and appreciated.'

This catalogue also included titles in French and German such as *Cambridge en un Jour* by Ruth Mellanby.

Transcriptions of lectures were also published by Heffers. The 1968–69 catalogue lists the *Churchill College Overseas Fellowship Lectures*, with this description:

'Each year a number of distinguished scholars are invited as Overseas Fellows to Churchill College, Cambridge. During the course of their Fellowship they are asked to give a lecture in their special field but designed to appeal to a wide audience. Some of these lectures are being made available in permanent form.'

Ruth Mellanby's *Cambridge en un Jour* was first published by Heffers in 1955.

97

One of the lectures was, *Why Literary Criticism is Not an Exact Science* by Harry Levin, Irving Babbitt Professor of Comparative Literature, Harvard University.

In September 1975 the staff newsletter, *Trinity Street News*, stated:

> 'The dismantlement of Heffer publishing – necessary, but inevitably tinged with a little sadness and much nostalgia – has continued efficiently and with financial success. It has been particularly gratifying to find good homes for many of our long-established best-sellers in the fields of medicine and language teaching. Houses like Macmillan and Cambridge University Press will keep some of our titles in print and in the course of time will publish new editions. This is very good news for us and for the heirs and assigns of the original authors.'

PERIODICALS

As a printer and publisher, Heffers also produced many periodicals. The 1968–69 catalogue included the titles *Antiquity*; *The Chartered Secretary; English Philological Studies*; *History of Science*; *Italian Studies*; *The Medico-Legal Journal*; *The Music Review*; and *Newcomen Society Transactions*. The firm also acted as distributing agent for a number of other journals, such as the *Journal of the International Folk Music Council*.

The Periodicals department, which had handled subscriptions to learned journals of all kinds, closed in June 1979. In 1980, the management combed through all the magazines and journals that the firm had acquired over the years and 'firmly' took the stand that Heffers are '*book* sellers only'. Sandra Thompson (*née* Hornsby) worked in the Periodicals department in the early 1960s, when hundreds of obscure or academic titles were produced and sent all over the world. Although profitable at the time, it was closed because the net trading margin was small, the running costs were escalating and it was not an economic proposition to invest in computerising the department. This decision was taken two years after the firm had acquired its first computer system. As with many firms during this period, computerisation would become a major factor affecting business profitability.

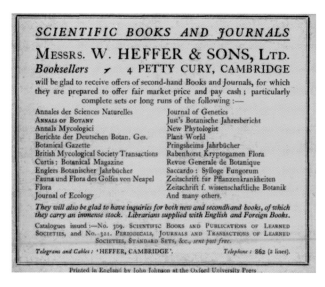

THE CAMBRIDGE REVIEW

Reuben Heffer is credited with saving *The Cambridge Review* (*A Journal of University Life and Thought*) in 1939, when its publisher, Fabb and Tyler, was forced to close. The journal, first issued in 1879, was a fixture of Cambridge academia. Citing Heffers' publishing diary, Frank Collieson in *Remembering Reuben* relates the moment when father and son were poised by the telephone,

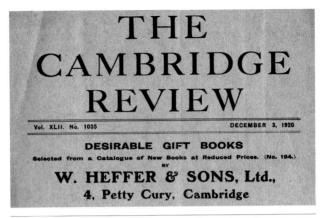

Part of the 1920 *Cambridge Review* verse supplement (green) cover.

awaiting a call from the Cambridge scholar Bernard Manning to confirm whether or not the firm's offer to publish not only the attendant list of *Resident Members* (which John Austin Fabb himself instigated in 1890) but the full *Review*, was accepted. The answer was yes, and the first edition published and printed by Heffers was issued on 14th October 1939. That issue's editorial stated:

'Mr E. J. A. Fabb

It is with real regret that we have to record the closing of the firm of Fabb and Tyler, the home of The Review since its birth sixty year ago. The many friends of Mr E. J. A. Fabb, while expressing their sympathy with him in the loss of his business, will wish him all prosperity in his new work with Messrs. Heffer, who have undertaken the publishing of The Review, and a hope that he will continue to interest himself in the journal which can never be dissociated from the name he bears. To his late father and himself our thanks are due for the never-failing care and enthusiasm bestowed by them upon the weekly appearance of our pages throughout so many generations of academic life.'

The *Cambridge Daily News* reported the change on 7th October 1939, in Robin Goodfellow's 'Table Talk', saying, 'War brings many changes to Cambridge we know, but I had a real shock this morning when I learned that the priceless institution, the "Cambridge Review" is affected.' Addressing those who, 'had grown attached to the old style', Goodfellow quoted assurances from Heffers that there will be 'no forgetting' the dignities of tradition, 'while it is hoped that the new form may attract the interest of some who have never thought to penetrate the familiar light blue covers'. Cambridge without *The Cambridge Review* was deemed unthinkable.

It is recorded in the publishing diary that Ernest was keen to publish the attendant list of *Resident Members* as a separate venture and that Reuben felt it was a mistake to miss the *Review*, 'that we ought to have it'. The distinction between the two different features of the publication was brought out much later, by Homberger, Janeway and Schama in their anthology of the *Review*, issued to mark its 90th birthday in 1970. While it has acted as a forum of debate about the work and future of the University itself, it has always been, 'much more than a dons' house magazine'. *The Cambridge Review* continued for many years after the Heffers acquisition and, after 119 volumes in total, finally ceased publication in 1998.

HEFFERS AS PRINTERS

In 1909, Heffers had been keen to promote the services of the Eagle printing works, a small Cambridge firm based in Hobson's Passage that had been acquired by the firm and which, by that time, was managed by Frank Heffer. In 1911 they also acquired the Black Bear Press (Dixon's Printing Works Ltd) at 104 Hills Road, Cambridge. Under the terms of that sale, Heffers were not permitted to use the title, 'Black Bear Press', as the 'Goodwill' had not been included in the purchase. (They had been offered the business, including the Goodwill for a sum of £3,500 but in the end bought the machinery and plant only, for £1,875 – £200,000 at today's value.) Both operations were amalgamated to form Heffers printing works, employing thirty people. Sidney Heffer says in his biography that 'William had no experience of printing. Nevertheless, the matter interested him, and it opened up great possibilities. He therefore decided to launch out in the printing world.' George Newman was appointed works manager in 1916: he later became a director of Heffers.

The printing business expanded rapidly between the wars and strong connections were developed with learned societies and trade associations, for whom a wide range of periodicals, books and ephemera were produced. Clients included local businesses and the University of Cambridge. The expansion gathered pace and the premises had to be enlarged in 1923, rebuilt in 1935, and further extended in 1956. In 1955 Heffers had acquired the Cambridge Express Printing Company. The Express works at one time published a weekly newspaper which was eventually incorporated with the *Cambridge Weekly News*, which in turn amalgamated with the *Cambridge Independent Press* and *Chronicle*. In 1957 the company acquired R.I. Severs Ltd (established in 1940). In 1964, these two subsidiaries merged under the name of R.I. Severs and moved to new premises in King's Hedges Road.

Between 1939 and 1955 the company had purchased a number of properties adjoining the printing works site and these were in part taken over as employees' accommodation and offices. Construction of a new warehouse was completed in 1960. By this time, the printing works employed over 200 people.

Herbert Newman had joined his father in 1924, and Charles, son of Frank Heffer, came into the firm after the Second World War; both became directors. Herbert Newman took over the management of the printing works in 1953 on his father's retirement, and retired himself from the day-to-day affairs of the company in 1973.

Over the years, Heffers Printers won many awards for the quality of their printing and production. In 1971, Boyd & Hamilton's *Human Placenta*, a Heffers production, was chosen for the British Book Production Exhibition at the National Book League in London.

A corner of the composing room of the Eagle printing works in 1909.

In 1972 Heffers sold the Hills Road plant and the following year work commenced on extending the existing buildings on the King's Hedges site to accommodate the Hills Road workforce. Builders Johnson and Bailey Ltd, who built the Severs premises in 1964, carried out the construction work. Also in 1973, a new colour lithographic printing machine from Germany was installed. Originally priced at £37,000, it was reported that the firm ended up paying a total of £50,000 (£600,000 at today's value) for the equipment due to change in currency value, German export tax and VAT. At that time, Heffers changed their operations from 20 per cent lithographic printing and 80 per cent letterpress to 60 per cent litho and 40 per cent letterpress. The firm won a 'Highly commended' award in 1974 for the quality of the printing of *Ballet and its Music* (by Judyth Knight and published by Schott and Co.). Ironically, the firm's first award for a litho print job was for a black and white production.

A glossy 1973 brochure declared:

Letterpress typesetting at Heffers printing works in 1973.

'We have absorbed the successive advances in printing technology and combined them with the proud craftsmanship of our calling. We know about and fully use the special understanding, interpretive flair, and organisational skill of our production and administrative back-up people. In our 40,000 sq. ft. of modern plant we provide a useful range of services from creative design through production to finishing and mailing.'

'What of the future? We are quietly proud of the achievements of several generations of Heffers printers. We can look back with affection to the solid accomplishments from which we have drawn our inspiration and forward to an exciting future that our heritage enables us to face with vigour and confidence.'

In the same brochure, Heffers writes about the benefits of letterpress, 'the oldest and possibly the most flexible of all printing processes … Printing direct from type is the cheapest and simplest way of producing many kinds of work, especially the technical, scientific, and learned texts in which we have a particular expertise.'

The 1970s and '80s was a difficult time for the printing trade in general. In 1975 Heffers Printers had to make eleven workers redundant following the loss of a contract to print a fortnightly electronics magazine with a controlled circulation of 25,000. This was not the main issue, however, despite the unfortunate job losses. Interviewed by the *Cambridgeshire, Huntingdon & Peterborough Life* in 1979, John Heffer declared, "Printing has changed dramatically in the last few years. Processes are becoming quicker, customers more demanding and their requirements more complex. So, unless one changes with the times, there is a certainty of losing out." From the late 1970s the tides of change swept through the printing works.

In 1979 a development plan was announced for the introduction of computerised photo-composition, involving capital expenditure of about £750,000. At the same time the firm introduced a policy of directing the work towards larger orders, moving away from journal work and towards specialist book and commercial work. It was always going to be delicate balance, with the loss of

Bryan Anstee working on page layouts in 1973.

profit from the periodicals and the impact of introducing new technology. The management team was restructured in 1982 with a view to meeting the new technical, operational and marketing challenges. In February1983 the Cambridge press reported, 'New computer is key to Heffers' flexibility', as the firm invested further in photo-composition and typesetting, along with data management, using a general purpose computer. About 45 per cent of the company's work was on books and booklets, and 35 per cent with dated journals and periodicals, from the academic to news and pictorial products. The remainder was general printing. Heffers also ran a comprehensive design service. The cost of these changes meant that in 1983 the printers had 'a very difficult year but managed a small profit'.

In 1984 the firm withdrew from hot-metal composition and from letterpress printing with seven employees being made redundant as a consequence. An Aurelia four-colour press, installed in August 1984 at the cost of about £165,000, was another capital expenditure that needed to be offset by results. In 1986, manager Richard Laming reported on the firm's ability to deal with highly technical productions such as *The Analyst*, a monthly journal for the Society of Analytical Chemists, a client since 1922. Coping with extremely complex texts like this, plus many diagrams, was routine for Heffers.

In the latter half of the 1980s, it became clear that, due to the constant need for major capital expenditure, the printing works division was in danger of damaging the profitability of the Heffers group as whole. In 1987 the board sold the printing business for around £600,000 (£1.6m at today's value) to a management buyout team headed by Richard Laming, who renamed it Black Bear Press Ltd. Other members of the team were John Sidaway, Mike Hallam, David Street and Andrew Grigor; with a total number of print staff of 140. Heffers retained the freehold of the site in King's Hedges Road and leased it to the new company.

The printing works at King's Hedges Road in 1973.

Personalised Stationery

For many years Heffers offered personalised stationery and materials, all printed at the firm's own printing works. Customers could commission specially designed cards such as the example here of the Old Mill House, produced in 1959.

Delivery note (*top*), letterpress printing block with reversed image (*centre*) and printed card.

Private Greeting Cards

In 1944 Oldfield gave this description of the printing works in the *Stationery Trade Review*:

> 'A fine modern factory with all the latest machinery for printing and binding ...
> Their Cantabrigia Series of cards is also printed and made there. So from the very
> humble beginnings in 1876 there has resulted a large and flourishing business,
> with infinite possibilities for the future.'

From as early as 1898, the firm sent typewritten circulars and postcards to customers, offering the opportunity to select their Christmas cards, private or ordinary, at their houses. From 1901 these were accompanied by catalogues which were met with, 'general appreciation' as recorded in the firm's minute book, and promotion of the 'private' and 'ordinary' cards were separated. These clearly had different customers. Department stores also purchased quantities of the cards. Prices ranged from 7s 6d to 12s 6d per dozen, or up to 70s for 100. Selfridge & Co. Ltd, Harrods Ltd, Fortnum and Mason, John Lewis & Co., and W.H. Smith & Co. were all regular puchasers, as were the Heffers Sidney Street and Petty Cury shops.

Described as 'designs of distinction and of real artistic merit', this small selection from the Cantabrigia war time catalogue features the best selling ones.

A selection of artwork for greetings cards, probably from the 1930s, commissioned by Heffers.

Another artwork from the 1930s used by Heffers on a greetings card. This illustrates life in a different era. Mother and father dress the tree while cook works in the kitchen and nanny puts the little ones to bed.

8

OFF THE SHOP FLOOR

LIBRARIES AROUND THE WORLD AND AT HOME

In 1903 Heffers offered £205 (£22,750 at today's value) for the library of the late Sir George Gabriel Stokes, physicist and mathematician. We do not know if the offer was accepted. In 1929 Heffers handled the sale of the library of the late Sir Edmund Gosse (1849–1928). It was the first of several such commissions, some of which had hidden dangers. After the death of physicist Professor Ernest Rutherford in 1937, Frank Stoakley valued his library. In Bradley's oral history of the book trade, Frank recalls what happened subsequently,

> "Two or three of his books went to America, where they tried them on a Geiger counter and it jumped all over the place. The Americans phoned Rutherford's department and spoke to the librarian: 'Who bought Rutherford's library?' 'Mr Stoakley at Heffers.' 'Is he still alive?' 'Why?' 'Whoever bought them ought to be dead. They're absolutely lousy with the radium.' So I went to see my doctor and told him what had happened. I said, 'I know George Crowe, Rutherford's assistant, because he goes fishing and shooting with my father, and he's lost two fingers from his right hand getting stuff ready for the professor to work on.' I handled those books for two weeks when I was valuing them, then when I got them to the shop it took me three days to price them up. The whole lot had gone in a fortnight – people came from all over the place for them, and they were scattered everywhere." [37]

As he lived to the grand age of 101, it would seem Frank was unharmed by the exposure. Frank also recalled an incident when books from an Egyptian medical library caused strange warts to break out all over his hands. He had to have hospital treatment every other day for month. Eve Stafford worked in the Second-hand and Antiquarian department for a while and recalls her manager, Cyril Mansfield, valuing libraries for probate. The valuation and sale of the late E.M. Forster's library in 1971, is a notable example.

The catalogue cover, which declares, 'This book belongs to E. M. Forster', reproduces, within a border, the small bookplate which appeared in the front each of Forster's books. The code word of this catalogue for cabling purposes was ABINGER. The introduction is by A.N.L. Munby, Litt.D., Fellow and Librarian of King's College, Cambridge, who says:

> 'My friend Reuben Heffer has asked me, as custodian of the main group of the late E.M. Forster's books and manuscripts at King's College to contribute a prefatory note to this catalogue of the residue of his library; and I welcome the opportunity to set down for the record certain facts which may elucidate the provenance of some of the books and be of assistance to those who study Forster and his works.'

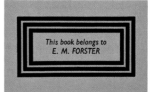

Portrait, by Edward Leigh of Cambridge, of Forster, from the catalogue. Reproduction of Forster's bookplate from the catalogue cover (*top*) and (*below*) his signature, as it appears on the back cover.

In the 1960s American scholar Steven L. Isenberg visited four British writers, W.H. Auden, Philip Larkin, William Empson and E.M. Forster. Looking back on the experience of visiting Forster in 1966, Isenberg says:

'At some point Forster began to remark on things he loved about particular colleges – their gardens and parts of the river. I followed his lead, and we wound up walking down the main street of the town; soon we were in front of Heffer's, the university's bookstore. Only then did I realize I hadn't brought a book for him to sign. I asked him if I could run in and buy one. He said, "Yes," and that he would wait outside. I ran in, totally unfamiliar with the store and suddenly worried about leaving Forster in the street alone. I don't know what I thought would happen, but I imagined headlines reporting an accident: "Forster Accompanied and Then Abandoned by a Visiting American Student." I couldn't find the novels section, but I caught sight of a hardbound edition of Lionel Trilling's book on Forster and bought it in a desperate rush. We then walked back to King's and up to his room. "Now it is time for me to go," I said, and I told him how grateful I was for his kindness. He asked where I would go, and I said back to Oxford. He said, "Let me sign your book," and without explanation, I showed him the Trilling. He smiled and drew a line through the title – his name – and signed his name.' [38]

Large scholarly collections had been more prominent in the first half of the twentieth century, and when they became available, a catalogue was prepared. Clive Cornell remembers going round to St John's College to view the library of Professor Norman Brooke Jopson (1890–1969). Clive received a call from George Porter (of Galloway & Porter), who had viewed the library and didn't think there was much there for him. George invited Clive for tea to talk about it. Clive says, "George Porter's idea of a cup of tea was a whisky bottle he kept in the filing cabinet. So we had a drink."

Heffers also, of course, sold books to libraries, locally and overseas. The Cambridge University college libraries generally had extensive budgets and whilst Heffers was (and still is) a supplier, this was not on an exclusive basis. Clive Cornell recalls that the smaller rivals Galloway & Porter had a very good share of the college library business in Cambridge. "The college librarians could walk into two or three hostelries in Cambridge, have a beer and put it on Mr Porter's account." For many years the libraries supplied were mainly academic and specialist, in colleges and universities throughout the world. Clive says: "the more specialised the books you were involved with, the more likely you had customers who'd been at Cambridge and then moved on. We had a lot of university library business in North America. I remember sitting at home writing out the addresses of American universities."

Alison Blair-Underwood, senior manager from 1974 to 2003, recalls the firm's vast turnover in library business during the 1970s and '80s, supplying, for example, the whole of Riyadh's new university: "The libraries were new and sparkling and wonderful, stuffed full of books. The packing cases couldn't be recycled and the Riyadh streets were full of them. It was a very interesting period." Alison's first manager, Robert Machesney, was chosen to learn Arabic so he could travel to the Middle East where he secured a lot of business. In 1972 Robert had undertaken the firm's first retail journey overseas, visiting university libraries in Canada. The objectives of these overseas visits were to meet many customers that the firm had previously known only by correspondence, make new customers and retrieve former customers that had been lost over the years.

Ronald Hall, Market Development manager from 1986 to 1994, also travelled widely. The idea was that he should contact all sorts of higher education establishments and offer to supply books more quickly and more cheaply than their local suppliers. The Market Development team which at one time had five representatives, regularly visited university and college libraries and international schools in many countries including Kenya, Nigeria, Singapore, Hong Kong, Ethiopia, Egypt, Iraq, Canada, Iran, France, Spain, Zambia, Germany, Ireland, Lebanon, USA, Belgium, Austria, Syria, South Africa and Switzerland. During 1989, Heffers maintained a consistent presence in Maiduguri, north-eastern Nigeria, with the intention of being well placed when the World Bank and other agencies provided aid for the refurbishment of university libraries in Nigeria.

Stephen Heffer often visited libraries abroad. His visits would be followed up by letter on his return, and then reviewed every six months. In 1982 he visited eight universities, three public libraries and several specialist libraries in Texas and found a need for the type of service which Heffers offered, with much interest in the academic catalogues. In November 1996, following his sad early death, the *Cambridge Evening News* described his career at the firm, which had begun in 1971 and had included visits to libraries across Europe and the USA. Stephen had left the firm in 1986 to pursue a career as an artist but had remained a non-executive director.

In 1989, Heffers' Market Development team reported on the firm's attempts to enter the Chinese library market. Competition from the Americans and other major UK booksellers

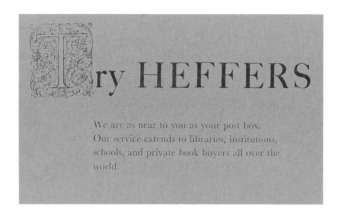

ry HEFFERS

We are as near to you as your post box. Our service extends to libraries, institutions, schools, and private book buyers all over the world.

was formidable but a new account was opened with the Shanghai Medical University Library. The library asked if Heffers would take their Foreign Publications Acquisition Librarian for training and the subsequent visit proved beneficial for both parties. Heffers had several letters written in Mandarin to use in a direct mail campaign and gained a much clearer idea of the ways in which Chinese academic libraries were allowed to use their budgets. Their guest wrote a letter of appreciation saying, 'Your endless efforts meant that I have brought back with me to China a treasure-house of information about how libraries and booksellers go about their business in England … I will tell everyone I can in China that Heffers is a first-rate organisation.'

Julian Sedgwick says he loved doing the stock pick at Trinity Street in the 1990s, and seeing the far-flung universities and libraries all over the world who would be receiving that day's orders: "It really felt like a global business then."

Heffers also supplied public libraries in the UK. In 1970 the firm acquired the Lucas Bookselling Service, based in Bootle, Lancashire, from Elwyn Jones. The business supplied thirteen major libraries in the UK, mainly in the north west. In 1972, Heffers introduced 'Heffer Selector', a blanket order service designed to automatically supply selected books to libraries. In the early 1980s, the firm agreed to 'service' the books they were supplying to Cambridgeshire, Suffolk, Essex, Northamptonshire and Hertfordshire County Libraries. This meant providing plastic jackets, labels, issuing slips, reinforcing paperbacks and so on. As a consequence, librarians regularly visited to pick from the shelves and were delighted to access the range of stock. Initially, the idea was to regulate the number of libraries serviced in this way in order to manage the process in the most economic way possible.

In 1990, Heffers acquired the institutional customers of Baker Books, supplying children's books to libraries in London and the Home Counties, and to schools in Spain. During the early 1990s, more and more local authority public libraries wanted to select material from Heffers' wide-ranging stock. Becky Proctor remembers, "we took a lot of hardbacks because libraries would come. They would go with a trolley and a footstool and you might have five librarians picking books all day." It seemed that the traditional suppliers to public libraries could not match such a range of titles in their showrooms. Librarians were also invited to view Heffers' order processing facilities. Librarian Chris Jakes, says:

> "I would visit Heffers with a list but then I'd come out with that list plus, because I'd spotted other items that I'd no idea had been published, or topics related to Cambridge and Cambridgeshire that Heffers have come at from a different angle … Personally, being a book lover, browsing is always great fun."

A Bookshop in Britain
with customers all over the world

In 1990 Heffers acquired a small library supply business called Dickinson Books, based in Blackburn, Lancashire. Dickinson Books had been suppliers to public, academic, industrial and medical libraries in the North of England, giving a personal standard of service. As a result of the acquisition, Roger Dickinson, the proprietor, became a director of the bookselling division of Heffers, bringing with him his public library supply knowhow and giving Heffers a depot in Blackburn together with a staff skilled in servicing books for libraries. Armed with this new facility, this area of the business quickly expanded and soon representatives were appointed to call on and promote it to other public libraries. The expertise and reputation for selling children's books, together with the new facility, provided an opportunity to provide a bookselling service to the Children's Library Services in many of the London boroughs, amongst other places.

Library trade throughout the 1980s and the early 1990s was strong. The directors' Annual Reports in 1983 and 1984 recorded an increase in overseas sales, and to academic and public libraries in the UK (the bookselling profits rose by 19.8 per cent and 23 per cent in those years respectively). In 1984, computer equipment was installed to handle the library servicing in the Book and Orders Handling departments. In 1987, sales showed a good increase again, although at a slower rate. According to the Annual Report for that year, cuts in funds for libraries worldwide made export sales harder to achieve and the same applied in the home market: 'Nevertheless, with two senior staff travelling at home and abroad and our continuing excellent service, we have expanded our markets. During the past year we have, in two separate months and for the first time in our history, sold over one million pounds' worth of books in a single month.'

In the mid-1990s, a severe drop in UK library sales was experienced by all library suppliers as a result of budget cutbacks and re-organisation in public libraries. Heffers took a number of actions to reduce costs, including the closure of the Blackburn depot in August 1996. Another issue was the demand from libraries for catalogue records to be provided in MARC format (i.e. machine readable form), particularly overseas – a demand which at that time Heffers' computer system could not provide, and so sales to some libraries began to decline.

Heffers retained a 'trade library', available to all staff which contained useful and interesting information on the book trade. Staff were also permitted, and indeed encouraged, to use the whole Heffers stock as a free library. Up to three books were loaned for periods of one month at a time. This perhaps mirrors Sarah Burton's view of the Trinity Street shop when she said, "Heffers has the comfort of a library."

READING CLUBS

In 1975 Heffers launched its Bookworm Club. This was not a UK first. Penguin had set up the Puffin Club (in 1967) and publisher Scholastic had also created clubs (TAB – Teen Age Book Club, Arrow, Lucy and See-Saw). Bookworm was the brainchild of John Welch, assisted by

ISSUE No3
January 1976

The Bookworm Club is a paperback club for schools run by
Heffers of Cambridge and E J Arnold of Leeds

Frank Collieson, John Cheshire, Robert Machesney and Stephen Heffer. A paperback club for schools, Bookworm was a collaboration between Heffers, educational publisher E.J. Arnold & Son of Leeds, and four leading trade publishers – Collins (Amanda/Lions), Pan (Piccolo), Hodder and Stoughton (Knight) and Transworld (Carousel/How and Why). In the first mailing, 22,000 schools received information about the club, with the first selection of twenty titles. Six bulletins a year were issued to teachers, with free stickers and bookmarks. An early flyer in 1976 declared: 'We believe that children like and need to have books of their own to increase their confidence in reading ... Bookworm also provides a basis for class discussion of books, and produces parent involvement.'

School children (initially aged eight to twelve years and then extended to include five to eight years) chose books and a club organiser collated the order, collected the children's money and sent it the club. The books were sold at the same price as in the shops but the school received 10 per cent of the value of all sales, to use as they saw fit. For the first few years, the orders were despatched by E.J. Arnold from their book distribution centre at Cumbernauld, Glasgow. In 1983, Heffers became the sole owner of the club, believing it to be a valuable acquisition that could increase the profitability of the bookselling division. Clive Cornell says: "It was quite a clever idea, in that a news-type letter was published, quite frequently and there would be selections of good children's writing in there ... riddles and giggles. They always sold first and best."

During the 1970s and '80s, the club grew from strength to strength. *Trinity Street News* reported at the time that the success was due to the splendidly original and colourful bulletins, and to the care and experience which went into selecting the right titles, and not just the obviously pot-boiling books. In 1981, the club's seventh year, Bulletin 37 went to nearly 7,000 schools and the editorial team comprised John Welch, Stephen Heffer, John Cheshire and Fiona Waters, all of whom read and selected the books. Frank Collieson wrote the copy and gave 'such excellent style to the bulletins'. That year a new club, READ ON!, targeted at teenagers, was formed in response to demand from teachers, parents and children. Michelle Kavenagh, who worked as an invoice typist for the firm in 1984/5, would sometimes go down to the warehouse to help pack books for the Bookworm Club and remembers seeing the bulletins at her own school. She still has the books she bought via the club.

The most successful Bookworm year was 1986, when over 530,000 books were sold. For the first time the club gave away pens, glove puppets, membership stickers and posters. A new club, Early Worm, specifically for children up to the age of seven, was also launched. The under-fives was a fast developing area of the children's book market and details of the new club went to 16,000 pre-school playgroups and nursery schools in addition to all the infant schools. Unlike the

Bookworm Club poster.

books in Bookworm, which were mainly bought by the children with their pocket-money, Early Worm was used by parents and teachers.

In 1994, the Bookworm Club was re-launched with a revised format. By this time, there were several similar bookselling operations run by other companies, including the Usborne Party Plans and the Red House, and the school book fairs run by Scholastic and School Book Fairs. The new look Heffers 'Club News', designed by Ben Taylor and printed by Black Bear Press, was sent to all 26,000 primary and middle schools in the UK, plus around 1,000 international schools overseas. As always, all books had to be read before they could be selected. Certain 'taboos' were avoided – 'witches, violence, bad language and sex'.

The book jacket was considered to be important. *Heffers Bookselling News* declared, 'There is no point in selecting a book if the jacket is not going to stand out on the page; it doesn't matter what we write about the book, it is the visual image that children will choose from.' A specially produced Bookworm Club Year Planner was sent with all orders and for those orders over £50, a special PVC bag; and children received a sticker with every book they bought. Heffers account holders were also targeted and a home/family club mailing list was created. All the orders were processed at the Book and Orders Handling departments (by the 1990s located at Rustat House – *see p.140*). After Heffers was bought by Blackwell's in 1999, the book clubs were sold.

The following feature, some content of which would almost certainly be considered 'politically incorrect' today, appeared in the spoof newsletter, *Trinity Street Blues*, in 1986:

CAN OF WORMS
Following up the success of our recent onslaught on the Early-Reading and Pre-Reading sectors of the children's market, we are pleased to announce a diversification of our campaign. Months of market research involving

interviews with thousands of under-fives in the Isle of Ely have enabled us to identify a number of customer profiles in the specialised areas. Each will now receive its own tailor-made 'worm' with a back-up staff of dozens of specialists meeting every fifteen minutes here at Trinity Street to select the most suitable books.

For instance: EARTHWORM will be aimed at the ecology-conscious child, whose parents shop at Arjuna. GLOWORM will be for that perennial pest, the precocious brat. Its counterpart will be the WOODWORM – specially designed for the child as thick as two short planks. The next grade up will be catered for by SLOWORM – for the E.S.N. In a brave attempt to counteract physical prejudice in schools, we are introducing LUGWORM – for the child with embarrassingly large ears. RAGWORM will cater for the designer-scruffy end of the market, while BLINDWORM will be printed in Braille. FLAWORM needs no description from us, and any other suggestion of likely Nematoda will be warmly welcomed. Wriggle, wriggle.

RINGWORM – Dial-a-bedtime-story. (Subject to negotiation with British Telecom).
THREADWORM – Ingeniously cross-referenced volumes for youngsters who are always losing it.
MEALWORM – Recipe books for aspiring young cooks.
LOBWORM For the hyperactive child/sports enthusiast.
CASEWORM – Whodunnits for young adults.
ROOKWORM – Tattily produced books at exorbitant prices for children with more pocket money than sense.
ROUNDWORM – For the chubby child.
SILKWORM – Casebooks for the aspiring young advocate.
WIREWORM – Books that get the message across quickly.

THE FIRST CHILDREN'S CATALOGUE

Claire Brown, who set up Heffers Children's Bookshop in 1968, also compiled the first Heffers Children's Catalogue. Claire held strong views (and still does) on child and adult reading, as demonstrated by this letter she wrote to her prospective in-laws on 27th August 1969:

In my opinion (and experience, as far as it goes) the really well-read and intelligent child, with access to unlimited books, will read just books, *choosing the subjects that appeal to him, whatsoever the author, and whatever the supposed age group of the book. For this reason, I obviously think it is equally ridiculous for adults to restrict themselves to 'adult' books: if a book is well-written, you miss an appalling amount – almost being lop-sided – if you reject it simply because it has been classified as 'children's'. I do dislike classifications ... I always disagree with those who say that 'Narnia' or 'Hobbit' are 'not really children's books, are they? More for adults, really' – they are very well written books, that is enough. That's why in this shop I have Graham Greene and Evelyn Waugh and P.G. Wodehouse in profusion, to mention only a few: all these authors are enjoyed by the elevens and indeed, by some nines.*

The catalogue was divided into several sections: Picture and story books for small children; Folk and Fairy Tales; Poetry; Religion; General Fiction; Biography; Careers; French; History; Hobbies; Horses; Music; Nature; Plays; Reference; Science; Travel and Crime and Adventure. In another letter (1st July 1969), Claire introduces her creation to her prospective in-laws:

> *Just a quick note to usher my brain-child into the continent of Africa. This modest offering has just been printed and I feel like a young mother, for it lists all my likes – just look at items 255 on – and I wrote all the blurbs most lovingly. You can tell the books I don't much care for (not that there are many of those: only the non-fiction, science books) because I have written no highly prejudiced synopsis for them. I chose the picture for the cover, I did all the reading, choosing and researching: the only thing I am not responsible for is the grammatical error in no. 19. Do read it, for my sake, even if children's books bore you pallid.*

Cover of Heffers first children's catalogue, 1969.

The selections Claire made for this catalogue, and her synopses, reflect her views on reading and on the chosen books. Included are E. Gordon's, *Miracle on the River Kwai*, a 'true story of the faith that grew in the hearts of the starving prisoners on the Kwai. By one of them', 15 shillings (£11.75 at today's value), and Charles Chaplin's *My Autobiography*: 'The first quarter of Chaplin's autobiography is of particular interest, describing as it does the life of poor children of London at the end of the last Century, 10/6d.' Others listed are:

NORTON, M. *Bedknobs and Broomsticks*. Miss Price, the ladylike witch, and her exploits with three children who regard her powers as more infallible than they in fact are. 16/-

STREATFIELD, N. *The Circus Is Coming*. Peter and Santa, two slightly priggish children, romantically run away to join the circus where their uncle is a clown. They are forced to revise many of their ideas, but finally find useful careers within the circus. 15/6

TOLKIEN, J.R.R. *The Hobbit*. Bilbo Baggins, a quiet conventional hobbit, finds himself caught up in an outlandish adventure involving dwarfs, dragons and gold, of which he thoroughly disapproves, but during which he discovers in himself a capacity for rising to occasions which he was unaware he possessed. 20/-

"BRIDGE" BOOKS TO HELP MAKE THE TRANSITION FROM READING CHILDREN'S TO ADULT BOOKS

DURRELL, G. *My Family and Other Animals*. Gerald Durrell's hilarious reminiscences of his childhood on the Island of Corfu. 25/-

Author and illustrator Thomas Taylor worked for Heffers from 1995 to 2000, in the Children's Bookshop, under shop manager Kate Agnew. During this time he received his first cover art commission, for J.K. Rowling's *Harry Potter and the Philosopher's Stone*, published by Bloomsbury. At Heffers, Thomas worked with several colleagues who went on to become authors and illustrators, including award-winning authors Julian Sedgwick and Marcus Sedgwick, and illustrator Adrian Reynolds. Working with such people helped Thomas' own creativity and working closely with children's books helped him to understand better the publishing environment. All still collaborate from time to time.

Over the years, a number of leading illustrators were invited to illustrate the children's catalogue covers.

Page 118, Raymond Briggs (*bottom left*), Quentin Blake (*bottom right*). Antony Browne (*above left*), Helen Oxenbury (above right), Jan Pienkowski (*below left*), and David McKee (*below right*).

"A CATALOGUING TIME"

In 1898, Heffers produced 250 copies of a catalogue, 'Books for the Preliminary Examination' and, later, in 1903, it was decided that the 'Cury business' (the Petty Cury shop) would benefit from a catalogue of second-hand books. None of the employees could do this job and so the firm advertised for a 'cataloguer'. In 1905 the firm decided that Sidney Street would be given 'an impetus' by the production of a catalogue. The production of catalogues gradually built up over the years and in 1909, Heffers posted out some 60,000 copies, involving a postal charge of over £200 (£21,700 at today's value). These included lists of 'School and College Text Books'; 'Recent Second-Hand Purchases'; 'Reference Catalogue of Reduced Price Books'; 'New Books'; and 'Books, New and Second-hand, suitable for Christmas presents'. The firm continued over several decades to produce and circulate catalogues on a wide range of topics to their 50,000-plus account holders worldwide.

The ladies working in the top-floor office at Petty Cury in the 1950s and '60s loved 'stuffing envelopes' when the catalogues went out because it meant they could chat. They often had to work overtime, sometimes until nine o'clock at night to get them all out in time. The only drawback was using the Graphotype and Addressograph machines to produce the address labels. Ann Kidman managed to become an expert on the Graphotype, cutting the metal plates, working at quite a speed. Susan Nunn (*née* Fakes) recalls how the plates would frequently get stuck and buckle whilst producing the labels.

Diane Allinson (*née* Bass) was at Heffers from 1960 to 1969, starting at the age of fifteen, when she was put in charge of the 'damper' machine, with the job of changing the rollers (the machine was for sealing gummed envelopes). Ingrid Bane (*née* Ochotny), a junior clerk in the Sales Ledger office at Hills Road from 1968, had a few of her own tussles with the technology whilst packing the monthly statements for account holders to be sent all over the world. The "ultra-modern machinery of the day" that folded the statements and put them into envelopes, would more often than not get jammed, which resulted in Ingrid being knee-deep in shredded and screwed-up statements and envelopes. She says, "Thank

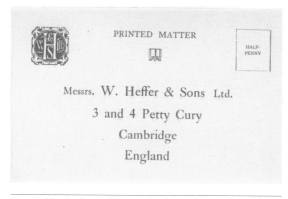

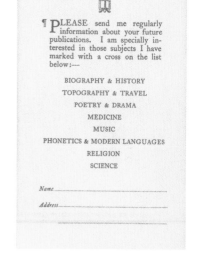

Front and back of an early promotion for catalogues. The card would have been inserted in each book sold.

God there was no window as the management would have had nightmares if they had seen some of the disorder I would be in."

Frank Collieson recalled the 1960s and '70s as "generally in the trade a cataloguing time … always Spring and Autumn lists. Some of the simpler ones were publishers' announcements. Then we did so much more. When we moved to Trinity Street in 1970 we went back to number one [catalogue numbering] and Will Carter designed the cover."

In 1974, the firm established a special cataloguing unit, overseen by a small committee and serving all departments. Every catalogue contained meticulous details of ways to pay, for customers all over the world. Frank and Clive spent many hours designing the order forms, getting it right. Frank recalled that "It was hard to explain to some colleagues. I think it all paid off and I'm very proud of it all. We looked at everything critically but with a sense of humour."

Alison Blair-Underwood acknowledges Frank's wit and style – and his extensive connections in the book trade. "Frank spent a lot of his time being in meetings with a glass of wine and did a great deal of networking." Frank also put many 'Heffers Book Adviser' lists together, designing the covers and writing the introductions. These catalogues promoted popular history and general interest books. Alison herself covered literature and gardening and recalls the competitions:

> "We used to love it, thousands would go out and the money would start coming in. It was absolutely great. We used to have in-house competitions to see whose catalogue would make the most money. I used to miss out because literature was always small-value books. Something like linguistics and oriental studies did well. All our staff could talk knowledgeably about their subject."

Catalogue front and back covers celebrating the bicentary of the French Revolution.

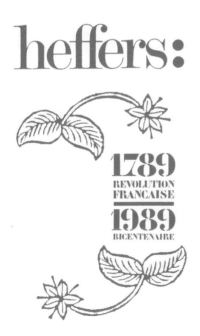

LOUIS XVI: C'est une révolte?
LA ROCHEFOUCAULD–LIANCOURT: Non, Sire, c'est une révolution.

Get it right at **heffers:**
a cut above the rest.

Heffers Booksellers 20 Trinity Street Cambridge England

Clive Cornell concedes that among other bookshops, none – not even Blackwell's Norrington Room in Oxford – had quite the same style as Heffers. "A lot was down to Frank, who added an extra dimension to the world of books in Cambridge."

Richard Reynolds has a story about the production of one catalogue that went slightly awry. Heffers produced catalogues well into the 1990s and Richard's *Bodies in the Bookshop*

Like all the catalogues over the years, this Celtic Studies list (*right*) announced, 'We sell books by post to universities, libraries and individual customers throughout the world ... we can supply any book in print anywhere in the world.'

Heffer Books Second-hand & Antiquarian Catalogue 868, Summer 1969, 'Librarians and students are invited to send their list of Desiderata' (*below left*).

Heffer Catalogue 159, 'Evolution' to commemorate the centenary of the death of Charles Darwin in 1982, a selection of books on Evolution and related areas of study (*below right*).

CELTIC STUDIES
1996

heffers:
Booksellers
Cambridge

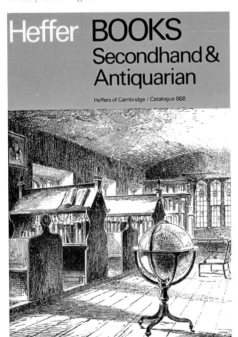

series was the last. Before Richard became the Heffers crime specialist, however, he looked after the travel section. His last travel catalogue was produced by a marketing team at Rustat House who were really good at securing sponsored advertising. For this particular catalogue, entitled *A Greater Sense of Place*, the team were delighted to get guide book publisher Baedeker on board with a large advert. It wasn't until it was published that the problem was spotted and Rustat House received an angry letter from Eva Baedeker. None of the Baedeker Guides were listed in the catalogue. They had been omitted because the booksellers didn't actually like them.

A selection of other Heffers catalogue covers – including the first *Bodies in the Bookshop* catalogue.

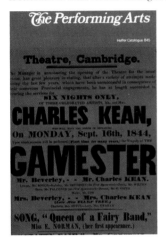

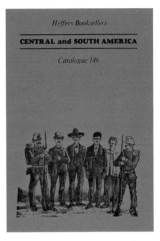

'KNOWN ALL OVER THE WORLD'

As the firm's reputation grew during the 1900s, the catalogues began to proclaim proudly, 'The bookshop known all over the World'. In December 1908, the *Cambridge Independent Press* reported under the heading, 'A WELL KNOWN FIRM', that a letter addressed only to 'Messrs Heffer and Sons, England' from Free Town, Sierra Leone had just been successfully delivered through the post to Messrs Heffer and Sons, Sidney Street, Cambridge. In a May 1923 feature marking the diamond wedding anniversary of William and Mary Heffer, the *Cambridge Chronicle* mused on 'Curiosities of Literature', stating it was a triumph for Heffers as well as the Post Office when a letter addressed to 'Esser, England' from Nigeria reached the firm. These are just two of many examples.

In that same 1923 feature, the *Cambridge Chronicle* observed that Heffers frequently received curious letters in their daily post, 'from the distant places of the earth'. One pupil of a missionary school intimated that if he was sent a catalogue, his order for books would, 'entail a severe strain on the staff' (presumably due to the weight of his order). This letter dated 13th August 1946, from the Gold Coast, West Africa, arrived at Heffers on 16th September:

> *Dear Hefer,*
> *I am exedingly of having a golden opportunity to communicate with you to day.*
> *And as opportunity has present it self to me I there fore pen you these words,*
> *before I write one to two words I am first asking you about your health … I am*
> *fourteen years of age … I am about 5ft tall, I have brown hairs … Try and send*
> *me one fountain pen because I bought some and some body stoled it so this time*
> *I haven't got one yet … I am prospecting no longer days of your reply. More news*
> *are wanted from you as cool water needed to a thirsty soil.*
>
> *I beg to remain,*
>
> *Samuel*

Letters were also received from other customers who, for very different reasons, were unable to visit Cambridge in person. Clive Cornell recalls occasionally seeing letters in the post tray from prisoners, bearing HM Prisons' stamps, which had obviously been censored before being posted. One such customer was Alfred Weston, a serial fraudster whose appeal to the Home Office against one of his sentences achieved some newspaper coverage in the mid-1960s. Weston had a criminal record dating back to 1943, and had been the subject of eighty-one charges of dishonesty, spending many years in and out of prison. During his time inside he had, as one Home Office minister put it, 'applied himself with the utmost determination in prison to improve his education'.

Weston was eventually awarded a PhD, prompting the Home Office to declare: 'It is undisputed that this man is now a brilliant designer, engineer and inventor, worthy of, and able to hold, a high ranking post in his own field.' [39] His rehabilitation was in part thanks to Heffers, in particular Win Anstee (at Heffers from 1947 to 1973), from whom Weston had ordered several books. The service he received must have made an impression upon him, as that Christmas he took the trouble to send Win a card, sincerely thanking her for her assistance. She kept it, noting, 'sent to me at Heffers. I helped with scientific books he needed in prison.'

938 BEL AIR ROAD
WEST LOS ANGELES, 90024

BEL AIR, 20 DECEMBER, 1971

MISS ZSA ZSA GABOR

HEFFERS BOOKSTORE
TRINITY STREET
CAMBRIDGE, ENGLAND

DEAR SIRS,
THROUGH AN ARTICLE IN THE NEWSPAPER I HAVE LEARNED
THAT YOU CAN LOCATE ANY BOOK THAT HAS BEEN PUBLISHED.
I WOULD LIKE YOU TO FIND A BOOK FOR ME AND TO LET ME KNOW
AS SOON AS POSSIBLE IF IT IS AVAILABLE AND HOW MUCH IT WILL
COST. THE COVER OF THE BOOK IS AS FOLLOWS:

DIE ZARIN
SCHWANSPIEL IN DREI AUFZUGEN
VON
MELCHIOR LENGYEL UND LUDWIG BIRO
1912
MUNCHEN BEI GEORG MULLER

PLEASE REPLY IMMERDIATELY AS THIS BOOK IS VERY
IMPORTANT TO ME. I PLAN TO USE THE BOOK IN PREPARATION

938 BEL AIR ROAD
WEST LOS ANGELES, 90024

2.

OF A NEW PLAY AND MUST HAVE IT AS SOON AS POSSIBLE.

THANK YOU FOR YOUR ATTENTION TO THIS MATTER.
I HOPE TO HEAR FROM YOU VERY SOON.

SINCERELY,

ZSA ZSA GABOR

Heffers' worldwide reputation drew enquiries from a broad spectrum of potential customers including celebrities, for example, actress Zsa Zsa Gabor, who wrote to the firm in 1971, requesting their services.

Besides Heffers' name being known in all quarters, it has, on occasion, been observed in unexpected places. In 1990, *The Bookseller* published a photograph taken by broadcaster John Simpson, on one of his trips abroad as BBC Foreign Affairs Editor, of Mujahidin outside Kabul, Afghanistan, clearly seen holding a Heffers carrier bag.

IT'S IN THE POST

Books as well as catalogues were distributed to customers by post (*see also The Unpacking and Packing department p.41*). Dudley Davenport, in the Science department at Petty Cury in the 1950s, recalls a big demand from Nigeria for medical books: "We used to send the books and they used to pay as they could." Postage labels were colour-coded for 'foreign', Great Britain and local destinations. Robert Hill recalls regular orders from a huge library in Kirkuk, northern Iraq during that time, and lots of customers in North America. Overseas order trade was quite important to the firm, especially for the Science department. Every now and again, Rosemarie Hill might be sent out to local bookshops to buy stock to complete a large order. Mistakes inevitably occurred. Eve Stafford once sent a parcel to Melbourne, Australia; it was returned as not known at this address and 'try Melbourn, Royston' scrawled across the package (Royston is twelve miles from Cambridge!).

Julian Sedgwick, in the Oriental department, remembers ordering pamphlets and books from remote ashrams and foundations on the Indian subcontinent, and the frequent use of the cumbersome and massive *Indian Books in Print*. To his amazement the books almost always arrived, usually six to eight months later, although it could take considerably longer: "One bewildered customer came to me to say he couldn't remember ordering a book. We worked out it had been on order for eleven years."

In 1971 Heffers ceased all post-free concessions, apart from for a few key accounts. From then on, standard packing and insurance charges were added to the cost of postage. A 'binning' service was also in operation. Binning involved the despatch of regular and large customer orders in economically-sized consignments, saving up to 10 per cent on postage and packing charges. The books were collected together in a 'bin' until they made up one consignment. In 1973 the firm had 160 permanent 'binning' arrangements for delivering to more significant customers all over the world. At that time the Sidney Street van was still making local deliveries to customers within the Cambridge city boundary and to a handful of villages beyond.

In July 1977 Robert Webb was transferred from the shop floor to what he describes as the "cramped, windowless Trinity Street basement", to work in Orders Handling – the office that dealt with customers' orders sent in from all over the world. In those days, long before email and the internet, this was a manual task. Dozens of orders and letters arrived every day in the mail and were distributed to 'Post Editors' who annotated them with full bibliographic information. The order process mostly required researching through various bibliographic resources, with only *Books in Print*, the UK publishing database, available on microfiche. The annotated paper orders were then passed to the 'input girls', who typed up the orders on official Heffers forms for dispatch to the relevant publishers. Robert handled the History orders to begin with, but soon moved over to Science.

By 1977, the Orders Handling department was pressed for space at Trinity Street. Along with Book Handling (goods in and out), the entire ordering operation was relocated just before Christmas that year to new offices at St Tibbs Row, off Downing Street, behind the original Lion Yard redevelopment, and a new computerised ordering system was also installed (*see p.135*). This building, now demolished, was shared with a branch of the Norwich Union insurance company, and Heffers occupied 17,000 square feet over four floors (Periodicals, Packing and the telephone/telex services were also transferred from Trinity Street to St Tibbs Row).

Under his manager, John Gregory, Robert carried on the same work here as part of a small team, editing customer orders. The biggest change during this period was the computerisation of the ordering process, which meant the installation of a large mainframe and 'VDUs' (visual display units) scattered around the office. The flickering green screen was quite a novelty and Robert's first introduction to computers.

For a while from 1982, Heffers operated a 'Post-a-book' service. This was a promotional scheme developed by the Post Office in association with the Book Marketing Council and the Booksellers Association. The idea was to encourage the purchase of books as gifts by offering the customer immediate postal facilities, 'the book trade answer to "Interflora"', as declared in *Trinity Street News*. Customers selected books, paid for them and then took them to the Information Desk where a pre-stamped pack could be purchased. The customer addressed the package and then left

it for Heffers to take to the Trinity Street Post Office. As well as the 'Post-a-book' service, at this time, generally, the turn-around time for orders received on the telephone or through the post was 24 hours.

In October 1995, a new scheme, 'Heffers by Post', was launched with a selection of current books and CDs, video, Filofax and stationery that could be ordered. Notices about the new service were sent to most customers all over the world and copies of the catalogue were distributed through the shops.

On 6th November 1997 Heffers website was launched, with 1.9 million titles on its database. The site offered free post and packing (post-free clearly being back on by this time). On the same day the *Cambridge Evening News*, under the heading 'Users can read between the lines', reported that Heffers, which now had eight Cambridge shops carrying around 300,000 titles, plus 30,000 other products, already boasted 50,000 mail-order customers worldwide. Nicholas Heffer was quoted as saying, 'Our aim was to combine the strengths of traditional bookshops … with the convenience and speed of the internet.'

ADVERTISING AND MARKETING

From very early days, Heffers made use of advertising opportunities in local publications. In 1898 the firm's first full page advertisement, in the *Members List* of *The Cambridge Review*, secured a favourable response from members of the University who were already benefitting from William's controversial discount policy. In 1939, *The Cambridge Review* Commentator wrote, 'Fortunately, most of us still preserve sufficient presence of mind to be able occasionally to leave war-thoughts behind and turn to our bookshelves. At the bookshops *War and Peace* has been in great demand from those "who have always been meaning to tackle it, and have never before found the time." At such period as this there is comfort in length. One desires a really substantial world into which to escape.'

A 1931 Heffers advertisement from the *Bury Free Press*.

You can Buy Gifts for them all at

W. HEFFER & SONS LTD.

SIDNEY ST., CAMBRIDGE
Together with CHRISTMAS CARDS, CALENDARS and DIARIES.

HEFFERS Petty Cury Bookshop. Five Floors of Books and nothing but Books.

Be sure to stock

BURNHAM ABBEY AND CANTABRIGIA

CHRISTMAS CARDS AND CALENDARS
(RELIGIOUS & SECULAR)

Designs of distinction and of real artistic merit.

If our representative does not call on you, kindly send us a post-card.

W. HEFFER & SONS LIMITED
CAMBRIDGE

HEFFER'S

W.HEFFER & SONS LTD.

BOOKSHOP
FOR ALL BOOKS IN ANY LANGUAGE

¶ A List of all the new Books is issued monthly.

✗ Send for Secondhand Text-book Catalogue.

¶ Also send us your lists of Books Wanted. Quotations by return.

Are you on our Mailing List?

W. HEFFER & SONS, LTD.
3 & 4 PETTY CURY, CAMBRIDGE
England. Telephone 862.

As near as the nearest mail box

Advert for greetings cards etc. (*above*) from the 1934 *British Stationer*. (*Top right*) 1937 Heffers advertisement which was enclosed with a letter sent from a customer in Lagos who requested a French language book, and ' my coronation present!'.

Wartime created new advertising themes, as seen in these 1939 examples from the *Cambridge Daily News*.

. An *Infallible* Medicine for Those Who Are Anxious:—

"A GOOD BOOK"
Books wisely chosen can Stimulate, Dope, or Steady the mind.

In the moment of stress, don't get alarmed, but get a Book—a good Book—and Read.

This is a far better plan than that which drives you, for consolation and stimulus, to conversation with the " other man "—who knows no more than you do.

A Book can be bought for a few pence or a few shillings, and it will be **your** Book—a possession which doesn't deteriorate, which requires no battery to energise or switch to manipulate ; it is always ready to work, and it doesn't answer back, unless you deserve it, and that will be part of the cure.

If you don't know of suitable Books, ask Heffer's ; they know what . Books to recommend for all occasions.

W. HEFFER & SONS
LTD.
Petty Cury and Sidney Street, CAMBRIDGE.

A letter a day while he's away!

Waterman's Ink prevents Ink-clog.

Waterman's

W. HEFFER & SONS
LTD.,
SIDNEY STREET, CAMBRIDGE.

In fact gold stickers had been used well before 1975. The example above, together with the bookmark, were in a copy of *A Christmas Carol* by Charles Dickens purchased from Sidney Street during the 1940s.

In 1975 it was announced in *Trinity Street News* that the Promotions department had had some nicely designed, easy to apply, gold labels produced for putting into the inside cover of books sold. The newsletter stated, 'We have been rather reluctant to do this immediately we receive the books because of the problem of eventual possible returns to publishers.' For libraries, prizes and 'bin' accounts the labels could of course be inserted immediately.

In 1984, Heffers played a major role in the Book Marketing Council's campaign, *The Best Novels of our Time*. The campaign featured displays in 3,000 bookshops and nearly all libraries in the UK. A sales drive, the aim was to sell one million books – and rekindle public interest in good literature. Thirteen novels of outstanding literary merit first published in English since May 1945 were selected by four judges, Sir Peter Parker, Dr Richard Hoggart, Elizabeth Jane Howard and John Welch. Following on from the Council's previous campaigns, *Best of British Novelists* (1982) and *Best of the Young British Novelists* (1983), this initiative caused much controversy. *The Spectator* called it a 'fatuous' campaign and novelists, Anthony Burgess and Graham Greene (not included on the list) set about devising their own list of favourites. The campaigns, widely advertised and featured in the broadsheets and colour supplements, appeared to benefit from the controversy. In 1985, two of the 'best' young British novelists, Adam Mars-Jones and Kazuo Ishiguro participated in a reading at Trinity Street as part of a Faber event.

In 1986, the spoof newsletter, *Trinity Street Blues*, contained a feature on the 'Book Marginalising Council', 'based on the sound principle that reading and buying books is an elitist occupation and should remain so ... History shows us that ideas are generally bad for people and books do give people ideas.'

Heffers regularly ran competitions. Gerald Criddle recalls the annual Heffers Rowney Painting Competition for schools. It was a popular event and dinner for the judges was hosted by John and Bunty Heffer at their home in Barton Road, Cambridge.

In 1989, the firm's directors reported that the book trade had been going through, and continues to go through, a time of great turmoil: 'Many publishers and booksellers have been amalgamating and changing ownership; some of this has followed the development of chains of bookshops that have been growing at a rapid rate in the very questionable belief that the market for books can be hugely expanded. Heffers Booksellers continue to concentrate on doing the things we know how to do well.' The arrival of Dillons in Cambridge in 1988 (next door to the Sidney Street shop) was a significant development, although it was reported that the impact on shop sales had been less than anticipated. The directors put this down to the firm's long experience with the local market and to the efforts of the newly created Marketing Department, overseeing major advertising initiatives. Suzanne Jones recalls the Heffers *R Campaign*, aimed a reinforcing the Heffers name throughout Cambridge via television advertising, commercial radio, ITV and *Cambridge Evening News* pull-out supplements. The *R Campaign* was run just before Dillons opened, and featured promotional clothing in blue and jade green – Heffers sweatshirt, umbrella, mug, tie and jacket and children's tee-shirt. (In 1989, a signing for Jeffrey Archer's *A Twist in the Tale* was advertised on Anglia Television's Oracle teletext service, under 'Community Information'. Archer was greeted by a large crowd and over 200 copies were sold that day.)

Themes and related events, such as *Bodies in the Bookshop*, instigated by Richard Reynolds (with the encouragement of Alison Blair-Underwood who was managing the Literature department at the time) have proved to be enormously successful in helping the firm to build positive relationships with customers, writers and publishers. The first event in 1991 involved five authors and a two-week long promotion. As a competition prize, the winner could produce the screen for one night only at a performance of *The Mousetrap*. Richard says: "We have a lot of people who come in, a lot of elderly people who like the traditional murder mysteries. People come back for recommendations."

Finally, Reuben always did his bit by leaving Heffers bags on the beach when on holiday in France.

Like bananas,

heffers:

BOOKSHOP contains highly nutritious pulp. It's the best of the bunch.

20 Trinity Street, Cambridge

20 Trinity Street Cambridge

When you sell a man a book you don't sell him just twelve ounces of paper and ink and glue — you sell him a whole new life.
CHRISTOPHER MORLEY

Live again with

heffers:

wherever you live.

We post books all over the world. Write to **Heffers Bookshop, 20 Trinity Street, Cambridge, England**

Two further examples of advertisements with slogans devised by Frank Collieson (*above and top*).

Celebrities endorsed book selections such as Kenneth More (*above*), and Heffers produced their own branding for useful objects such as this paperweight and tapemeasure. In 1984 the firm produced a *Book of Answers* containing very useful information about stationery such as paper sizes. Colourful broachures were produced for various shops and departments.

Where are we?

Stationery Shop
Sidney Street
Cambridge, CB2 3HL

Office machines and
systems
Retail stationery
Art gallery and books

Commercial Warehouse
Kilmaine Close
Kings Hedges Road
Cambridge, CB4 2PH

Furniture showroom
Commercial stationery
(See page 21)

Drawing office equipment
Graphic design materials
Survey equipment

Artists' materials
Papers
Boards

Large scale
Ordnance Survey
Maps
Guide books

(0223) 58241

What are we?

From a humble beginning as a small Stationery Shop
opened in 1876 by an East Anglian ostler,
we have expanded to our present size on the sound principles
of service and quality merchandise.

On a Heffers account you can charge anything from any of
our 10 shop premises. You could:

have your
Queen's Award
to Industry framed

decorate for
the firm's
Christmas
party

buy a gift for the
typist who's leaving
to be married
(superb wrapping
papers and an
excellent range of
gift cards as well)

select a print or
painting for
the boardroom

pick up helpful
reference books and
maps for the office,
or paperbacks for
the library

treat your
secretary, or
yourself, to the
latest in a
typewriter,
calculator or
dictating machine

print new
letterheads

buy paints and
brushes, fine papers,
boards, Letraset . . .
in short, anything
an artist or
draughtsman might
need

refurnish the office

Heffers service is not only available in East Anglia;
we will pack and export for you to almost anywhere in the world.

3

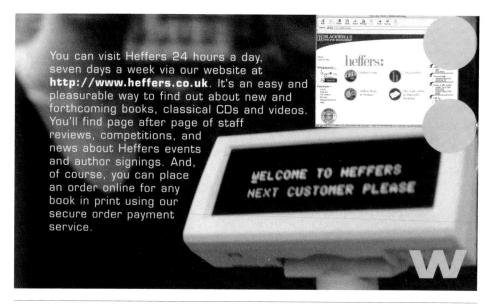

You can visit Heffers 24 hours a day, seven days a week via our website at **http://www.heffers.co.uk**. It's an easy and pleasurable way to find out about new and forthcoming books, classical CDs and videos. You'll find page after page of staff reviews, competitions, and news about Heffers events and author signings. And, of course, you can place an order online for any book in print using our secure order payment service.

Page from a Heffers brochure entitled, *Discover the Difference.*

9

INFORMATION TECHNOLOGY AND HQ

*'Much is going on with the development of all our
computer systems ...'*

Heffers Bookselling News, October 1989

The early 1980s saw a number of technological innovations at the firm. For a hundred years or so Heffers had relied on manual systems for stock control and managing customer accounts, sales and purchases. It was now clear that computers were needed for monitoring customer orders and accounts, stock management and control, responding to bibliographic enquiries, compiling catalogues, dealing with 'point of sale' transactions in the shop, taking orders 'out of hours' and so on. *Trinity Street News* announced a forthcoming important step in the computerisation of the firm's clerical operation for customer order cards:

> 'This will resolve many problems, remove much drudgery and enable us to take on much more business with comfort. Our present clerical system has been most carefully evolved and has proved itself admirably. It will "translate" very smoothly to highly sophisticated and amazingly fast machine operation ... we hope to be in operation quickly – probably in January 1978.'

'COMPUTER FOR CITY SHOP'

The acquisition of a £200,000 (£1.3 million at today's value) mainframe computer for Heffers in 1977 was a significant milestone in the history of the firm. So much so that it was announced in the *Cambridge Evening News*. It was installed by Telecomputing Ltd of Oxford, to handle book ordering for British and overseas customers. By the start of 1978 the entire Book and Orders Handling and Accounts departments had moved from Trinity Street to St Tibbs Row, where the computerised ordering system was installed. In January 1979 *Trinity Street News* declared: 'It cannot have escaped anyone's notice that during 1978 we quietly introduced an ICL 2903 computer ... anything that reduces human drudgery must be a bonus and we believe that the very large investment involved will keep Heffers as one of the leading booksellers in the world.'

John Heffer, in his 1978 Chairman's Report declared a record year in sales and profits; the Group's turnover increased by 24.5 per cent, and net profit was up by 31.6 per cent. Whilst the increased expenditure was acknowledged, the installation of the ICL 2903 was hailed as 'the greatest innovation', transforming the whole book-handling operation. The following year the continuing increase in book sale profits was absorbed by the first full year of the extra costs of the new computer installation and the new office building. The process of computerisation was reported as 'most successful'.

By 1981 the stationery side of the business was benefitting from an office supply order system, enabling the division to compete more effectively for bulk supplies of stationery products to large users. In 1983 the ordering and stock control systems of the commercial stationery side of the business had been computerised and in 1984 the main computer used by both the stationers and booksellers was replaced with a bespoke system (by 1982 Heffers already had their own book file with 115,000 titles and over 5,000 publishers listed). The directors' 1984 Annual Report says: 'Advances in technology make it possible and economic to have our own programs for these systems and obviously new programs can be more flexible and efficient than those written about fourteen years ago.' A reduction in profits was predicted, affected by, amongst other things, the special computer costs.

Keeping track of the 40,000 or more customer accounts was a major task. In 1971 cardboard account cards had been introduced and despatched to all account customers (plastic cards were issued much later, in 1987). Heffers decided that only by using account cards could they ensure that a customer actually had an account when they asked for books to be charged. At that time a very high proportion of accounts were used by customers who spent less than £5 a year and so a minimum annual spend of £10 was stipulated as a condition of opening a credit account.

Computer technology had in fact been in use by Heffers for some time. In 1969 the firm began producing computerised statements for account customers, using Cambridge Computer Services (owned by Geest Computer Services from 1976). Customer accounts were, therefore, computerised before any other part of the firm: certainly before the major acquisition of the mainframe computer in 1977. The customer accounts index went 'live' on the computer at St Tibbs Row in 1983. This signalled the end of the era of the card index, which had also been created in 1969 when all customer accounts were first given numbers and sorted into alphabetical order (the card index system had originally consisted of three desks with three large card wheels to accommodate the many thousands of accounts).

Writing in *Trinity Street News* in 1982, under the heading of 'The Forgotten Army', Monica Sarll described the Customer Accounts department at St Tibbs Row, 'where most paper ends its life'. Data from daily record sheets was fed into the computer and stored on floppy discs.

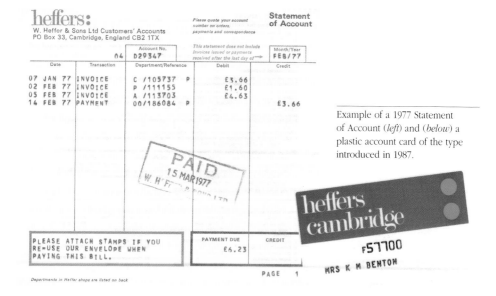

Example of a 1977 Statement of Account (*left*) and (*below*) a plastic account card of the type introduced in 1987.

Once a week, this information and Sidney Street sales were sent via a telephone connection in the Accounts department to Geest Computer Services. In 1985 the firm installed Kodak's Oracle microfilm system for storing customer account folders and associated files. Documents were retrieved using a machine-readable barcode.

In 1982 Heffers established a computer loan scheme for staff to borrow small computers for use at home. These included the Sinclair ZX81 and Sinclair Spectrum (Sinclair was a Cambridge based company). These early home computers used a television set as a VDU. 1982 was 'Information Technology Year' and Nicholas Heffer stated to staff that 'a number of you may be interested in finding out more about computers by experimenting with them yourself'.

Also in 1982 an 'Ansafone' service was installed, 'for all those people who want to buy a book at midnight having just seen the latest T.V. programme or only just realised they want it for a birthday next week', as *Trinity Street News* reported. The first order, received in February 1983, was for *Snow White and the Seven Dwarfs*.

In September 1983, it was announced that the firm was planning to introduce both Access and Visa credit card payment facilities in all shops, having previously resisted doing so (Barclaycard/Visa had been in the UK since the late 1960s; Access since 1972). Credit card payment was finally introduced in 1984. Also in 1983, Trinity Street and St Tibbs Row became fully up-to-date in office automation with Olivetti electronic typewriters and two 'videotypers', connecting a screen and disk-drive unit to one of the typewriters to provide a word processing facility that stored information, which could be modified and printed out as required.

In 1982 the firm's new Bookfile system had 115,000 titles spread amongst 5,249 publishers and this continued to grow. Computer terminals for the use of booksellers on the shop floor were not seen at Trinity Street until 1985, by which time the main computer was being replaced. Clive Cornell recalls the card index system for stock control for bookselling in use up until then, with files arranged alphabetically by subject. This system had been introduced at Trinity Street, the Paperback shop, the Children's Bookshop and the Penguin shop in 1971. The sales record for each publication was recorded manually on the cards and an additional card created for 'continuation works' where, for example, the volume was part of several such as an encyclopaedia or other reference work. Whilst the system was never 100 per cent accurate, booksellers could check stock levels and when the next volume was due. Clive also remembers doing other tasks manually, such as using a slide-rule to convert foreign prices into sterling.

Richard Reynolds recalls using Whitaker's *Books in Print*, the annual reference catalogue of current literature, available in hard copy and on microfiche. *Trinity Street News* noted in July 1982 the growing number of publishers who were sending updated microfiche lists of their books in print. Despite the advances of technology, Richard remained very attached to the index cards, which were still being used even when the computers were coming in: "A lot of us hung onto our cards. I took mine home because never again would I have so much information." Of course, any database

Microfiche reader at Trinity Street.

relies on human compilation and may suffer some degree of inaccuracy. In 1986, a spoof staff newsletter, *Heifers: Trinity Street Blues*, included this 'music hall' joke,

"I say, I say, I say, how to do you get 18,000 publishers on a publisher file?"
"I don't know. How to do you get 18,000 publishers on a publisher file?"
"It's quite easy: you start off with 3,000 and spell them each six different ways"

In 1985 *Trinity Street News* announced the provision of three terminals which were linked to a new ICL ME29 computer at St Tibbs Row: 'The most frequent uses will be checking the status of a customer's order, and checking details such as price and the ISBN on our Bookfile.' There was no facility to amend details on the computer via the keyboard and booksellers still had to fill in an amendment form, kept next to the terminals. The directors' Annual Report in 1985 acknowledged the negative impact on profit of the phased replacement of the main retail computer and the introduction of new programs. The continuing development of the firm's own Book File was cited as a 'vital element', with over 400,000 titles listed.

Whilst the computers did make things easier, it was a big change for some booksellers. Richard says, "the good thing about the card system was that you retained much more information. It was laborious in a sense. You can remember whole swathes of publisher prefixes." In 1992 Becky Proctor, who had used a computer in a previous job at Dillons, remembers not only using Whitaker's on microfiche at Heffers but also index cards for stock-keeping whilst the new computer system was being phased in. (And it was in 1992, that Mark Wait, the new Managing Director who replaced John Welch, declared IT to be a priority and announced that he would be getting rid of the stock cards in the shops.)

The firm's computer systems had continued to be controlled and operated by Telecomputing and, as stated in the 1986 Annual Report, developments were 'always under consideration'. Expenditure on computer facilities continued over subsequent years with investments in both systems and staff. The Bibliographic Unit was further developed and a full-time training manager was recruited in the late 1980s. In 1988, investigations into stock control and electronic point-of-sale systems (EPOS) led to a pilot system being installed in the Paperback shop. A list of bestsellers could be accessed via the computer. Writing about the Children's Bookshop in *Bookselling News* in 1991, manager Lindsay Fraser describes the process of asking the computer for the shop's 100 bestsellers for the past twelve months. To no-one's surprise, it was Roald Dahl's *Matilda* (1988), selling 433 copies. Number two was Eric Carle's *The Very Hungry Caterpillar* (1970).

By 1992 an Information Systems manager had been appointed to, 'review, replace and extend the group's computer systems'. Rapid developments followed. A new computer was installed alongside the existing one (the ME29), which at that point had been in use for seven years. All applications were then to be transferred to the new computer over a period of eighteen to twenty-four months, and an EPOS system was installed at Trinity Street. Barcoding had begun in Trinity Street and Rustat House, implemented by a new department, BH3, initially created to barcode but then to do other systems-related tasks as well. Hand-held bar-code readers were also introduced. The editorial of *The Magazine*, under the heading, 'I.T. comes to Heffers', declared,

'Everyone will be learning something new ... The system is designed to be used by us, not to replace staff, or the essential contact between bookperson and customer. The system will free those with book knowledge to use that knowledge in more valuable (economic and intellectual) ways ... All this means that Heffers will be entering the 21st Century with all the technological infrastructure in place to help it carry on doing what it does best, selling books.'

The total cost of the equipment, financed by leasing, was around £600,000. These changes took place during a recession when trading was proving particularly difficult and redundancies occurred. Nicholas Heffer, in his Chairman's letter to shareholders, stated,

'It is usual for me to give some forecast for the current year. However, on this occasion I find it impossible to tell you what the outcome will be for the year to 31 March 1993. I can only tell you that we have great strengths within the Company and will be well placed to recover when the national economy does so. It is this confidence which enables us to press ahead with our current investment in information systems ... I sincerely hope that in another twelve months' time the picture will be brighter, both for us and for the economy.'

The new information systems were extended to the Accounts department, the Stationers' commercial operations, the Children's Bookshop, the Paperback and Video shops and the Art & Graphics shop, giving staff access to the central bibliographic database. Staff in these shops could check the titles held in Trinity Street and vice-versa. The system enabled staff to order books directly, and to gather information about books ordered by the firm. The Bibliographic Unit, based at Rustat House, comprised a team of three staff and a number of microcomputers that were used to interrogate various bibliographic databases, such as Whitaker's and Bowker ('American Books in Print'). The HMSO (Her Majesty's Stationery Office) catalogue was also available in this way from 1989.

Nicholas reported to shareholders in 1994 that the continuing increase in information 'is proving invaluable to customers, staff and management. Customers can often get better and quicker answers to enquiries, which helps them to buy more books. Staff have more detailed information than ever before for controlling their stocks of books, and management are benefitting from more and better knowledge of the whole business.' Alison Blair-Underwood recalls, "we had a wonderful system that was totally bespoke but it was too expensive".

The investment certainly didn't end with this latest outlay. In 1996 the directors reported problems with the new computer system for the commercial stationers, which resulted in profit being considerably below budget. And there were further developments: 'The replacement of all our current Information Systems is still not completed but should not take much longer. There continues to be much activity in connecting local libraries into our system so that they can examine our stocks on-line and place orders.' Suzanne Jones recalls getting a computer on her desk in the late 1990s and the exasperation everyone felt at having to 'input' everything. By this time, electronic tills had been installed throughout the Sidney Street shop and in the Art & Graphics shop and Heffers Sound. All the shops were now linked up and total sales information instantly available. In addition, new stock computerised control systems were being introduced on three floors at Sidney Street.

For both 1996 and 1997, the directors reported a year when 'substantial further investment was made in information systems'. In 1998 Heffers, like many other businesses, began to address the question of 'Year 2000' compliance. A review of the firm's information systems ensued and further investment in a new integrated sales and stock management system was authorised. At the same time, expenditure on redundant software totalling over £500,000 had to be written off.

HEFFERS HQ

In October 1986, it was reported in *Trinity Street News* that Heffers Booksellers, for the first time, sold over £1 million worth of books in one month and £50,000 worth of books on one Saturday (by the time of the Blackwell's takeover in 1999, the firm was selling over a million books a year).

Towards the end of 1986, the Heffers board decided that more office space was needed. New premises of 34,000 square feet on two storeys were secured just outside Cambridge city centre, at 60 Clifton Road, and the leases for St Tibbs Row were disposed of. The *Cambridge Evening News* reported that Heffers had agreed to take over the Clifton Road building, which had stood empty for two years after being leased to Sir Clive Sinclair before his Cambridgeshire-based company ran into difficulties. [40] Architects Austin-Smith:Lord (who had worked on the Trinity Street shop) were employed to plan the space, which was to accommodate Book and Orders Handling, Binning and Library Services. It was also to house the new computer department, Cataloguing and Promotion – including a machine for shrink-wrapping catalogues, the Book Clubs, Accounts departments, Wages Office and senior management.

Heffers held a staff competition with a prize of £100 for the best suggestion of a new name for the building and over a hundred were submitted. A spoof staff newsletter, *Heifers: Trinity Street Blues*, shared some ideas such as, Hefferopolis, Dundrinkin (withdrawn), Packer's Paradise, Blindworm House, A House for Mr Heffer, and Bookhandling Buchhandlung. Nicholas and John Welch decided on the name 'Rustat House', announcing that they wanted something short and individual to Cambridge, that 'would not suffer from alteration in daily parlance' and that, being close to Rustat Road, had a local connection to the site. [41]

The opening of the new headquarters was celebrated with a large and lavish reception. Open days were also held for staff and for invited visitors from publishing and other suppliers.

We Sell More Books!
A Special Eight-Page Advertising Supplement
Thursday October 6th, 1988
Cambridge

Cover of an eight page advertising supplement in the *Cambridge Weekly News*, 1988

Back in 1970, the new Trinity Street management suite had a men's toilet only. By 1986 the senior management team included women too. This photograph shows managers at Rustat House: (*left to right seated*) Alison Rimmer (now Blair-Underwood), Nicholas Heffer, John Welch, Linda Wright; (*left to right standing*) Clive Cornell, Keith Crossley, David Watson, Frank Collieson, John Cheshire, Simon Larbey, John Gregory, Pippa Clegg, Pauline Sutton, Michael Fuller and Geoff Fowler.

The Cambridge press coverage of the opening described Heffers as, 'one of the leading stockholding booksellers … the largest issuer of catalogues of any stockholding bookseller anywhere in the world.' The open days were described as an opportunity to see how Heffers' 'other half' works; the operation that deals with worldwide postal sales which account for 47 per cent of the bookselling operation's £11 million turnover. In 1995, the firm took advantage of a break clause in the lease for Rustat House and bought the freehold from landlord, Scottish Life Assurance. In 1999, after the Blackwell's takeover, Rustat House was sold.

Bibliographical researchers at work in Rustat House.

Photograpic portrait of Ernest Heffer taken by Olive Edis Galsworthy FRPS, and given by him to Mrs Anstee, widow of Frederick, in the summer of 1948.

10

HEFFER LIFE

DRESS CODE

Whilst the dress code at Heffers, for the office or shop, was perhaps not always expressed in formal terms, on a day-to-day basis, certain conventions were (or were not) observed. It was about more than just never having your hands in your pockets (although at Sidney Street the gentlemen never did). In 1933, Ernest Heffer declared, 'A bookseller is brought into such close relationship with his customers that he cannot be too particular about his personal appearance.'

The managers helped to set the tone. For example, John Heffer would come into Sidney Street in his RAF uniform when he started back after his service in the Second World War. Thereafter, he would always be immaculately attired in a gleaming suit. Although also wearing a suit, in comparison, Reuben Heffer would appear more nonchalantly dressed.

Rosemarie Hill, who had come to work at Petty Cury from the much more formal Swiss environment in 1955, could hardly believe the sight of Reuben with leather elbow patches on the sleeves of his jacket, cycling home for lunch. Lucy Heffer, also at Petty Cury, always wore brown skirts, cardigans and sensible shoes. Rupert Boasten, a Petty Cury manager who came from Blackwell's (long before the takeover), always wore what the staff described as an 'ice-cream' jacket, which seems appropriate for a manager who is remembered for having freely given, or secured, pay-rises (treats all round?) And then there were the idiosyncratic touches. Miss Dudley-Hay who ran the Church Supplies department at Sidney Street in the 1950s, cut holes in her shoes to make room for her bunions. Hopefully she always stood behind a counter.

At Petty Cury, up until the 1960s, ladies were not permitted to wear trousers or high heels and the cramped offices gave hardly enough room to swing those voluminous skirts that became very fashionable during the post-war years. They were also not supposed to wear jewellery and would occasionally be ticked-off for touching up their lipstick. One young lady wore a plunging V-neck sweater and was told most firmly not to come to work in such inappropriate garb. Ingrid Bane, a fifteen-year-old junior clerk in the Sales Ledger Office at Hills Road in 1968, described herself as a bit of teenybopper, wearing mini skits that her mother described as nothing more than an extended belt. Ingrid's attire didn't get her into trouble and she was allowed to adorn the office wall near her desk with posters of pop groups Marmalade and Amen Corner. (Ingrid was also helped out by an older female colleague, Evelyn, when she got into scrapes; one evening Evelyn smuggled Ingrid out of work in the back seat of her Morris Minor with a blanket over her head, to avoid a boy who was waiting at the top of the printing works driveway.)

Navy blue overalls were provided at Petty Cury for specific tasks such as 'chaining' the heavy sales ledgers down the stairs to the safe in the basement at the end of the day and then back up first thing the next morning before the shop opened. An overall was also worn in the Packing department by any ladies who occasionally helped out there, as well as by the gentlemen who worked full time in that department.

Suzanne Jones, who began her thirty-four year career at Heffers in Trinity Street in 1974, believed the aim was for the staff to look more like the students customers they served. She felt that jeans and T-shirts, despite being frowned upon at times, did the trick. Even Suzanne, however, would not go as far as emulating a regular academic customer, who always came into the shop wearing a life jacket.

Heffers gold and black enamel staff badge.

The question of 'KNOWING WHO'S WHO', as the staff newsletter put it, was raised in August 1988, and management announced a new company policy, whereby all shop staff were required to wear a new Heffers badge from the beginning of the following term. 'In Heffers Booksellers we are lucky enough to have a fairly relaxed standard of dress, which I am sure is appreciated by all. The only problem that this inevitably causes is that very often you cannot tell who are the shop staff and who are the customers.' (A small enamel badge had been introduced in 1973, to help customers identify staff in the shop, but staff were only encouraged to wear the badge, rather than told to.) It took quite a few months for everyone to get into the habit of wearing their badge and reminders were still being issued in May, April and June 1989.

At the Sidney Street shop, ladies wore nylon overalls in dark red, navy or light blue before a new, much smarter, uniform was introduced; a blue suit with a green and white striped blouse for the ladies and grey flannels, a blue blazer, a green and white striped shirt and a blue tie for the gentlemen. It was neat and a real help to the business. Managers wore dark blue suits.

This would never have caught on at Trinity Street. A further comment was made in the May 1990 staff newsletter: 'Dress – the Summer weather problem of achieving the right balance between comfort and "professional" appearance …'. Indeed 1990 turned out to be a very hot. The summer of 1976 had also been very hot, and a spoof staff newsletter announced rules to keep you cool in 'high-temperature' bookselling including 'do feel free to unbutton your top button (only the top one of course)'.

In her early days at the firm, Suzanne Jones had a reputation for being "unsuitably dressed". One day in the 1970s, Reuben, noting her patched denim jeans with holes and her cheesecloth top, asked "do you have to wear those?" Suzanne's reply was that she did like them but she didn't *have* to wear them, to which Reuben declared, "Then you jolly well wear them". There were times, however, when ladies, including Suzanne, were sent home for wearing inappropriate dress on the Information Desk. As Alison Blair-Underwood believes, the firm in this respect had all the best of a patriarchal society and all the worst. Alison was once told to go home and change her knee-length boots to something more suitable.

All staff were permitted to dress down for stocktaking and for one gentleman, that meant wearing a cravat instead of a tie. Christopher South, writing in the *Cambridge Evening News* in 1984, quotes a staff member: 'I like the way people are a bit more informal on stocktaking day. I don't have to worry if my blouse is a bit creased.' (Stocktaking at Sidney Street, presumably.) [42]

For the gentleman, hair was a particular bone of contention. According to Ernest in 1933, 'hair will be brushed and oiled, though of course not over done, according to the latest fashion'. Long after Ernest's time, Stephen Perry arrived at Sidney Street in the late 1960s. Stephen described himself as a bit of a teenage tearaway with very long hair. He always wore a suit (being a bit of a mod) but his hair was definitely too long. One day he had a call from John Heffer who asked to see him in the boardroom but didn't say what it was about. When Stephen entered, John told him to sit down and said, "Don't you think it's about time you had your haircut, young man?" Stephen immediately went to get a haircut, and did so regularly for a while, but after slipping back into his old ways he would receive the message, "Mr John wishes to see you in the boardroom now please Stephen". Called in, for the same misdemeanour several times over the years, the firm but non-threatening suggestion was that Stephen had let himself and Heffers down. On one occasion John even asked him it would be helpful if Heffers paid for the haircut.

John Skelton, at Trinity Street from 1973 to 1976, observed that "smart casual" might exaggerate the average sartorial effort of his colleagues. Also one who wore his hair rather long, John would often pass for a customer, and at times would cause surprise when someone asked to see the manager, and he responded, "That's me". John was not advised to get his hair cut but he was not at Sidney Street.

Stephen at his wedding on 1st September 1973. He married Veronica, who also worked at Sidney Street. Veronica always says she found him in Fancy Goods.

Interviewed and offered a job at Heffers Sound in 2001 by Tony McGeorge, Mark Jones reflected on something his father had said about him having no chance of getting the job because of his long, straggly hair. Even though his father's prediction was wrong, Mark decided to get a short back and sides at Mr Polito's Barber Shop the day before he started work. Tony greeted Mark on his first day with dismay, "What on earth have you done to your hair?" He had only given Mark the job because his hair made him "look interesting". It had been a toss between him and another candidate and the hair had swung it. That too would not have happened at Sidney Street.

OPENING THE POST

There was a daily morning ritual of opening the post at Petty Cury, which continued after the move to Trinity Street. Frank Collieson recalled the tall figure of Rupert Boasten standing at Reuben Heffer's desk in the Petty Cury shop, where the post was opened. Clive Cornell remembers the secretaries coming into the office to open the envelopes and stamp the correspondence. Marion Davenport recalls doing this: "When I first started it was quite daunting to go in this room with Mr Reuben and the other managers to open the post. I didn't take the letters out, just slit the envelopes open." (Recalling her previous employment at Blackwell's, Claire Brown remembers one secretary there who was a former prisoner of war, and who would burn the post from time to time because she thought it contained German propaganda.)

After examining the post, either Reuben or Rupert Boasten (or sometimes both) would walk around the building, handing the mail to the various departments for them to deal with the orders. The girls on the top floor would type the invoices, weigh the books and calculate the postal charge. After the move to Trinity Street the ritual would take place in the new boardroom, supervised by John Welch. At Trinity Street there were two machines on hand; one dispensing coffee and the other, small memos ("bloody bus tickets", as Frank would call them) on which John Welch wrote instructions and then attached to the various items. Instead of using memos, Reuben had a large, thick pencil, which he used to write on the correspondence.

There was a similar mail routine at Sidney Street, overseen by John Heffer. Norman Biggs recalls:

"If you saw the post coming in, you very quickly got a good idea of what was going on. The post all came in centrally, we opened the lot and looked at it. You learned a great deal from it. You'd see an invoice for £1,000 and then one for

£7,000 and you'd phone the buyer and ask what it was about … You could put things right very quickly."

This mirrors Suzanne Jones' recollection of the Trinity Street routine, when eight senior managers would gather together every morning to examine the post: "You did know what was going on and everybody would discuss it." In 1975 *Trinity Street News* reported:

> 'Mr Reuben, particularly because he enjoys the post himself, feels that some of the compliments and jokes, not the brickbats, might be more equally shared out and I am therefore going to put a few of these from time to time on the Notice Board. You will have to take the not so nice letters for granted.'

And under the heading, 'Philately':

> 'Will students of this civilised pastime please steel themselves against the temptation to remove stamps from incoming unopened parcels. This is particularly necessary in the case of books being returned by customers, involving as it quite often does, the amount of postage to be finally credited to account. Friendly editors we are sure will pass on to devotees all unwanted Penny Blacks.'

TIME OUT

It would seem there was always time for tea at Heffers. Refreshments were provided either free or at cost for many years and, indeed, there were periods of great abundance. The working day at Heffers included morning and afternoon breaks of fifteen minutes and, until 1971, a one-and-a-quarter-hour break for lunch. From May that year the shop opening time was put back from 8.45 a.m. to 9 a.m. and the lunch break was reduced to one hour. This change applied to all locations except for Sidney Street, where the shop closed for three quarters of an hour and the staff staggered their one and a quarter hour lunch break. The few who still wished to go home for lunch were permitted to continue with the longer break and make up the time at the beginning or end of the day.

Cycling home for lunch had been a routine for many staff at Petty Cury during the post-war decades. Dudley and Marion Davenport occasionally cycled home for lunch in the 1950s. Susan Nunn had to go home during the 1960s because her mother only cooked at lunchtime. If she didn't go home then, she didn't get a cooked meal. On summer's days in the 1940s, Ernest would occasionally invite staff to his garden for lemonade and apples. Audrey Coleman recalls walking to his house during her lunch break. In the summer it could get really hot in

Cycles have always been a very popular mode of transport around the city's busy streets.

146

the top office and the ladies would sometimes climb out of the window, walk along the parapet and cool off on the roof of the building.

The tearooms at Petty Cury, located at the top of the building, were segregated between ladies and gentlemen, separated by a small kitchen so that "never the twain shall meet" (however, it seems this arrangement was flouted from time to time). There was also a small sick room upstairs, in the annex, accessed from the Oriental department. Barbara Shorter operated the telephone switchboard from a small cubicle up in that annex.

Staff on the Petty Cury rooftop. Sheila Reuben (*née* Howe) stands fourth from left with Ann Kidman (*née* Warren) on her right.

Described as tiny and often smoke-filled, the ladies' tearoom overlooked Petty Cury and the gentlemen's room overlooked the rear of the building. The ladies would wave to their counterparts at Dolcis shoe shop across the Cury. Eve Stafford remembers the tearoom as a good place for a tête-à-tête in times of trouble. Win Anstee, also a typist, would signal to her when she needed a few minutes with her upstairs. Privacy was not always afforded to those who desired it in such cramped conditions, and people's foibles had to be abided at close quarters. There were times when Eve and Win would be irritated by the very precise way a colleague consumed her genteel sandwiches – they so very much wanted to say, "go on, take a big bite, rip it apart!" Clive Cornell remembers his colleague John Webb eating small, jam sandwiches with his tea every day. John, like many others, would cycle home for hot food at lunchtime.

The tearooms at Petty Cury were serviced by tea-ladies, a different one in the morning and afternoon. (The morning tea-lady's husband's Christian names were apparently 'Kent, Essex, Middlesex', his parents having been keen on cricket.) Mrs Hall, in the afternoon, could always be relied upon to have the tea poured out ready for latecomers.

In the 1980s, a married couple ran the Sidney Street canteen. The facilities, accessed on the first floor through the Book department, were also described as tiny, or "pokey". At least they were not segregated and could seat around fifteen people. In earlier years a tea-lady, Mrs Lilley, made the tea and lunches. Staff who lived out of town would appreciate a meal in the middle of the day. In the 1950s Sidney Heffer would arrive by taxi to have morning coffee with his son, John, in the boardroom. Veronica Perry had to fill in as tea-lady a few times and, as a young girl, found it quite scary to be preparing refreshments for so many people (there were over eighty staff at Sidney Street).

Rosemarie Hill was unaccustomed to a morning coffee tradition before her arrival at Petty Cury in 1955, but soon fell into the routine. Staff at both Petty Cury and Sidney Street were expected to provide their own sugar. Morning coffee was not always taken on the premises, however. Employees would also frequent nearby cafés. Dudley and Marion Davenport recall:

"All of us used to traipse to the Lyons Coffee House or the Civic Restaurant. And we went round the back of Heffers to the Dugout." (The Dugout was a milk-and-billiards bar in Guildhall Street.) One lady regularly accompanied two close colleagues to the Arts Theatre Roof Garden Café where she would order a cold sausage for sixpence, to consume with her morning coffee. Another, described as a bit of a "gay girl", would ring gentlemen friends using the Petty Cury switchboard and then meet her illicit lover for coffee at the Eaden Lilley department store whenever opportunity arose. Sandra Thompson, a typist in the late 1960s, remembers fun times at Petty Cury; she was once challenged to eat a whole Swiss roll by her colleague, Guy Edwards. The Davenports remember the 1950s as "a very civilised way of working".

In the 1950s and '60s, William Heffer's daughter Pom was a regular visitor to the Petty Cury shop and would arrive on her bicycle at the side door with her parrot, Joey, chained to her basket. She would go to Lyons for coffee with Miss Edwards and Miss King from Accounts, every Thursday morning. One week, as they went in, Joey slipped his chain and caused a bit of a flutter.

In 1968, at the Hills Road offices, Ingrid Bane was responsible for taking orders for freshly-prepared rolls, making the morning coffee and afternoon tea and then washing-up all the cups:

> "Nowadays any young girl would look down on this task as rather demeaning but I enjoyed it and this helped this young nervous junior get to know all the girls in the department when going round taking the orders – and with my confidence, in having to go to the pub next door to take and collect the order for the rolls for the girls' lunch, also dealing with all the money to pay for them."

The Civic Restaurant, a popular venue at the St Andrews Street end of Petty Cury, was large and inexpensive. When Robert, the school-age son of History department manager John Webb, called in to see his father at Petty Cury on a Saturday, he would be taken to the Civic for an orange squash and a packet of Smith's Salt 'n' Shake crisps.

While Sidney Street was undergoing another refurbishment, staff were given a voucher to buy their lunch at the Civic. Mr Court, manager at Sidney Street, one day asked Gerald Criddle for assistance during one lunch hour, and offered to pay for his lunch by way of compensation. Seeing this as an opportunity to dine somewhere nice, Gerald popped to the Dorothy Ballroom next door and had a three-course lunch for 6s 6d. Unsurprisingly, the firm refused to meet more than half the bill. (Gerald would often attend trade fairs at Earls Court in London or Birmingham, with Mr Court or Mr Biggs. These also involved dining out but, as Gerald recalls, he would be the only one drinking as both his managers were teetotal.)

The Dorothy next door to Heffers. The picture was taken in 1953 – the Dorothy closed in 1972.

In May 1971 a professional caterer was contracted to take over responsibility for providing tea and coffee at Trinity Street and to provide a variety of hot dishes for lunch. The staff continued to pay for the food but at cost. Free evening meals were provided for those who worked at locations that opened late during the Christmas period. There was a separate ladies' restroom at Trinity Street well into the 1970s, next to the main tearoom, mainly used by the clerical staff and the secretaries.

Richard Reynolds believes that 'Mrs M' who worked in the main canteen felt sorry for all the bachelors, as she would often give them more than two biscuits and a bigger helping of lunch. Senior managers would sometimes forget they were due to attend a boardroom lunch and, having already eaten in the canteen, would get a call and, off they would have to go for their second lunch that day. Becky Proctor was amazed by the catering on offer in the Trinity Street tea-room; toast and cakes for the morning and afternoon breaks, and popular hot lunches, all prepared by two ladies.

In March 1971, the staff newsletter, *New Shop News*, noted some congestion at tea-time and announced staggered set times of fifteen-minute sittings in order to allow caterer Mrs Veasey time to clear-up between sittings. There were regular reminders for people to phase their breaks. Consequently, not everyone stayed on the premises for their allotted fifteen-minute break. Robert Webb liked to spend his at one of the local cafes; the Whim, Belinda's, or his favourite, the Coffee Pot, round the corner in Green Street.

There were also regular reminders about time keeping. In October 1990, the management declared: 'It would be invidious to mention names and we hope that this statement, which really ought to be unnecessary, will at least reach the conscience of people who are persistently arriving late and taking too long for coffee.' Julian Sedgwick remembers the laid-back atmosphere and pace at Trinity Street, "Some very long tea and lunch breaks taken, and many of those lunches with [publishers' sales] reps being reasonably drink-fuelled. Not quite Madison Avenue standard, but at times the early years felt more like a social club where occasionally you had to tidy the library shelves." The Baron, the Mitre and the Maypole public houses were well within reach. Robert Webb recalls that in the late 1970s, the Blue Boar hotel in Trinity Street was also a regular lunchtime haunt for Science department staff. During 1977 Britain experienced occasional power-cuts, a forerunner of the Winter of Discontent, one of which closed the Trinity Street shop and sent Robert and colleagues off to the Mitre for an extended lunch break.

When the Orders and Book Handling departments moved out of Trinity Street to St Tibbs Row in 1977, office staff there had to make do with a hot drinks vending machine on each floor. Bob Cox-Wrightson (at Heffers for a year from 1998) was impressed by the facilities at the firm's later headquarters in Clifton Road. The on-site canteen served a full range of meals, including freshly-baked scones for the morning and afternoon breaks: "Any place which serves a subsidised cheese scone, I thought to myself, is a civilised place to work!"

Author Pippa Goodhart, whilst working at the Children's Bookshop in the late 1970s, would drop the takings over the road at the main bookshop in Trinity Street and return with biscuits and milk for the staff (not for the children). An Induction Pack given to Lisa Newman in 1988 confirmed the free coffee, tea and biscuits plus a free drink with lunch. Lisa remembers the delivery drivers dropping off tins of biscuits with the books at the Paperback shop in St Andrews Street, "We got told off on more than one occasion because we used to get through the biscuits too quickly, usually within a day or two." Mark Jones represented Heffers Sound at the Staff Forum and recalls good company, debates about whether the male staff should be permitted to wear shorts in summertime, and great biscuits. In July 1989 the management expressed concern in the staff newsletter about the considerable cost of the free refreshments: 'Please can everyone consume them in moderation so that this free amenity can continue for everyone.' Eventually, having calculated that the free biscuits were costing the firm £3,000 a year (£7,260 at today's value), Heffers withdrew the perk.

Eating 'on the go', for Sidney Thomas Munns (a compositor's apprentice at Heffers Printers), many years earlier in 1914, had tragic consequences. The fifteen year old sadly died of acute congestion of the lungs, probably caused by hurrying on his bicycle to County Hall after having eaten a pint of walnuts. He was delivering a Heffers parcel. [43]

Management would occasionally treat the staff. John would buy everyone at Sidney Street an ice-cream; Lucy would send someone out for Chelsea buns from Fitzbillies. A spoof staff newsletter, issued at the height of a scorching 1976 summer, advised everyone to look out for the specially trained HEFFERETTES in blue and green, handing out Coca-Cola and ice-creams.

Catering was also provided on specific occasions when staff were required to work unsocial hours. Late-evening staff meetings were introduced, where 'as many staff as wish may meet informally with the General Managers'. In September 1975, a young John Skelton suitably impressed his colleague Francesca Pearson with his chutzpah in putting forward his bookselling ideas to the managing director, John Welch. So much so, that they got together and married two years later.

Besides these informal meetings, stocktaking days were also catered for. John Skelton recalls, at Trinity Street a young Stephen Heffer in charge of the trolley bringing round free drinks and snacks during stocktaking day. (Pippa Goodhart remembers how Stephen Heffer would always circulate with plastic cups and wine on Christmas Eve, making sure that everyone was included in the festive spirit.) When the stocktaking was finished a staff party ensued, with hot and cold food provided. Christopher South described the 1984 stocktaking after-party as a 'sedate and appropriately scholarly knees-up'. Suzanne Jones, who lived out of town, recalls a somewhat different affair: "Someone would go out an order more pizza than you could carry. There'd always be wine and beer. It was always wise to stay over."

There was a time when staff were permitted to smoke inside the buildings and many did. Smokers were asked to keep their distance from the ceiling smoke detectors after these had been fitted. Julian Sedgwick remembers the impenetrable fug of smoke in the "fishbowl" canteen at Trinity Street at lunchtimes that generally sent him out for fresh air. The canteen window at Sidney Street was also rarely opened. Julian recalls his colleague Ian Catchpole, manager of the Oriental department at Trinity Street, lighting his pipe at the end of each workday, sending up clouds of blue-grey smoke with a satisfied puff.

STAFF PARTY

Immediately after stock-taking on Monday, 1 April, there will be a Party in the shop, to which everyone is invited. The Canteen staff will be preparing hot & cold food, and so that they know how many to cater for, would you please tell your Senior Manager by 15 March if you won't be able to make it.

FAMILY TRADITION

Many of the former employees who contributed memories for this book remember the firm as a place where you were looked after by the managers and where colleagues were generally very kind. As Claire Brown recalls, "it was a place where you could be yourself and everyone looked out for everyone". Even John Heffer, whose management style was in many ways more formal and "scary" than Reuben's, is remembered with affection. As a constant floorwalker, John liked to give staff an impromptu spelling test – "spell chrysanthemum!" Scary indeed! Bunty Heffer remembers the atmosphere of the shops as being very personal. She can picture "Uncle Ernest" standing at the top of the stairs at Petty Cury, greeting everyone as they arrived in the morning. Clive Cornell remembers seeing members of the Heffer family every day.

On special birthdays staff, were invited to 'choose something' from the stock. Audrey Coleman chose *Mrs Beeton's Everyday Cookery* for her twenty-first birthday in 1947. It was inscribed by Ernest.

In the 1960s, the children of long-serving employees were offered a book each Christmas, until they reached the age of ten or so. Robert Webb, whose father John ran the History department at Petty Cury, still has the first book he was given, one with farmyard pictures on thick, cardboard pages.

All staff enjoyed a discount of a third on books, 10 per cent on non-net books and 25 per cent on stationery. Writing in *Trinity Street News* in 1973, John Welch states: 'Because books are special and because they are our business, we should like to encourage the ownership of books by staff as much as possible.' Occasionally employees from other firms, such as Cambridge University Press, would come into Trinity Street asking for a courtesy trade discount and were politely refused.

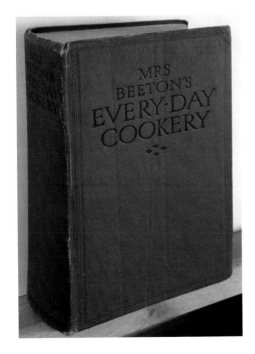

MRS. BEETON'S
EVERYDAY COOKERY

The 21st birthday gift inscribed by Ernest Heffer chosen by Audrey Coleman (*née* Wright).

Petty Cury in the 1950s and '60s (when Reuben was in charge) had a familial atmosphere, remembered as very positive. Frank Collieson wrote about Reuben: 'His charm and his unshowy concern for the happiness of his staff and the contentment of his customers won him immediate affection.' [44] John Welch wrote: 'He was not at home with detail or administration or planning, but he was always meticulous in valuing and thanking those of his colleagues who undertook those chores on his behalf; he was a good master.' [45]

As a young student bookseller from Switzerland new to the country, Rosemarie Hill was advised by Reuben to "be patient" with herself. Despite the staff not knowing what to do with her on her first day (they didn't seem to know that she was coming), Rosemarie found it a very friendly place. Soon after her arrival she was invited by staff to their homes; by Ian Catchpole and his wife, and by Paul Klauber and his friend Arthur.

Norman Biggs, at Sidney Street, also describes the firm as being "family oriented". For Bob Cox-Wrightson, the firm's history gave it "family feel", reinforced, he recalls, when he received his Heffers staff badge.

Marion Davenport (*née* Mynott) remembers how, like many large families, the firm supported its staff during difficult times at home, "When I started in 1948 my mum was taken ill and had to go into hospital. They let me have quite a bit of time off to help my dad look after my younger brother. Mr Reuben was very good." When Peggy Green's father became ill in the 1950s with just a few weeks to live, he wanted to come home from hospital. Reuben gave Peggy time off so she could help her mother to look after him and didn't stop her wages. Much later, after Peggy's mother had died, Nicholas gave her extended paid leave to visit relatives in Canada. Robert Webb remembers that when his father, John, died in 1979, while still employed by the firm, Stephen Heffer called on his family personally to offer condolences on behalf of the Heffer family: "That was so much appreciated at a difficult time. My dad had been at Heffers for over thirty years; it meant a lot to my mother especially." Every Christmas Reuben visited retired members of staff in Cambridge.

Being a 'family' may not have suited everyone, and the atmosphere could at times be cloying. Whilst acknowledging that it could be an enclosed community with tensions, "to which I contributed", Frank Collieson recalled how remarkably well everyone got on, considering they were thrown together on the shop premises every day: "Trying times were overcome" – as with many families, it seems. There were certainly times when a bit of light relief was most welcome. Julian Sedgwick remembers a lot of laughter, prank calls from other staff and even publishers' reps, and in-jokes that ran for days. Peggy Leeming, a former gang-show trooper who oversaw training and pastoral care, would show everyone how to tap-dance up and down the stairs at Trinity Street. Relief also came in the form of social occasions and activities.

SPORTS AND SOCIAL

Before the Second World War, Heffers ran a Sports and Social Club which organised regular dances at Cambridge venues such as the Dorothy and the Rex ballrooms. These occasions were big enough events to warrant coverage by the local press. Many staff liked to socialise, as Dudley Davenport recalls: "Then it was a close knit thing. You got to know each other. Go out for a drink. We had some good times." Eve Stafford enjoyed the staff Christmas parties, held at the Guildhall during the 1950s and '60s. Although he was far too polite to express it, Eve sensed Charles Heffer's regret at asking her for a dance one year, only to discover that his young partner could not quickstep and would much rather jive. It was the first dance of the evening, and their last. Charles should have chosen Peggy Green from Accounts, a keen dancer and founder, with colleagues from Sidney Street, of the Cambridge Dancing Club.

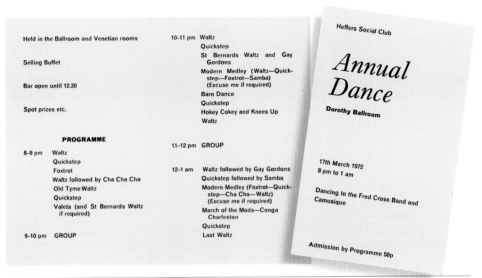

Held in the Ballroom and Venetian rooms

Selling Buffet

Bar open until 12.30

Spot prizes etc.

PROGRAMME

8-9 pm   Waltz
          Quickstep
          Foxtrot
          Waltz followed by Cha Cha Cha
          Old Tyme Waltz
          Quickstep
          Valeta (and St Bernards Waltz
            if required)

9-10 pm   GROUP

10-11 pm Waltz
          Quickstep
          St Bernards Waltz and Gay
            Gordons
          Modern Medley (Waltz—Quick-
            step—Foxtrot—Samba)
          (Excuse me if required)
          Barn Dance
          Quickstep
          Hokey Cokey and Knees Up
          Waltz

11-12 pm GROUP

12-1 am   Waltz followed by Gay Gordons
          Quickstep followed by Samba
          Modern Medley (Foxtrot—Quick-
            step—Cha Cha—Waltz)
          (Excuse me if required)
          March of the Mods—Conga
          Charleston
          Quickstep
          Last Waltz

Heffers Social Club

Annual Dance

Dorothy Ballroom

17th March 1972
8 pm to 1 am

Dancing to the Fred Cross Band and
Camusique

Admission by Programme 50p

This Heffers Social Club dance programme from 1972 shows a wide selection of dances.

At the dances, Eve would be astounded by her colleagues who would rush to pile up their plates as soon as the buffet was announced, as though they hadn't eaten for weeks. At one of the dances, not wanting to appear greedy, she and her friend Gill initially took a modest amount and went back for seconds – only to be mortified when someone loudly exclaimed, "Evelyn and Gillian, don't be afraid of your big appetites!"

Although shop-floor staff frequently worked on Saturdays, the Thursday half-day early closing had its benefits. Together with colleagues, Gerald Criddle would occasionally attend theatrical performances in London on these afternoons. These were paid for by a subscription of one shilling a week and organised by Miss Star on the pen counter and Mrs Snell. In the 1950s and '60s it was possible to travel to London, go to the theatre and have dinner, all for 25 shillings (£26 at today's value).

Time out was also taken in aid of good causes. The firm sponsored University Rag Week events. Sandra Thompson was sold in a slave market for one Rag Day in the 1960s. For several years Heffers sponsored the Rag Week Bed Race twelve-mile relay. In 1977 the 'Heffers Trinity Bed' came a respectable fifth place.

Relaxing on a theatre trip to London in 1962. Vanessa Rule (*née* Phillips) is on the left, next to her is Dudley Davenport. At the table (*rear*) is Dudley's wife, Marion. Eve Stafford is fourth from the right. On her left is Terry Rule and on his left is Mrs Hall, the Petty Cury afternoon tealady.

In the early years, sports were encouraged. Heffers Printers had a cricket team in the 1920 Cambridgeshire Cricket Association Junior Cup Competition and a darts team in the 1939 Cambridge Social Clubs League. Games and sports were also very much encouraged in the 1980s – angling, cricket, badminton, bar-billiards, squash, football, five-a-side football, tennis, hockey, rounders, ten-pin bowling (team name, the 'Bookworms') and darts. A sponsored cycle ride in 1989 raised £250 in aid of Action Research for the Crippled Child. As well as inter-company teams, competitors included other retailers and publishers, such as Stopshops, Robert Sayle, Unicam and the Michael Joseph XI.

OUTINGS

Heffers has always had a sense of fun and a sense of occasion. Many employees and members of the Heffer family participated in annual outings and gatherings to mark special dates in the calendar. The 'works outing' was not of course exclusive to Heffers. Many firms, particularly in the 1950s and '60s, arranged annual day trips for their staff. The purpose was to have fun and, from all accounts, that was what people did. The Heffers outing was a popular day in the works' calendar and most, although not all, staff went. For a couple of years, one bookseller claimed he got the date wrong and didn't go on the outing or into the office that day. Eventually, he was rumbled.

The outings were arranged by an organising committee, with representatives from the Heffer family and the bookselling and stationery divisions, and often took place during May Ball Week in June on a Thursday (that being the half-day). As Norman Biggs recalls: "In many ways people didn't mind where they went. It was a jolly day out."

The evening meal rounding off the day was usually within an easy reach of Cambridge and involved speeches. Bunty Heffer remembers enjoying the outings but recalls her husband John's concern about getting to the destination and back in time: "It was always so worrying, to manage to get wherever we were going back to [in order to] have the evening meal, with speeches ... fitting in with that and getting back on time was a real do." Someone had to be selected from Petty Cury and from Sidney Street to make thank-you speeches on behalf of the employees. Members of the Heffer family who could not attend would send a telegram to be read out.

The outings are remembered as "good and happy" events. One year, Eve Stafford took a photograph of John Heffer landing at the bottom of a slide at an amusement park. He phoned Eve to thank her but she didn't work in the afternoons. Having tried to speak with her a number of times and failing to do so, he resorted to writing a thank-you memo in which he remarked, 'you must be the only member of staff who only turns out for the staff outings'.

Audrey Coleman recalls that everyone was in their "Sunday best" for the outings, although the gentlemen were probably in the same suits they would have worn on a normal working day. There was no dressing down, not even for the beach, where trousers had to be rolled up for a paddle – apart, it seems, with one exception: Stephen Perry from Sidney Street. Fortunately, according to Stephen, no photograph exists of him lying on Great Yarmouth beach with bare chest and leather jacket.

In the 1950s and '60s, limited car ownership may have contributed to the popularity of these trips. Well over a hundred employees would usually go along. Children did not attend Heffers outings, although husbands and wives who didn't work at the firm could join in. The atmosphere on the coaches was jolly, with people singing "rude songs". Eve recalls that Paul Klauber from the Petty Cury Packing department, who had a great sense of fun –"such a colourful character of a man" – would always make the most of the day out. Unlike the King's College staff outings (as Eve, who worked at both Heffers and King's recalls), alcohol was not permitted on the coach (perhaps in honour of William Heffer's temperance views?).

The various destinations included Windsor (1948 and 1954 – and Blenheim Palace), Oxford and Stratford-upon-Avon (1949), Norfolk (1950), the Festival of Britain in London (1951), Felixstowe (1953), the Cotswolds (1955), Clacton (1956) and Boulogne (1961).

On 14th September 1950, 137 employees and their guests toured the picturesque parts of Norfolk, starting with Hunstanton – 'sunny Hunny'. The weather was exceptionally sunny and the party visited Cromer, Great Yarmouth, Lowestoft and the Norfolk Broads. Dinner was at the Samson and Hercules hotel in Norwich.

On 14th June 1951 five full coaches departed from outside the Senate House, Cambridge and headed for London's South Bank for the Festival of Britain. On arrival the party split up and people attended the various Festival attractions, including an afternoon concert in the Festival Hall and a river trip to the Battersea Pleasure Gardens. Dinner on the way home was at the Hendon Way Hotel, Hendon. Sidney Heffer and his wife joined the party for dinner and speeches. The outing was organised by Miss Edwards, Mrs Snell, Mr Brown, Mr Sharp and Mr Elwood. It was on this outing that Dudley and Marion Davenport's courtship began. Marion began work in the office at Petty Cury in 1948, straight from school, and left in 1955 when they started a family.

A party of 150 attended the Windsor outing in September 1954, which included a three-hour ride on a river steamer in glorious sunshine through Datchet and Staines to Chertsey. Dinner on the way home was again at the Hendon Way Hotel.

In 1961 the firm was feeling adventurous and scheduled an outing by air to Boulogne, France, with a charge to employees of £10 (£208 at today's value) per head. Many had never flown before. Susan Nunn was petrified. Gerald Criddle (who went on fifteen staff outings in all), recalls the firm were so anxious about safety, that husbands and wives were asked to travel on separate planes. Some of the older ladies were full of trepidation but in the end thoroughly enjoyed it. At Boulogne they lunched in a casino and took a walk along the sea front. Dinner on the way home was at Stowmarket in Suffolk. As everyone disembarked the coach at the end of a long day they were reminded not to be late for work in the morning.

The outings came to an end in the late 1960s. Norman Biggs reflects, "It ended when the six-day opening came in. You couldn't really close for a whole day. Also, the idea of outings had gone. The world had changed."

The printing works had their own separate day trips. Such an outing in the printing industry is known as a 'wayzgoose'. In 1974, a printed programme was found for a 1938 Heffers wayzgoose to Llandudno, and was featured the local newspaper. The press report stated:

> 'The 106-strong party left Cambridge LMS station at 5.15 a.m. on June 18 and arrived at Llandudno at 10.40 a.m. A great deal of eating, drinking and walking seems to have gone on until the train left for Cambridge at 10 p.m. Happy days, when listening to a banjo on the pier could be a highlight of a day out.' [46]

On 18th June 1987, the discovery of an even earlier programme was reported, for a 1927 wayzgoose to Margate. The programme stated: 'A word of advice for those tempted to go for a swim, sail, row or paddle – yes, even paddle; ladies' knees are now constantly on view so there is no need to be shy.' [47]

Pom, John, Nesta, Reuben & Lucy Heffer (*above left to right*) and employees enjoying an ice-cream (*below*).

Nesta, Ernest & Lucy Heffer (*above left to right*) and Reuben (*below*) taking a photograph.

Coaches transported well over a hundred employees and their partners to a destination each year, and in 1961 they boarded two planes and flew to Boulogne, France. Everyone went in their Sunday best. There was no dressing down, not even for the beach, apart from removing one's shoes and rolling up trousers.

SPECIAL OCCASIONS

"If there was an occasion, we'd throw a party."

Alison Blair-Underwood

The annual general meetings (AGMs) and various new shop openings also provided opportunities for a 'do'. The AGMs were big occasions, held in Cambridge at the University Arms, the Garden House and, more latterly, the Post House hotel (now the Holiday Inn) at Histon. Reuben Heffer prided himself on getting through the business in under five minutes.

The Trinity Street shop was formally opened on the first day of a new university term and year in September 1970, by Lord Butler, Master of Trinity College. It was a significant event, attended by the great and the good, including the Vice-Chancellor, Professor Owen Chadwick and Mrs Chadwick, and by the Lord Mayor and Mayoress of Cambridge. A month after the event, Dr J.R.G.

Bradfield, Senior Bursar of Trinity College, sent the architect, Peter Lord, a copy of the notes he had prepared for Lord Butler's speech. He says in the covering letter that Lord Butler could not follow the notes exactly because of the presence of 'Plum'

Reuben addressing the staff (*left*) before the celebration dinner, 18th September 1970. The dinner (*below*) was held at Trinity College.

Warner, his old friend and the head of rival bookshop Bowes & Bowes. This prevented him from saying Heffers was the best bookshop in Cambridge. Lord Butler did talk about the suitability for the street: "The trade fits perfectly with this part of the City", and the "admirable piece of collaboration … between Town and Gown" and the College's delight in being associated in this way, "with an old and distinguished Cambridge family firm". What he chose not to say was:

> 'We have long had the finest Cambridge College library <u>inside</u> our walls. And now we have the best Cambridge bookshop just <u>outside</u>. Indeed not only the best in Cambridge, but probably the best in the whole country – for whereas Blackwell's at Oxford previously had the edge on Heffers, we think the position is now reversed.'

On September 18th, the night before the shop opened for business, a formal staff dinner was held at Trinity College and was attended by 140 employees. Reuben addressed the staff from the top of the stairs in the shop, before going over the road to Trinity. Shortly before his death in 2016, Frank Collieson recalled this event as though it was, "only yesterday in a way, I remember getting ready for it all".

Trinity College also hosted the firm's centenary celebration, in an outdoor reception at Nevile's Court, on 23rd June 1976. Pippa Goodhart, who first worked at Heffers as a Saturday girl and was invited to the centenary party, recalls: "The fireworks ended with the word, HEFFERS lit up and everybody cheered. I was standing around gawping at everybody and feeling very shy." Robert Webb, who had

heffers:

1876-1976

William Heffer
opened his first shop
in Cambridge
in July 1876

Stephen Heffer (*below, centre*) and colleagues with balloons celebrating the centenary. A gold bookmark was produced (*right*) for the centenary.

Outdoor reception at Nevile's Court, 23rd June 1976.

only left school the previous summer, recalls buying his first three-piece suit for the occasion ("brown pinstripes and wide lapels") and feeling similarly awkward at the party.

Later that month a letter appeared in the *Cambridge Evening News* from a resident, Mrs Helen S. Monro, complaining about the noise from the firework displays:

> *The junketings with fireworks between 10 pm and 10.30 pm on June 23 were part of Heffer's Centenary Anniversary celebrations at a private party … Trinity College should have refused permission for the fireworks display in their grounds at that hour of night … Who knows how many potential scholars or buyers have been lost because his or her sleep was disturbed so that Heffers might celebrate.* [48]

Mrs Sheila Sear responded by writing:

> *If her son or daughter who is taking exams was put off by a mere half an hour of fireworks I hate to think how he or she will find the strength to live for the next 50 years or so in this noisy world of ours … As to the old people being frightened, we have a large number on this estate, and on asking them if they were frightened, they laughed and replied they have lived through two world wars and it takes more than a few fireworks to scare them.* [49]

Each employee was given a keepsake of the centenary – a print, produced by Heffers Printers, of A.C. Pugin's illustration for *Ackermann's Cambridge* (1815). This was also made available to customers.

Gifts presented to employee Frederick Anstee in the 1920s.

Frank Collieson MA (*centre*) on
the day he received his award,
2nd May 1987 with his wife,
Mary, and Dr Frank Stubbings,
fellow member of the Cambridge
Bibliographical Society.

Gifts were made to employees to mark significant occasions. The following year, a silver
crown issued by the Royal Mint to mark the Queen's Silver Jubilee was given to all staff in a
presentation box.

Other events were more personal. In 1987, bookseller and bibliophile Frank Collieson was
awarded an honorary MA by the University of Cambridge.

Frank recalled the great thrill of being sixty and receiving a letter from the Vice-Chancellor
saying the University wanted to grant him the award: "Some people said it should be a
doctorate. I thought, ah, doctors are ten a penny. To be an honorary Cambridge Master of Arts,
I couldn't have been more happy." The firm bought Frank's gown and provided the champagne
for the celebration. The oration given at the award ceremony stated:

> 'The public at large admires his handiwork in the windows and catalogues of
> Heffers, where, with his sure sense for what is visually right, he takes charge
> of typography, displays and exhibitions. Still others have experienced his
> inexhaustible grace and charm as master of ceremonies at those celebrated
> parties which have done so much to establish Heffers as not only a bookshop
> but also a meeting place of scholars and booklovers.'

WEDDING ANNIVERSARIES AND A FUNERAL

In 1913 William and Mary Heffer celebrated their golden wedding anniversary with a supper and
social evening at the Masonic Hall, Cambridge. The guests numbered 114 and the employees
presented a gift to the couple of a silver salver. The catering was by Eaden Lilley and the
entertainment provided by the Black Pom Troupe and a magician, Mr Laurie Sydney.

In 1923 the Heffers celebrated their diamond wedding, again at the Masonic Hall. On this
occasion they received a congratulatory telegram from HRH George V and Queen Mary. The
Cambridge press observed: 'There is no doubt that Mr and Mrs Heffer have endeared themselves
not only to a large circle of friends, but to their large band of employees, this good relationship
being in no small way responsible for the firm's success.'

During the afternoon William and Mary were 'at home' at the Masonic Hall to a large number
of invited guests, including the Mayor and Mayoress of Cambridge, Councillor and Mrs Lavender
and the Chief Constable, Mr R.J. Pearson. Music was provided by Messrs Millers' orchestra.

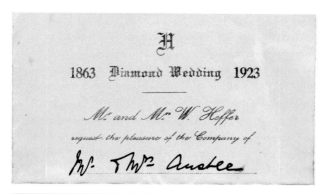

Invitation to William and Mary Heffer's Diamond Wedding celebration. The printed programme for the event included the Toast List and Concert (*below left*) and a Programme of Dances which included several 'Valses', 'Fox Trots', 'One Steps' and a 'Sir Roger'. There was a four course menu accompanied by beer and iced still lemonade.

TOAST LIST & CONCERT

The King, The Queen, Queen Alexandra, The Prince of Wales, and the Royal Family.

SONG	MISS M. MILLER

OUR GUESTS.

To propose	MR. HEFFER
To respond	MR. R. D. LITTLECHILD

OPENING OF SOUVENIRS

SONG	MR. T. KEMPTON

MR. & MRS. HEFFER.

To propose	MR. F. J. SEBLY
	MR. R. S. DIGBY
	MR. G. NEWMAN
To respond	MR. HEFFER

SONG	MR. T. KEMPTON

THE DIRECTORS.

To propose	CAPT. W. R. ELWORTHY, O.B.E.
To respond	MR. E. W. HEFFER

SONG	MISS M. MILLER

Amongst the presents was a handsomely-bound book containing an expression of good wishes and the names of all the employees, accompanied by a silver clock. In the evening, there was a supper at the hall for 160 employees and their spouses. The toast of the evening was proposed by Heffers' oldest employee, Mr F.J. Sebley, supported by Mr R.S. Digby from Sidney Street and Mr G. Newman of the printing works. William's own toast was responded to by Mr R.D. Littlechild. Each employee was presented with a pair of candlesticks. The evening's entertainment involved dancing and a whist drive.

In 1928, on the occasion of another special wedding anniversary, the employees presented William and Mary with a handsome, beaten-silver fruit bowl on an ebony stand, with an accompanying scroll bearing the words:

'We, the employees of the firm, as members of your family in a lesser degree, feel we cannot let the occasion of the 65th anniversary of your wedding pass without some small token of our affectionate esteem and regard. We therefore ask your kind acceptance of the accompanying fruit stand, together with our sincere wishes for continued years of good health and happiness.'

By way of thanks, William and Mary issued a note to all the staff stating,

'We would like to thank personally each and every one of the Staff ... but as this is impossible we ask the recipient of this letter to try and realise the feeling of joy and pride and affection which was ours when your representatives of our large "family" came to us yesterday bearing your tokens of remembrance, and we hope that the happiness that has been ours may be equally yours.'

William died later that year. Even for such sad occasions as Heffer family funerals, many employees would attend to show their respect. Some of the funerals were large gatherings, also attended by the dignitaries of Cambridge. William Heffer's, in August, was held at Christ Church, after which he was interred at Mill Road Cemetery. The Cambridge press reported that the service had a total absence of gloom, something that would have delighted William. The hymns were *Fight the Good Fight* and *Now Thank We All Our God*. The newspaper observed that William was a driven man with a forceful personality: 'He had something more than learning: a dominant personality, a character which was never swerved from the goal that it had set itself: and he achieved in spite of enormous difficulties, where perhaps many others would have failed.'

William and Mary Heffer at home.

Three Men in a Bookshop.

Need people?[1]
Then Bummel along to

heffers:

20 Trinity Street.
[1](Not to mention the dog.)

Advertisement devised by Frank Collieson in the programme for 'Jerome K. Jerome at the Union Society Debating Chamber' at the Cambridge Festival 1981. A selection from the works, familiar and unfamiliar, of the great humourist, devised and presented by Gabriel Woolf in association with Heffers Booksellers.

11

HEFFER PEOPLE

"I went into a bookshop and life followed me there.
Interesting people and events."

Alison Blair-Underwood

EVERYDAY FOLK AT HEFFERS

The phrase 'nowt so queer as folk' seems appropriate when it comes to depicting everyday folk at Heffers – the staff (often referred to as 'Hefferites') and the customers. As several former employees observed, the shops were a haven for many 'characters' and eccentrics. According to Richard Reynolds, the Trinity Street staff were all, in their way, eccentric. Perhaps this can be said about the book trade in general.

Claire Brown, who began her career at Blackwell's in Oxford, before being invited by John Welch to join Heffers in 1968, remembers the generation of booksellers who had been through the war. People who had more than just a career, who knew a lot and who had style: "You knew that you might be frightfully clever and aged twenty-five but there were other people who were frightfully clever and aged fifty-five who knew a very great deal." David Wilkerson describes the bookselling side as being "more edgy". The outside shops did, however, have their fair share of eccentrics. Sarah Burton recalls that Tony McGeorge would hire interesting people at Heffers Sound, "eccentrics and geeks – people who were passionate about their subject". Mark Jones, also at Heffers Sound, was told that some of the bookshop staff thought the Sound staff a bit eccentric (rather like the pots calling the kettles black, it seems). Certainly the different Heffers locations had their own distinctive cultures, very much separate worlds. As Norman Biggs acknowledges: "We had our moments ... It makes life interesting, characters in the firm and in the customers."

Like their customers, some booksellers would take a dislike to a particular book or author. Janet Tinling, who ran the Children's department at Petty Cury, refused to stock *Where the Wild Things Are* by Maurice Sendak, a best-selling 1963 American picture book. Duncan Littlechild, a strong pacifist, disapproved of Winston Churchill and actively discouraged customers from buying Churchill's *A History of the English-Speaking Peoples* in the 1950s: "you don't want to buy that old rogue", he would say. Considered 'old school' by then, colleagues would often observe Mr Littlechild 'kowtowing' to academic customers on the telephone. Littlechild began his fifty-four-year career at the firm as an apprentice in 1903. During the First World War he had a spell as a prisoner of war and in November 1917, the *Cambridge Independent* reported:

'LANCE-CORPL. R. D. LITTECHILD – Mr. E. Littlechild, 2, Park-parade, has received the following letter from an officer regarding his son, Lance-Corpl. R. D. Littlechild of the Royal Scots: 'I regret to be the bearer of news which will cause you great anxiety and suspense, but your son, Lance-Corpl. R. D. Littlechild, went into an attack on the 2nd of this month, and it has been so far impossible to ascertain anything definite regarding his fate. None of the company who arrived saw him hit, but several fell in to the hands of the enemy. You will have to wait patiently, perhaps several months, before hearing news. He was a cheerful and brave soldier, and a highly efficient N.C.O.' Lance-Corpl. Littlechild had been in France since June. He was formerly employed by Messrs. Heffer and Son, Petty-cury.'

After the war ended he returned to employment with Heffers. On Mr Littlechild's retirement from the firm, the Cambridge press reported that generations of publishers' 'travellers' (sales representatives) had called on him and he always liked to remember the more leisurely days of the early part of the century when the traveller would call in his silk hat and with his bag of books pushed on a barrow from the station by an outside porter. Perhaps a more incongruous memory is that of Mr Littlechild in regular conversation with a favourite customer of his, English comedian and actor, Cyril Fletcher, who, for many years, appeared as the Pantomime Dame in the Arts Theatre every Christmas.

Suzanne Jones once overheard a bookseller's response to a request from a customer to purchase a particular volume, "if you must, you must but it's absolute crap": not something that Suzanne, as a seventeen-year-old new member of staff, had expected to hear.

On the other hand, some booksellers took an inordinate liking not just to particular books, but to reading in general (and who can blame them?). Marion and Dudley Davenport remember a colleague at Petty Cury in the 1950s and '60s who sat in a corner of his section reading for most of the time. Another would occasionally lose his temper at a particular book and flail around with it, knocking other books off the shelves. There were moments when colleagues seemed to forget that they were there to provide a service, but then you might say that this was no different to any other organisation. Perhaps at Heffers, it was question of the extent to which idiosyncrasies were accommodated; as indeed many were. Some staff may have found it very difficult to work anywhere else; perhaps that is why so many spent their entire working lives at the firm. In the second half of the 1950s, after joining the firm, Gerald Criddle and Norman Biggs noticed the predominance at all Heffers locations of unmarried ladies who had been there since leaving school (conversely, of course, some employees left overnight and were never heard from again).

One Sidney Street manager, 'Barmy' Clarke, who ran the Maps and Guidebooks department in the 1950s, had perfected a way of avoiding customers. From his counter he could see the front door and when he saw someone approaching the shop he didn't wish to serve, he would niftily step out the side door and re-enter from the front. Now, behind the customer, he was able to go up to them and say, "Are you being served? Oh, I see you're being taken care of."

Another Sidney Street assistant, while generally affable in his dealings with customers, was always on the edge of sarcasm. Being in the General Stationery department on the ground floor, he would regularly have to re-direct customers who wanted to purchase envelopes, sold in Office Equipment on the second floor. On one occasion he told a customer to, "go out of the front door, turn left and you'll find a drainpipe. Climb up that to the second floor and you'll find Office Equipment".

Then there were managers who had their own habits and favourite sayings. Clive Cornell remembers Tiny Copping in the Second-hand department; every time you saw him he asked, "had all your holiday yet?" Frank Cowell, manager of the Classics department at Petty Cury, would always play the King's College Chapel Carol Service in the office on Christmas Eve and break out a bottle of brown ale to mark the beginning of the festive season. Paul Klauber in the Packing department would frequently break into song, usually *The Foggy Foggy Dew* or, for Rosemarie Hill, *Oh Rose Marie I Love You*. Frank Collieson recalled Fred Sharp, manager of the Oriental department, who whistled a tune, "which we could always remember because it was tuneless." Fred certainly whistled while he worked and it was usually hymn tunes. He worked for Heffers for over sixty years and sadly died just three weeks after his retirement at the age of eighty-one. He had set up the Oriental department after finding a collection in Eire while serving there during the First World War.

At the time of his retirement in 1993 after spending twenty-nine years with the firm (having joined when Reuben asked, "Would you come here on a handshake?"), John Cheshire recalled that one of his first jobs in the old premises in Petty Cury was in the theology section, where his first customer was the Archbishop of York. The team of which John became a part was affectionately known as the Crazy Gang. John also reflected on the customers,

> "One of the things I shall remember in retirement is the assortment of characters we have met over the years – including a shoplifter named Fiddler and a drunk who was lying on the floor of the music shop," he said. "Frank Collieson, by then a fellow director said, 'Put on some Elgar – that should make him stand up!'" [50]

Reuben had a habit of putting up his hands and saying "don't tell me now", when staff approached him. Not that he was unapproachable; far from it. There were of course times when he was busy with duties elsewhere. Sheila Reuben, in the Petty Cury Invoice Office, remembers being asked to take a letter down for Reuben Heffer to sign. On entering his office, she was told by his secretary that he was on the bench. Sheila thought he must be having a bit of a lie-down, not realising he was in fact officiating as a magistrate.

Every Wednesday, Reuben, accompanied by Frank Collieson, would walk over to the printing works to see what was going on there. In his 1985 obituary, *The Times* declared that Reuben, 'Spending a great amount of his time on the "shop floor" … was always ready for an informed gossip with any member of the university.' [51] It is apparent that, unlike John, Reuben's style of management was more 'hands off', although he was actually very involved with overseeing the business and concerned with the welfare of the staff. He would pre-arrange a telephone call, to be made one hour into board meetings, as a very judicious solution to excessively lengthy meetings. His son, William, remembers that his father's happiest days were spent signing cheques for authors. John Heffer's habit, apart from giving instantaneous spelling tests, was rearranging things on the counters at Sidney Street. Reuben, instead, would share his excitement about finding a new word. Rosemarie Hill remembers him telling her about the word 'tiliaceus', meaning a shrubby tree.

Frank Collieson cited a 1964 *New Yorker* survey of the British book trade:

> 'The scholarly atmosphere of the Petty Cury establishment is due at least partly to R. G. Heffer, a rather easygoing product of Corpus Christi College, Cambridge, who became the overseer of the firm when his father died, in 1948 … R. Heffer takes pride in being deficient in drive and ambition, and preens himself on certain archaic features of his bookshop.' [52]

In 1964 Reuben had what many have described as foresight when he appointed John Welch as general manager of the bookselling division. By then, it was clear that someone was

John Welch.

needed to project manage the exit from the premises at Petty Cury, which was on the horizon. John Welch was not, however, the first 'outsider' to be in a senior position in the firm. There had been other non-family directors such as Mr Court, Mr Edge and Mr Newman. While the chairmanship was always reserved for a family member, non-family members were not prevented from holding other senior roles. Alison Blair-Underwood believes John Welch, while "totally Machiavellian", acted as great buffer between Heffers as an old family institution and Heffers as a modern firm. Perhaps his strength was a particular blend of enterprise and innovation. It was a huge business and he pulled it into the twentieth century.

Richard Reynolds recalls that John Welch would often have a look through the stock boxes. On one occasion the stocks included the *History of Jesus College* by Gray and Brittain. Richard had written on the card, only order in tens via John Welch or 'through Jesus'. John Welch then scrawled on the card after 'Jesus', the word 'College'. On being asked why he had made that change, he said he didn't want any confusion. On another occasion Mr Welch said he wanted every edition of Jane Austen brought upstairs to the boardroom. Suddenly boxes were being moved and two ladies took a barrow-load of books up, having removed them all from the shelves. One wonders if that was what he really meant. The ladies didn't share his reaction.

John Welch was also one of the best managers that Alison had ever worked for and he did have a sense of humour that may not have been apparent to everyone. Eve Stafford remembers his reaction to an April Fools joke she once played on a colleague, Les Palmer. She typed up a spoof memorandum from John Welch, announcing that he had decided to have various members of staff to tea in his office each morning and that Les would be the first. The note requested staff to bring a cream bun. On entering Mr Welch's office, Les apologised for not having a cream bun with him, much to everyone's subsequent amusement, including John Welch.

On a less humorous note, like many organisations certainly at the time, some male colleagues had what was then termed 'wandering hands', giving the phrase 'hands on' a somewhat different and unpleasant meaning, particularly for the ladies. It would not be appropriate to deny that this occurred, as so many have mentioned it when interviewed for this book, but it would also be inappropriate to name the alleged culprits, who are now long gone. Needless to say, for some ladies, taking dictation could be a hazardous chore, when they were trapped between the wall and their manager. For others, there were certain amenities best avoided, so not to give a gentleman colleague an opportunity to get too close. John Welch was made aware of certain issues on his arrival in 1964 and his response, not untypical of the time, was, "we all have our little idiosyncrasies".

Former Heffers staff have met many memorable customers and there are notable incidents that have stuck in the memory. As already suggested, some staff seemed to view customers as an interruption to their bibliographic pleasure and pastime – although bookshop customers, in the main, shared that passion for reading. One such regular, Professsor Hersch Lauterpacht QC FBA LLD, Whewell Professor of International Law and a member of the International Court of Justice, had an extensive private library at his house in Cambridge and would occasionally invite Heffers staff round to view it. Professor Lauterpacht came into Petty Cury every two or three weeks and would take away a pile of books on 'appro' (on approval). On one occasion, Robert Hill was invited for a visit and went along on Thursday after half-day closing. He remembers the house being packed with meticulously catalogued books and an amazing cross-reference system that the professor had devised himself. He also remembers being treated most graciously by the professor, who served coffee with cream.

Liz Davies recalls assisting a very "posh" lady, dressed in beautiful furs, asking for the "self-help divorce" books at Trinity Street. Directed downstairs to the Law department, she later reappeared and thanked Liz warmly, adding "and you know the best bit – I put it on HIS account!" Becky Proctor particularly remembers offbeat customers seeking self-help books. One well-groomed gentleman, dressed from head to toe in white denim, was looking for a book on confidence but his retort to every suggestion was, "I've got that one". Another would always stand on a footstool, looking for the books on her list and, finding them, would drop each selection on the floor. On another occasion, a customer came into the Sociology department asking for a book that he didn't have the title or author for. He did have a description: A4, quite thin with a green cover. Becky spent a long time trying to locate the book with nothing much to go on, but to no avail. As he left in a huff the customer shouted back, "this is the kind of service I've come to expect at Heffers?!" Other customers were far more relaxed. In the 1970s the Children's Bookshop had a big round red seat, which one gentleman customer liked to curl up on and go to sleep. Another would play the violin at Trinity Street: it seems that Reuben didn't mind.

One enquiry at Heffers Sound, put to Mark Jones, was: "Heard a fabulous piece of music on the wireless a few months ago. Had a piano in it. At least I think it did. Might have been an oboe. Do you know what it was?" To which the only answer was an emphatic: "No." However, said Mark, if the customer could recall a short snatch of the music, there was a good chance they would be able to identify it. Mark's colleague Ali had an incredible talent for correctly "naming that tune", however tunelessly the customer performed it.

Over time, staff would get to know their customers' life stories and occasionally customers would express their appreciation for the interest and consideration given. Sarah Burton, also at Heffers Sound, once received a round of applause from customers who witnessed her dealing with a difficult customer on Christmas Eve. Heffers Sound frequently supplied customers with music to accompany life's most significant moments – baptisms, weddings and funerals. A gentleman once asked Mark Jones if he knew what the theme tune to *The Archers* radio show was called. Mark replied cheerfully, "Barwick Green; are you a fan?" "No, it's for my wife," came the reply. "She was … It's for her funeral." And the gentleman promptly burst into tears. Mark recalls similar reactions on a number of occasions when bereaved customers came searching for their late loved one's favourite music.

Mr Doggett makes himself at home in the Trinity Street shop. A picture taken some years ago – he still visits Heffers every Saturday.

Mr Doggett, a well-known regular customer for over thirty years, still comes into Trinity Street and is fondly regarded. Suzanne Jones recalls his love of David Lean films and Charles Dickens. Catherine Turner (*née* Hastings) always heard him from across the shop and remembers him helping himself to her colleagues' sandwiches. Jean Clarke (aka 'Jean the Bean') remembers Mr Doggett answering the phone if no-one was at the desk on the shop floor, shouting, "There's no-one here at the moment!" Very elderly, he still regularly asks if there are any jobs going at Heffers, talks about the 'Beard Law' and will stand at the front of the shop yelling the cast names from the 1947 film production of *Oliver Twist*.

Interestingly, a Mr Doggett was employed by the firm as a Clerk at Petty Cury in 1903, at a wage of 5 shillings a week. Not to be confused with his namesake the customer, John (Jack) Horace Doggett was gassed in the First World War but recovered and continued to work for Heffers after his return, in the Packing department (he died in 1971).

Julian Sedgwick fondly recalls Trinity Street when it was still flourishing as an academic bookseller. The parade of "influential, cosmopolitan, charming, grumpy, famous, notorious, odd and downright weird customers" intrigued him: "I made far more significant and stimulating friendships than at school or university." His most memorable customers included Chris Patten (now Lord Patten of Barnes), fresh from losing his seat in the 1992 general election, asking for advice on books about China. He was about to head off for Hong Kong, to oversee the transition to Chinese rule. He left with a stack of books. Then there was the President of Armenia, with his hefty bodyguards, bearing down on the Oriental department, asking to see the Caucasus section. They dutifully examined the twenty or so titles, but made no purchase. Julian also remembers surreptitiously watching Terry Waite while he quietly browsed the shelves in the basement following his release from captivity. His dignity and sense of calm fascinated Julian. Terry Waite (former Envoy for the Church of England, kidnapped and held captive in Lebanon from 1987 to 1991) did a signing for *Taken on Trust* at Trinity Street in 1993.

Not all customers were as dignified and some were not 'customers' at all. One, a serial shoplifter, had been plaguing Trinity Street for a few weeks. It took the booksellers of 'E' department a long time to work out that a regular was responsible for the disappearing books. Believing the security scanners to be operative he had lined a holdall with foil and was stealing ten monographs at a time, to order. Cameras were duly installed and, by instruction via various phone directions, Julian followed the suspect to the pavement outside, where he nabbed him. Caught red-handed the culprit was furious. There then followed an interminable interval in a back office with the managing director, waiting for the police to arrive. Julian recalls that after an awkward ten-minute silence his manager asked the shoplifter if he'd been on his holidays yet.

Norman Pittenger, Anglican theologian and regular Heffers customer with a great interest in crime fiction, might have given the impression of shoplifting. Disliking paper bags he would stuff the books he had just paid for into his pockets before departing the shop. Pittenger, who lived in Cambridge from 1966 until his death in 1997, was perhaps displaying 'green' credentials, such as those alluded to in a 1990 edition of *Trinity Street News*, which alerted staff to customers who objected to the use of any kind of wrapping in the 'present green environment'. Such foresight.

Librarian Chris Jakes has used Heffers all his professional life: "Heffers has always been grounded in its community. It has served both the academic and town communities and is as much part of the streetscape as Trinity College opposite." Others have observed a sense of ownership amongst the customers. Norman Biggs recalls: "People took a surprising interest in the firm. There were those who took a great interest in Heffers and treated it as their own. People used to talk about 'my bookshop'."

Mrs Cope, at Sidney Street in the early 1980s, worked on the ground floor and could see down Market Street from her department, and watch all the customers coming in: "People recognised you. It was so personal. Many regular customers." Helen Siedel, a regular customer at Petty Cury during early 1970, has very fond memories of Heffers:

> "A gracious and old-English-style store … Always a bit labyrinthine, and a delight to find 'whatever' by landing on the appropriate level and foraging. That old store left its mark on me, an American. It represented much of what I like about England, and is tied to my personal history in Cambridge. A wonderful atmosphere of treasures on many levels."

The American servicemen who visited Sidney Street thirty years earlier, in the 1940s, were friendly and loud. Joan Clark remembers that they didn't stand in front of the counter and would instead come and stand behind her while she typed their order.

One satisfied customer sent an appreciative postcard from Scandinavia in 1981,

> *Just want to express my appreciation of Heffers cooperative and friendly attitude as regards providing information and rapidly despatching books. I encountered great difficulties with Blackwell's and finally gave up. Thank you for the catalogue, I am now pondering some more titles. I have long wanted to know of a service of books in my own field.*
>
> *It is snowing here and winter is lightening its grasp.*

The booksellers' personal service would occasionally involve that something extra. Richard Reynolds remembers his visits to the widow of John Wilfred Linnett (former Vice-Chancellor of Cambridge University and Master of Sidney Sussex College). Mrs Linnett had been a regular customer, coming to Trinity Street with lists of the books that she wanted. When she became housebound, Richard started calling at her home. He would arrive at 6 p.m. and often stay until eleven, talking books. Each year she liked to choose a single title to send to friends and relatives at Christmas. Books were sent to friends such as the writer Charles Schulz and journalist Alistair

Cooke. One year, it was the novel *Sophie's World* by Jostein Gaarder. Richard thought perhaps her philosopher friends wouldn't want this particular book, but she insisted it would be fine.

Crime author Alison Bruce moved to the Cambridge area in 1998 and immediately made a beeline for Heffers. Richard provided encouragement and support as Alison embarked on her successful writing career. In the early days he read her drafts and suggested agents and publishers she could approach. Alison always acknowledges Richard's support:

> "He's been hugely generous with his time – for me and for other authors. He really knows what he's talking about and I was incredibly lucky to have that resource locally. I felt I was getting encouragement from someone who is part of a proper bookshop. It's that investment in people, readers and authors. It's more than a walk through the door. Heffers is a one-off."

Alison launched her first novel in 2005 at Heffers, and in 2016 published her eighth book, *The Promise*. As a sort of thank you to Heffers, she located one of the murders near the bookshop in Trinity Street. Alison can't imagine launching a book anywhere else, and not just because of the special relationship, "Heffers are very good at giving you window space, they have a substantial mailing list and a lot of people come to their events."

HERE COME THE FRESHMEN

> *'It is clear that the beginning of this Michaelmas term is perhaps the most important we have ever faced. We have the stocks to meet any demand and we have the staff to sell them; this is one of the most important months in the history of 20 Trinity Street.'*

> *Trinity Street News* September 1972

At the beginning of each academic year an invitation from Heffers was sent by post to every freshman at every Cambridge college. This tradition began in 1900 when the firm started sending a catalogue and circular to every freshman (first-year student) and second-year student. [53]

All freshmen were encouraged to open free accounts, and in doing so had to give their home as well as their college address. For many years, several hundred student accounts were set up at the beginning of each academic year. Whichever region or country the students came from, wherever they went after leaving Cambridge, their account went with them. Quoted in Bradley's oral history of the book trade, Nicholas said that in his father's and grandfather's day, if you were a student it was enough to give the name of your college when you applied for credit. At the end of every term, Heffers sent a list to the college tutor of every student who owed more than £20, because, according to a statute of Cambridge University, students had to pay all tradesmen's bills in town before they were allowed to take their degree. [54] Heffers were indeed trade, and their status as such was emphasised by some older academics who resented the imposition of monthly instead of quarterly account statements after 1964.

For the start of the academic year, at Petty Cury, non-academic stock was removed from the shop windows and replaced with a selection of books 'indicating the depth of our undergraduate stock'. No publishers' representatives were seen during the first two weeks of term and no Saturdays were allowed off for shop staff during October. Throughout Heffers

Students in the Trinity Street shop at the start of term in 1989.

– both bookselling and stationery – it was all hands on deck. Dudley and Marion Davenport remember the queues of students at Petty Cury, as they opened up the shop especially early: "It was mad at the start of term. It was the biggest bookshop in town. Galloway & Porter had the same thing, but not on the same scale."

Besides being the bookshop known all over the world, and supplying universities worldwide, Heffers is extremely well connected with the relatively small world of Cambridge academia. The custom that flowed from students, academics and libraries through links with the University has been very important to the growth of the business over many decades.

> 'We must see that proper attention is paid to Faculty Reading Lists and that we have the right text books for undergraduates; Managers will be making outward visits to Faculty Libraries and to Lecturers to seek their help and advice and to keep them informed as to what we are doing to provide books for them and their students.' *Trinity Street News, 1972*

Heffers supplied books, stationery, publishing and printing services to Cambridge University clients – and still today supplies many Cambridge colleges. Norman Biggs remembers the Sidney Street shop erupting at the beginning of each October with a huge influx of people. In the 1930s almost every undergraduate 'coming up' (starting university) had a printed visitor's card, but by the 1950s this aspect of the trade had more or less disappeared. Stephen and Veronica Perry, at Sidney Street from the late 1960s, remember that everything hinged on getting the students in. Nothing had to go wrong, nobody disappointed.

Shelley Lockwood, a fresher at Queen's College in 1983/4, remembers getting her Heffers account:

> "One of the most glamorous and grown-up things I did in my very first weeks in Cambridge was to open a Heffers account. As I recall, it was interest-free credit – an absolutely fatal temptation for an ardent bibliophile like myself! I did manage to rack up substantial debts and went in fear and trembling down to the basement of the Sidney Street store to pay off a little bit at a time when I could. Heffers is synonymous for me with my first years in Cambridge. I bought so many of what were then life's essentials; my diaries, the Lecture List, paper, pens, writing paper and envelopes, cards and wrapping paper, books, books and more books."

However, by the late 1980s students had begun to use personal computers and were not buying significant supplies of stationery materials.

In the 1950s Robert Hill at Petty Cury recalls he was able to recognise the students' colleges from their attire, as nearly all wore their college scarf. Many were very smartly dressed. Julian Sedgwick recalls a middle-aged German perpetual student with a duelling scar who would ask for incredibly obscure titles and then clip his heels together and give a neat bow. When Peggy Green and her friends started the Cambridge Dancing Club, they made it 'town and gown' as including "the University people" meant they always had partners. And sometimes a girl in the office would be invited to accompany a student to a May Ball. Peggy remembers students sitting and reading for hours on end in a corner of the shop and returning the next day to carry on. Other employees remember this also.

Undergraduates no longer buy a lot of books when they start their courses, although David Robinson, who manages Trinity Street today, says that students still appear to prefer physical books to e-books. And they do still read in different parts of the shop, although some are possibly taking photographs of the text on their smart phones. To David it is a joy to have the students in:

> "In a similar vein, so many shops in Cambridge say 'don't lean your bikes against the window'. I don't care if it slightly obscures the window, you're in Cambridge, what do you want? I don't mind if people bring their bikes in, and occasionally they do. That's what we're here for. We're a part of the community. If I could have twenty students a day sitting reading in the shop, that would be great."

David is very much reflecting Reuben's thoughts in 1970, when he declared that students can come and sit on the floor and, "study our books". There was a time during the three-day week in the 1970s (when business hours were limited in order to conserve electricity during a period of industrial action) that going into the shop was rather hazardous. Power-cuts meant the lights were out and staff had to take students downstairs two or three at a time, guided by a torch to search out textbooks. Catherine Turner at Trinity Street remembers special late opening of the shop for students; some had a book allowance from their college. However, many told Julian Sedgwick that they found the Trinity Street shop "intimidating". Perhaps it could be a little so, particularly for those who had never before encountered bookselling on this scale.

Becky Proctor remembers parents and students coming in during the early 1990s to buy A-level textbooks, particularly for Law, Psychology and Economics. Arriving at the till with books piled so high in their arms that you could only just see their nose, they were buying the entire reading list. David Wilkerson recalls textbooks piled around the floor everywhere. On occasions Heffers would receive a group visit from a school.

Many sixth-formers and undergraduates found part-time and temporary work at Heffers. Author Barbara Lorna Hudson read languages at Cambridge from 1959 to '62. She worked at Heffers in the holidays and insists she was never bored, even with having to spend time laboriously typing book titles and publishers' details on index cards in a dusty backroom at Petty Cury. But she was shocked at the demands of many customers who seemed to expect booksellers to have read everything in print and in any language. She was, however, very grateful to have been allowed to take books home and read them without buying them. It had never occurred to her that in doing so, she was a better resource for the firm.

Mark Jones, at Heffers Sound, remembers when a student colleague asked him what his plans were for the weekend. He replied rather smugly that he was just going to the pub with his mates. Looking forward to a three-night banquet of booze that would encompass trips to the Dobblers, Geldart and Cambridge Blue, and possibly the Live & Let Live, Mark hoped his colleague wouldn't be jealous. When asked in turn what he would be doing, his colleague replied, "Oh, I have to go on a course and learn how to shoot polar bears". It turned out he was preparing for an expedition to Greenland. Suddenly Mark's weekend crawl around the pubs off Mill Road didn't seem so impressive.

Another student colleague at Heffers Sound was once asked if they stocked any Massanet. She led the customer to the King's College Choir section and pulled out a Mozart CD. The customer protested. "But yes!" argued the student, "Mozart – Mass in A. Just as you asked." She also tried selling Mantovani to a man who had asked for Monteverdi.

THE HEFFER DIARY

For years, the Heffer Diary, a specially designed diary for the university year, was an essential item for many and was given free of charge to all those who could prove their undergraduate status. Every autumn Heffers printed and distributed around 10,000 copies, not just to students but also to colleges and libraries. The diaries were advertised in the *Cambridge Evening News* and in *Varsity*. Copies were issued and also sold from both Petty Cury and Sidney Street. Many townsfolk would buy a copy, and occasionally landladies of student accommodation would come in and demand a free copy for themselves. Copies would be piled up on the General Stationery counter at Sidney Street and Petty Cury's ground-floor cash desk. Eve Stafford recalls an occasion in the 1960s when the new girl on the desk had misheard a colleague telling her the diary was free. Thinking he had said "three", everybody she served that day was charged 3 shillings per copy. Gerald Criddle, who started his job at Sidney Street during the first week of term in 1955, remembers how frenetic it was. The policy was strictly one free diary per student and the price of the diary to those who had to pay was 2s 6d (£3 at today's value). Susan Green, working at both Sidney Street and Petty Cury in the 1960s, recalls students attempting to get a second copy by making up stories about friends outside who couldn't walk into the shop.

The Heffer Diary was not only useful with its Cambridge map and week-to-a-page layout; it was also a great advertisement for the firm. As Bunty Heffer acknowledges, it became a Cambridge tradition. Elaine Feinstein in her biography of Ted Hughes describes 1951 Cambridge and mentions the diaries: 'The gabled shops along Petty Cury bent forward like those in a children's fairy tale. Heffer's bookshop, with old-fashioned

AUTUMN, 1960

You are invited to ask at either shop for your free copy of the "Heffer", as our Diary, now in its 38th year, is known

The Bookshop	The Stationery Shop
3 & 4 PETTY CURY	18 & 19 SIDNEY STREET
UNIVERSITY TEXTBOOKS	NOTEBOOKS—BOUND & LOOSE LEAF
BOOKS OF GENERAL INTEREST	COLLEGE NOTEPAPER
SPECIALISED WORKS	FILES & CARD INDEXES
IN THE ARTS AND SCIENCES	FOUNTAIN PENS & REPAIRS
	TYPEWRITERS & REPAIRS
English and Foreign	DRAWING INSTRUMENTS
Secondhand and New	ARTISTS' MATERIALS

Printing Works : *Hills Road*
Heffers Penguin Bookshop : *Trumpington Street*

W. HEFFER & SONS LTD., Cambridge

Autumn 1960 student voucher for Heffer diary.

knobbed glass in its bay windows, offered free maroon leather pocket diaries, lecture lists and wall calendars to undergraduates.' [55] Heffers also sold the Cambridge Pocket Diary, the Cambridge University Handbook, the Varsity Handbook, the Residents List and the Cambridge University Reporter (the Michaelmas edition of the Reporter contained the Lecture Lists).

In 1971 it was decided that everyone, including students, should pay for their copy. The price was set at 10p (£1.40 at today's value) and, as announced in *Trinity Street News*: 'All freshmen this year will receive a note inviting them to buy their Heffer Diary and to open and account.' For a few subsequent years the diary was once again free to students who were then required to exchange a voucher for their copy, but eventually the practice was viewed as not financially viable and it had to stop.

Shelley Lockwood still has all her Heffer Diaries:

"The Desk Diary is the earliest one I have – the sixty-first, from 1983/4 – which was my first year at Queen's College where I was studying History. Looking at it takes me straight back to the intensity of it all: the weeks in term are crammed full of lectures, supervisions, 'squashes', Union Society debates, sherry with the tutor, Freshers' photos, films, trips to the pub – venturing out as far as the Elm Tree which I remember felt like a long walk – breakfasts at Waffles, the Seeley, the UL, essay crisis after essay crisis! But then the weeks of the vacations are completely blank because I packed my desk diary away in the locked cupboard in my student room – I had to empty and vacate the room at the end of every term. I am not at all surprised that I didn't choose to take it home for the holidays; it was very much a *Cambridge* diary, not for recording events anywhere else. I have a Heffer Desk Diary for every year that I was a student at Queen's and then a Research Fellow at Christ's, from 1983 to 1993. They, together with the Cambridge Pocket Diaries, also bought each year from Heffers, record my academic life in all its hard graft and busy glamour."

Shelley Lockwood's Heffer diary. The drawing is by Cambridge artist and illustrator, Jon Harris.

The Heffer diary today – remaining largely unchanged.

In 2000, the Pembroke College Winnie-the-Pooh Society wrote to Heffers to complain about the new policy to charge students for their diary, and a correspondence ensued. [56]

Pembroke College, Cambridge, CB2 1RF
8 October 2000
The Manager
Heffers Bookshop
20 Trinity Street
Cambridge

Dear Sir or Madam

As I am sure you are well aware, for the past few years you have been offering free diaries for students at the beginning of the academic year. Several of our members have taken advantage of this offer whilst buying their copy of 'Winnie-The-Pooh'.

You can probably imagine our horror, as we discovered that these diaries would now cost us £3. The dramatic repercussions of this have hit hard amongst the poorer students of the city. Personally, I have had to go through last year's diary with a pot of Tipp-Ex removing all the entries and altering the dates, but others are now begging on the streets without food or shelter, just because they did not have the funds to cover this.

We would therefore like to suggest that you reinstate your offer. Otherwise, you may force our members to shop elsewhere, causing a massive decline in the sales of books by A.A. Milne. However, if you should feel that offering free copies of 'Winnie-The-Pooh', by the aforementioned Mr Milne, would be a better solution, we would consider it a reasonable compromise.

A representative would of course be welcome to attend one of our weekly meetings, held every Saturday of full term, should you wish to discuss this matter further.

Thank you for taking the trouble to read this letter in such times of hardship.

Yours faithfully

Owen Barritt

Foreign Secretary

A reply, written by David Wilkerson, pointed to the spiralling production costs and an offer of the 'first bite of the cherry' for any diaries surplus to requirements. This offer was gladly accepted on behalf of the forty-four members of the Society.

The Heffer Diary has other literary connotations: it gets a mention in *Engleby* by Sebastian Faulks, when the protagonist uses the map in his diary to find Malcolm Street, Cambridge, so he could go and gatecrash a student party there. [57]

The diary is still produced today: the only significant change to the layout is that now the week starts on a Monday, instead of a Sunday as had been the style in earlier years.

CAMBRIDGE ACADEMIA

With its publishing, bookselling and stationery activities, Heffers' relationship with Cambridge academia was viewed as important and carefully nurtured. William Heffer, Reuben's younger son, says his father felt that putting people in touch at the University was his greatest social purpose.

Frank Collieson remembered Reuben as very easily occupying that middle ground between town and gown, as Reuben's father also had. One would often witness friendly banter between a mature Reuben and academic clients, such as, "Why, are you still alive?", an expression often exchanged with Joseph Needham CH, FRS, FBA, scientist, historian and sinologist.

In the way of college-courts and quiet scholastic porticoes, of gray-walled gardens and ivied nooks of study, in all the pictorial accidents of a great English university, Cambridge is delightfully and inexhaustibly rich.

HENRY JAMES

All this and

heffers:

too. Here's richness!

Advertisement devised by Frank Collieson in *The Cambridge Review*, May 1977.

As a Cambridge alumnus and businessman, Reuben was very well connected with University clients and would often introduce college bursars to each other. That was in the days when universities were generally less competitive. After the Second World War, Sidney Street appointed its first sales representative, who almost exclusively called on the colleges. They were treading in the footsteps of the founder, William Heffer, who first visited the colleges with his offer of Stone's Filing Boxes in the late nineteenth century. By the late 1960s, Sidney Street had four such reps. And the traffic was two-way: sometimes the wives of visiting academics would come and work in the Book department at Sidney Street.

Norman Biggs recalls some of the characters from the world of Cambridge academia who regularly used Sidney Street; and members of the University would often look in at Petty Cury and Trinity Street to check if their own publications were on sale. A number of them had an enduring relationship with the firm. One of the Proctors used to come into the Sidney Street shop early morning, soon after nine o'clock. He hadn't combed his hair, he

Award winning edition of Keynes' *Henry James in Cambridge* published by Heffers.

clearly hadn't shaved and his pyjamas were sticking out from the bottom of his corduroy trousers. Another time, an academic customer ended up running out of Sidney Street screaming because they could not find a particular type of stationery file that fitted his *exact* requirements from the hundreds of options available. For Julian Sedgwick, the regular academic visitors returning for conferences year after year further enriched the sense of family in the firm.

Heffers once received a letter of complaint from Sir Geoffrey Langdon Keynes because he thought the green doors on Sidney Street unattractive. Heffers was Keynes's publisher, having issued an award-winning edition of *Henry James in Cambridge* in 1967, produced and designed by Will and Sebastian Carter of Rampant Lions Press (Will Carter worked as a designer at Heffers from 1934 to 1949).

The firm also assisted with the sales of a publication written by Keynes's wife, Margaret, shortly before she died; a short history of the Darwin home in Cambridge (Margaret was Charles Darwin's granddaughter). *A House by the River: Newnham Grange to Darwin College* was published in 1976, under the imprint of Darwin College but printed by Heffers, who helped to sell around 950 copies within a year.

Julian Sedgwick remembers a King's College academic who would send one of his "boys" down for an urgent order, "Florid faced, his temper could be fierce and he was quite scary when he turned up in person. I remember him storming down the corridor looking for Michele [Julian's manager], shouting, 'Where's that BLOODY woman?!'" Clearly far from

Queen Mary and Westfield College
Mile End Road
London E1 4NS

Telephone: 071 975 5555 Ext 3410
Fax: 071 975 5500
Telex: 893750

1 August 1990

Dear Sir,

I write to congratulate Heffers most warmly on the recent display of Third World and Classical feminist and women's studies, mounted in the basement of the Trinity Street shop. I think it is quite remarkable that such a thoughtful and informed presentation could be produced within a bookshop (as opposed to an academic department at a University of Polytechnic). I bought a number of books from the display, which would otherwise have escaped my attention. And I confess that I returned a day or so later to add a number of other titles to my course reading list for the MA in my department here.

Bookshops are increasingly merely commercial outlets. Since I moved my academic affiliation from Cambridge to London I have become all too aware of the shortcomings of the average so-called 'academic' bookshop. I intend to retain my account with your shop even after I move my family to London, because I (and I am sure many others) value the real expertise which you offer.

When I made inquiries as to who was responsible for this particular display I was told that it was Ms Michele Thomas (who I remember well from the time when she used to be in charge of the feminist section of the shop). I wonder if you would be so good as to pass on to her my congratulations for the display?

Yours faithfully,

Professor Lisa Jardine
Head of Department, Mile End

Professor Jardine's letter praising Heffers and Michele Thomas.

incompetent, on another occasion, in 1990 Michele was highly praised by the eminent academic, the late Professor Lisa Jardine.

Julian also recalls the ageing Central Asian specialist whose lists were difficult to source and who had a temper always at the ready. The day before Julian's honeymoon, he was given a list including *Teubners, de Gruyter* and other far more obscure research foundation publications. All, of course, needed as soon as possible. When Julian explained that he would be away in Germany on honeymoon, his customer pointed out that he would be near most of the publishers and could "pop by" and pick up his orders.

For Julian, sometimes the job felt like an adjunct to the University. Academics, and particularly classicists, became friends and they gave him a great send-off party in the faculty when he left Heffers in 2003. He made a very close friendship with an ageing Japanese academic, Professor Yoshio Kanamaru, who filled his holiday from university in Tokyo by coming to Cambridge to study his real passion, classical tragedy. They were kindred spirits: one had grown up looking West and one looking East, and a deep bond developed. Julian ended up working for Professor Kanamaru in an unofficial capacity, travelling to Japan several times and essentially adopting him into the family. The professor became a kind of grandfather to Julian's two boys. Julian says, "if nothing else, this friendship alone made my whole time at Heffers worthwhile".

Sometimes, for the younger bookselling staff, working at Heffers felt almost like being at college. Robert Webb recalls a discussion with Professor H.C. Darby, an authority on fens and marshland, when he worked in the Life Sciences department in the late 1970s. "Why are you working here?" the professor enquired of the then-teenage Robert, hinting that perhaps he could be doing better for himself. "I love books and I love learning," Robert replied. It was impossible to work in a bookshop and not absorb knowledge.

12

VISITS, SIGNINGS AND CELEBRITIES

Over the years, Heffers have hosted many formal and informal signings, seminars, colloquiums, visits, receptions, parties, exhibitions, demonstrations and workshops. In the 1970s, '80s and '90s, especially, countless famous (and some latterly infamous) notables attended such events and many returned on a regular basis. Frank Collieson, who designed numerous exhibitions and displays, recalled the parties, speeches and refreshments "with marvellous and hospitable surroundings".

The exhibitions, usually on the 'platform' at Trinity Street (the mezzanine floor), often featured selected publishers. In 1972 a platform exhibition was held to mark André Deutsch's twenty-first publishing birthday. In 1984, a party was held to celebrate the first twenty titles of Polity Press, an imprint whose books were initiated and edited in Cambridge but produced and distributed by Blackwell's. The firm also made the most of significant anniversaries for exhibitions such as the 350th anniversary of birth of Samuel Pepys (1983), the bicentenary of Samuel Johnson's death (1984) (*Johnsononiana*) and the 200th anniversary of the French Revolution (1989, the topic also of a special catalogue). Heffers Sound had their own platform exhibitions, associated with live music performances and receptions.

Heffers also sponsored events at the Cambridge Union to coincide with significant occasions. For example, a display of *Eliotana* in July 1980 to mark George Eliot's centenary accompanied a Heffers sponsored reading in the Debating Chamber entitled *The Female Shakespeare, So To Speak* by Gabriel Woolf and Jill Balcon. In 1984, as a part of the Cambridge Festival, the firm sponsored an event at the Cambridge Union featuring Frank Delany, offering a selection from his personal literary diet.

National organisations occasionally had their activities featured on the platform, for example the National Association of Flower Arrangement Societies of Great Britain, British Waterways and

A selection of invitations to Heffers events, devised by Frank Collieson.

For I bless God
in the libraries
of the learned
and for all the
BOOKSELLERS
of the world.

An Invitation..

Books
are to be call'd for, and supplied, on
the assumption that the process of
reading is not a half sleep, but, in the
highest sense, an exercise, a gym-
nast's struggle; that the reader is to
do something for himself. WHITMAN

THIS BOOK IS ABOUT HEFFERS

**"Cambridge is the only town
where one can buy milk from
a Bull and ink from a Heffer."**
OLD SAYING

'The left leg of a frog'

Dissections from the Heffer
archive on exhibition in the
bookshop at 20 Trinity Street,
to mark the firm's first
hundred years.

Last few days! 9 to 5.30.

heffers:

1876-1976-

Time has no divisions to mark its passage,
there is never a thunder-storm or blare of
trumpets to announce the beginning of a new
month or year. Even when a new century
begins it is only we mortals who ring bells
and fire off pistols.

THOMAS MANN, *The Magic Mountain*

heffers:

Founded in Cambridge in 1876

Flyer for the firm's 1976 centenary exhibition and adertisement, devised by Frank Collieson.

Canals, and the Scrabble Society (who would play all-comers – copies of *The Official Scrabble Dictionary* were awarded as prizes to high scoring contestants). And there would be one-off exhibitions celebrating local institutions such as *Fulbourn Hospital Then and Now* (1975), with special emphasis on the work of the volunteers at the hospital. A very successful exhibition put on in 1993, with several authors including Jill Paton Walsh, Minette Walters and Lindsay Davis, as part of Richard Reynolds's *Bodies in the Bookshop* initiative which began in 1991, resulted in sales totalling £11,631 (£23,860 at today's value).

Demonstrations have been given – on flower arranging, airbrush art, knitting, stencilling, embroidery, sugar craft, lacemaking, graphology, Chinese brush painting and dream analysis. A wine tasting session with Malcolm Gluck of *Superplonk* proved to be very popular. In 1994, author Sybil Marshall sat for a lunchtime portrait demonstration at the Art shop by professional artist James Horten. There have been many artist demonstrations, as well as wall and window displays featuring artists and photographers. For example, watercolours of the Scott Polar expedition (1972) by Edward Wilson, the drawings by artist and biologist Jonathan Kingdon that featured in his publication *East African Mammals* (1982) and photographs from Charlie Waite's *Venice* (1989).

Heffers collaborated with academics from the University of Cambridge and other universities, and with the British Council, on seminars and colloquiums. For example, the 1982 British Council English Studies Seminar, chaired by Professor Malcolm Bradbury with guest speakers including Margaret Drabble, Geoffrey Hill and Doris Lessing. A reception for the attendees was held at Trinity Street. In 1987 the firm supported a successful Chekhov colloquium (which featured a visit to Trinity Street by Russian television) and a British Council course on *Conservation Crisis in Libraries*, organised by the Cambridge University Librarian. In 1988 Trinity Street hosted a Russian Soviet reception. This is perhaps what people mean when they say that bookselling is more than retail.

Heffers has been used as a film location. Robert Webb, an assistant in the Science department, remembers some excitement at Trinity Street when the BBC filmed actor Lee Montague, dressed as Charles Darwin, browsing the shelves for a *Horizon* programme, *Darwin's Dream*, in which the naturalist time-travelled to 1977 to explore twentieth-century advances in science. Staff were asked to keep out of shot. The programme was reviewed in *New Scientist*: 'Gathering up an armful of books on various aspects of evolution he retires to the quiet of the Linnean Society where he ponders the growth of the child he has fathered.'

Norman Biggs recalls that after the move from Petty Cury to Trinity Street, the events blossomed because the facilities were so much better: "There were quite a lot of evening parties with drinks and canapés ... Sometimes it was a signing and sometimes it was giving the public an opportunity to meet authors. We didn't do that at Sidney Street, it was a different world. We would occasionally have an artist evening." Clive Cornell recalls: "We used to have a combination of academics and showbiz people. And politicians." And Alison Blair-Underwood says: "We sat in Heffers and the world came to us."

Frank Collieson, who was in his element at Trinity Street, recalled some great occasions:

> "We had many very good evenings and launched all sorts of books with jokes and big parties. It began in 1973 ... There were one or two sticky guests but lots of lovely guests. [PD James was lovely but Ruth Rendell terrified everybody.] It was entertainment on a considerable scale. People poured into the shop. No-one went to Blackwell's in Oxford, who would ask, 'how do you get people to your parties?' I say, make them welcome, give them a good time!"

Much business at Heffers was conducted over a glass or two. As Frank Collieson acknowledged, "gin played a large part in the life of Heffers". Alison Blair-Underwood says, "I had the honour of being the wine mistress for years. I would go down to Berry Brothers and buy stuff. So many interesting events. It was great fun." The publishers' representatives, as well as the booksellers, enjoyed their drink. Dudley Davenport recalls that the reps would stay in town for three or four nights, as they couldn't get around all the Cambridge bookshops in one day. "They would invite you for a drink and a meal. A colleague at the Cambridge University Press used to take reps out for a meal every week, just for the company. Usually to the Blue Boar hotel in Trinity Street."

Bookseller Catherine Turner remembers being taken out to lunch by publishers' reps and one in

Raising a glass in the bookshop.

particular who would always regale her with stories about his hapless love life. But it wasn't always about the drink. Julian Sedgwick recalls the regular return of favourite reps and visiting academics. Over the years most booksellers made good friends with the longer-serving reps, "coffees, lunches and free books flowed".

Whilst these varied activities attracted wide attention and audiences, the real focus for the firm's events was the authors and their books. Although occasionally the subject matter suited the ambiance perfectly, as in 1993 when the chef Keith Floyd came along for an evening about his television series, *Far Flung Floyd*. According to the staff newsletter, 'Wine flowed, Bells flowed down Floyd, and a good time was had by all.' Sales of Floyd books on the night totalled £1,314.97 (£2,456 at today's value).

Suzanne Jones, who organised many events and author signings from the early 1980s, reflects on the days when people would queue from six o'clock in the morning to get their copy on the day a book was published. Many queued round the block and waited for hours to meet the author. Signings that stand out for Suzanne are Richard Adams's *Watership Down* (published 1972), Alan Aldridge's *The Butterfly Ball and the Grasshopper's Feast* (published 1973) and Aleksandr Solzhenitsyn's *The Gulag Archipelago* (published 1973). Robert Webb also recalls chatting to Alan Aldridge about his illustration work for the Beatles, while getting his copy of *The Butterfly Ball* signed.

Suzanne spent an inordinate amount of her time in the 1970s, '80s and '90s with publishers in order to see what was coming ahead and to make a pitch for authors to do signings. Frank Collieson is remembered as being adept at charming authors into doing signing sessions, but would occasionally forget to tell people that they were happening. At that time signings were special. According to Suzanne, "to get someone like Bill Bryson, or a politician, or Dirk Bogarde and Sir John Mills, would create a stir". Claire Brown also recalls the excitement when "it was somebody really big".

Suzanne also organised many visits. Different from the signings, these were occasions when an author would come for lunch. Suzanne remembers these as "very jolly affairs, with lots of wine and cheese". Every Saturday, she would get in supplies from Eaden Lilley for a lunch gathering at Trinity Street that was open to any authors who happened to be in town, "we always had the best that Eaden Lilley's could offer". The firm's senior managers would join in and use the time to chew over the events of the week. Amy Wilkerson, working in publishing today, says: "Heffers has a reputation as a good place to take authors. You know they'll be looked after and Heffers is well connected into the community."

Selling 100 copies of a book at a signing was considered a success. Some signings exceeded expectations and some disappointed. Richard Reynolds remembers John Mortimer's signing for *Clinging to the Wreckage* (1982). Despite being a hugely popular book, only a handful of people turned up. At least on that occasion the author was present, unlike the one arranged for another bestselling writer who, although living only three miles from Cambridge (not a mile more, not a mile less), failed to show. Perhaps there was some misunderstanding about the dates. When this particular author did actually turn up for a subsequent signing, he found the pen supplied unsuitable and a member of staff was duly despatched to purchase a replacement. In 1994, *Heffers Bookselling News* was delighted to report that twenty minutes into a very well-publicised event by the same author at the local Dillons, no-one was there.

Sometimes the book launches would involve something different. In 1994, air cadets formed a guard of honour for the author, and John Heffer, at the launch of Arthur Marshall's autobiography *The Arthur Marshall Story: A Century of Wings and Wheels*. In 1995, Heffers

A Lister Jaguar in the Trinity Street shop on the ocassion of the 1985 launch of Robert Edwards' *Archie and the Listers*, the story of Archie Scott Brown and Lister cars.

The Wilkerson family dressed up at the launch of the fifth Harry Potter instalment, *Harry Potter and the Order of the Phoenix* at Heffers in 2003. David Wilkerson, three times a Heffers bookseller and at Trinity Street from 1981 to 2003, met his wife, Alison, through the firm. Their children, Amy and Chris, spent much of their childhood in the Children's Bookshop and later both worked at Heffers.

hosted the official launch of Robert Edwards' *Archie and the Listers*, the story of Archie Scott Brown and Lister cars. For the occasion, Lister Jaguars were lined up and down Trinity Street. There was even one in the shop.

In 1990, Clive James had a Heffers event at the Arts Theatre – 'An Evening with Clive James', to launch the third part of his memoirs, *May Week Was in June*. "Clive James was always around," remembers Alison Blair-Underwood. The poem, 'Apotheosis at the Signing Table' (*see p.9*) shows that he clearly holds Heffers in his affections.

Events like these drew large crowds. In 1984, Jayne Torville and Christopher Dean (the British, European, Olympic and World champion ice dancers) had a signing at the Grafton Centre shop which was a manic event. Of course, in more recent times, the phenomenon that is J.K. Rowling's *Harry Potter* has been an extraordinary crowd puller for the launch of each book in the series. It is not unusual for the whole family to participate, dressing up to suit the occasion.

THE VISITOR BOOKS

The Heffer family enjoyed the events just as much as the staff. Here are Bunty, John and Stephen with comedian Arthur Askey at the signing session for his book, *Before Your Very Eyes – An Autobiography* in 1975.

Heffers kept a Visitors Book, from the first 1973 signing, by Lady Antonia Fraser for *Cromwell, Our Chief of Men*, until 2008. These (there are nine) are a valuable record of the hundreds of book signings that took place.

Claire Brown recalls the queue for a Joyce Grenfell event going on forever. She felt it was not right that an elderly author, who also happened to be blind in one eye, had to see so many people. When Claire herself reached the front of the line and proffered the book, the author asked if she would like her to write something special? "Not wanting to hold her up, I said, 'no thank you', but she replied saying, 'Oh, how dull, one so longs to know who it is for!' She did that for everybody." After a signing in December 1971, Joyce Grenfell wrote to Reuben,

> *I enjoyed that somewhat overwhelming signing on Dec 2. Thank you for asking me. And for the delicious foods that followed the endurance test! I never imagined that singing a book meant turning into a salesman too but it's a most pleasant way (for an entertainer) to meet the public and the affection and warmth is quite stunning at times. Doing it at Heffers is all pleasure. Can't say I feel quite the same about W.H.S or Boots at Brent Cross Shopping Centre!*

Joyce Grenfell left delightful sketches in the visitor book along with effusive thanks after each visit, including this self-portrait and a sketch of the queue in the shop at Trinity Street.

Alison Blair-Underwood has many memories of signings: "David Attenborough was lovely and kept coming back. Terry Pratchett never put a time limit on things and was so pleasant and lovely." In 1993 a Terry Pratchett signing attracted a very large crowd. He signed 548 books in two and a half hours that day, including street maps of Discworld, spoken-word cassettes and videos, generating total sales of £3,734.42 (£6,975 at today's value).

Suzanne Jones organised signings with Michael Palin at Cambridge, as she had at Blackwell's in Oxford. In 1992 his Trinity Street signing attracted a long queue round the corner into Green Street. The shop ran out of books and staff were sent to other shops scrabbling for more. Michael, she recalls, was charming and signed copies for everyone.

Heffers Booksellers News reported that Trinity Street was brought to a standstill in 1993 by a visit from Margaret Thatcher, to sign copies of her memoirs *The Downing Street Years*. Lady Thatcher signed over 600 books in just under two hours, some for people who had been queuing all afternoon. During that week Heffers sold a total of 1,017 copies. Thatcher wasn't the first Prime Minister to visit Heffers: Edward Heath signed his book *Music* at Trinity Street in 1976 and in 1969 Harold Macmillan had a signing at Petty Cury for the third part of his autobiography, *The Tides of Fortune*. (During the 1970s, '80s and '90s Heffers made a small annual donation to the Conservative Party as well as donations to charities.)

MARGARET, THE LADY THATCHER, O.M., P.C., F.R.S.

HOUSE OF LORDS

LONDON SW1A 0PW

27th October 1993

Dear Mr. Heffer

Thank you so much for organising the book signing at Heffers yesterday afternoon.

I was thrilled to be in Cambridge again and delighted to meet all the people who had queued for such a long time. I was also very encouraged to see so many undergraduates taking an interest in the book. I hope they will not only enjoy the book, but build on the achievements of the 1980's in the years ahead.

It was a wonderful afternoon and one I shall remember for a long time.

All best wishes

Yours sincerely

Margaret Thatcher

Nicholas Heffer Esq

The *Cambridge Evening News* declared on 27th October 1993, that Lady Thatcher had conquered Cambridge, 'Forget poll tax riots, Black Wednesdays, and her bitter exit from Number 10, this was Maggie's day'. Over six hundred members of the public waited for up to two hours to meet her. The average encounter lasted just nine seconds.

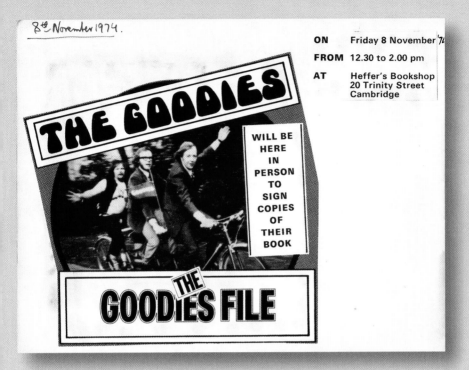

8ᵗʰ November 1974.

ON Friday 8 November '74

FROM 12.30 to 2.00 pm

AT Heffer's Bookshop
20 Trinity Street
Cambridge

THE GOODIES

WILL BE HERE IN PERSON TO SIGN COPIES OF THEIR BOOK

THE GOODIES FILE

Flyer for the Goodies book signing, 1974 (*above*).
The Goodies, Graeme Garden, Tim Brooke-Taylor and Bill Oddie (*below*).

With many thanks to
Heffer's for proving how
wrong we were not to shop
here when we were 'up'.

Goody wishes from

Graeme Garden

Tim Brooke-Taylor

& Bill Oddie
M.A. Cantab. 63.

P.S. "The Goodies" in case you don't
remember us now ....

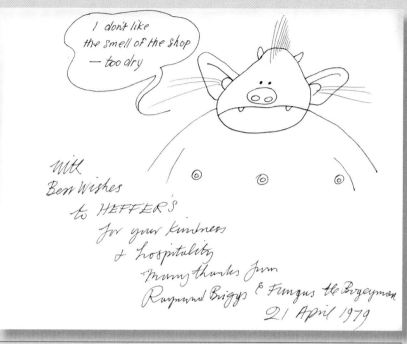

Raymond Briggs, 1979 (*above*).
Alistair Cooke, 1982 (*below*).

(The search for the Trojan War finally came full circle back to Trinity Street, and, fittingly enough, to Heffers'!)

Thank you for a splendid lunch, Michael Wood.

June 21st 1985.

Michael Wood, 1985 (*above*).
Sue Lawley, 1990 (*below*).

Thank you for the signing, the lunch AND the gossip!

Sue Lawley

November 1990

SUE LAWLEY'S
DESERT ISLAND DISCUSSIONS

To the educators of my youth,
the pleasure-providers of my maturity,
& (no doubt) the bankruptors of
my old age — assuming that I
live long enough to continue buying
Books at the very best bookshop
in the British Isles.
With thanks for your
company, in every sense,
John Simpson
7th Aug. '91

John Simpson, 1991 (*above*).
Michael Palin, 1992 (*below*).

Thankyou for a warm welcome at Heffers —
certainly warmer than the Poles !
and for a beautifully efficient production line —
Michael Palin
15:12:92

Stephen Fry was caused to suffer grievous callouses of the right middle finger this day, the 16th April 1994 — & was treated to soothing hob-nobs, buttered scones & jam, warming conversation by the unduly charming Heffers management —

love & thanks

Stephen Fry

16.iv.94

Stephen Fry, 1994 (*above*).
Michele Roberts, 1994 (*below*).

post-haste to Heffers
but never
post-feminist

thank you for your kind welcome
and hospitality —   Michele Roberts
                          Sept 194

Sue Townsend came here and signed
books and drank wine and smoked
five cigarettes. She also had a
good laugh and enjoyed herself.
Many thanks to the staff of Heffers.
Sue Townsend
(48½)

Sue Townsend came here, drank copious amounts of wine,
smudged the book with cigarette ash, and was
last seen heading towards Dillons with
a flame-thrower and a pyromaniacs glint
in her eyes.
Respectfully.
A. Mole Esq. (27¼)
(a.k.a. Nicholas Barnes)

Sue Townsend, 1994 (*above*).
Colin McNaughton, 1996 (*below*).

Preston looks into the future.

Colin McNaughton ♡ 1996—

Heffers chained me up for three hours and whipped me to sign all the books. Please send help or fresh whip.

Terry Pratchett, 1997 (*above*).
Shirley Hughes, 1998 (*below*).

To all at Heffers
with gratitude and very best wishes
Shirley Hughes
November 1998

Posy Simmonds, 1998 (*above*).
Anthony Browne, 2000 (*below*).

13

LAST WORDS

"Heffers is, must be, and always will be different"

Nicholas Heffer, 1991

The story of Heffers is a truly fascinating segment of Cambridge history. Reflecting author Penelope Lively's assessment of the book trade as a world of 'persons, of personalities, of personal relationships', [58] the 140 year chronicle of this remarkable firm, aspects of which are shared in this social history, has been shaped by all those who worked in and with Heffers, and by its patrons.

Ernest, in his 1933 address to young booksellers, declared that a bookshop is a 'microcosm of everything of importance which is happening in the world'. It is true that bookshops are close to the heart of our communities, and long may they remain so. Whilst the world may well be a different place today, Heffers (now owned by Blackwell's) is still a great Cambridge institution. Indeed, it is hard to imagine the city without Heffers.

The very last words are left to bookseller and bibliophile Frank Collieson (who sadly, in May 2016, passed away). Remembered by the Heffer family as a 'marvellously creative man', Frank had recently declared:

> "What Heffers means to me was a chance to be involved in something of value; all my life and all these books. My time at Heffers was the culmination of something totally civilised. This was where it was. Standards."

BIBLIOGRAPHY

Barham, J. (1986) *Backstairs Cambridge*, Ellisons' Editions, Orwell.

Black, M. (2011) *Learning to be a Publisher: Cambridge University Press, 1951–1987, Personal Reminiscences*, Cambridge University Press.

Bradley, S. (ed.) (2008) *The British Book Trade: An Oral History*, British Library.

Brittain, F. (1947) *Arthur Quiller-Couch: A Biographical Study of Q*, Cambridge University Press.

Chrimes, N. (2012) *Cambridge: Treasure Island in the Fens – The 800-year Story of the University and Town of Cambridge, 1209–2009*, Hobsaerie Publications, Cambridge.

Collieson, F. (May 1986) 'Remembering Reuben', *Cambridge Review*.

Faulks, S. (2008) *Engleby*, Vintage Books.

Feinstein, E. (2001) *Ted Hughes – The Life of a Poet*, Norton.

Heffer, E.W. (2011) *Instructions to the Young Bookseller*, Oleander Press.

Heffer, S. (1952) *William Heffer 1843-1928*, Heffers.

Homberger, E., Janeway, W. and Schama, S. (1970) *The Cambridge Mind: Ninety Years of The Cambridge Review 1879–1969*, Jonathan Cape.

Hylson-Smith, K. (1992) *Evangelicals in the Church of England, 1734–1984*, Bloomsbury.

Keynes, G. (1981) *The Gates of Memory*, Oxford, Clarendon Press.

Mann, S. (2005) *A Wonderful Thing for Cambridge: The Evelyn Hospital – 1921 to 2003*, Grant Editions.

McKitterick, D. (2004) *A History of Cambridge University Press: Volume 3. New Worlds for Learning 1873–1972*, Cambridge University Press.

Oldfield, M. (April 1944) 'Cambridge and its Stationers: An Unbroken Tradition of the Stationery Trade', *Stationery Trade Review*.

Petty, M. (2015) *A digital scrapbook comprising 4,000 pages of extracts from Cambridge newspapers relating to life in and around Cambridge, Cambridgeshire and the Fens, 1897–1989*.

Sanderson, J. (1964) 'Cambridge Bookshops', *The Private Library: The Quarterly Journal of the Private Libraries Association* Vol. 5 No. 4, October 1964.

Smith, J and Stray, C. (2001) *Teaching and Learning in Nineteenth-Century Cambridge (History of the University of Cambridge)*, Boydell Press.

Stubbings, F. (1991) *Bedders, Bulldogs and Bedells: A Cambridge ABC*, Emmanuel College, Cambridge.

Topham, J.R. (1998) *Two Centuries of Cambridge Publishing and Bookselling: A Brief History of Deighton Bell and Co., 1778–1998, With a Checklist of the Archives*, Cambridge Bibliographical Society, Transactions, 11.

Turner, R. and M. (July 1979) 'Family Businesses in Cambridge: An Interview with Mr John Heffer, Chairman of the Heffer Group of Companies', *Cambridgeshire, Huntingdon & Peterborough Life*, Vol. 13 No. 145.

W. Heffer & Sons Present with their Compliments, A Few Photographs of their Premises, A Brief Outline of their Business History, A Concise Catalogue of the Articles which may be Procured at each Department (1909).

Ward, Philip (1976) *Cambridgeshire Broadsheet, Heffers Centenary*.

Welch, J. (2004) 'Heffer, Reuben George (1908–1985)', *Oxford Dictionary of National Biography*, Oxford University Press.

Wilson, J. (2010) *Cambridge Grocer: The story of Matthew's of Trinity Street 1832–1952*, R.A. Wilson.

THOSE WHO KINDLY SHARED THEIR STORIES

Many shared their stories and generously loaned precious mementos of their association with Heffers. Everyone is listed here, including those who have not been quoted directly in the book. The years given beside the names indicate when they worked at Heffers.

Diane Allinson (*née* Bass) 1960–69
Jenny Ashman (*née* Langford) 1961–65; 1973–77
Ingrid Bane (*née* Ochotny) 1968–70
Kathy Benton 1950–54; 1977–97
Norman Biggs 1954–91
Alison Blair-Underwood (*née* Rimmer) 1974–2003
Claire Brown (*née* Johnston) 1968–69
Clive Brown, husband of Claire Brown
Alison Bruce, author
Beryl Brundish, customer
Sarah Burton 2000–07
Joan Clark (*née* Stubbings) 1941–49
Jean Clarke 1972–2006
Audrey Coleman (*née* Wright) 1944–54
Peter Coleman, worked on repairs after the 1946 fire at Petty Cury
Frank Collieson 1962–91
Mrs Cope 1981–82
Clive Cornell 1958–99
Bob Cox-Wrightson 1998–99
Gerald Criddle 1955–70
Hugh (Dudley) Davenport 1950–67
Marion Davenport (*née* Mynott) 1948–55
Liz Davies 1981–85
Naomi Davies, artist and illustrator
Triss Driver, granddaughter of Frederick Anstee
Lynda Feast (*née* Platt) 1978 to date
Pippa Goodhart (*née* Jennings) 1974–86
Susan Green (*née* Gilbert) 1962–68
Peggy Green 1953–83
Ronald (Andy) Hall 1986–94
Margaret E. (Bunty) Heffer, widow of William Heffer's grandson, John Heffer
Nicholas Heffer, Reuben's son and great-grandson of William Heffer
Richard Heffer, John's son and great-grandson of William Heffer
William Heffer, Reuben's son and great-grandson of William Heffer

Zillah Heffer, married to Nicholas Heffer
Robert Hill 1949–53; 1955–56
Rosemarie Hill (*née* Eicher) 1955–61
Barbara Lorna Hudson, 1959–62, author
Chris Jakes, librarian
Mark Jones 2001–05
Suzanne Jones (*née* Leonard) 1974–2008
Michelle Kavenagh 1984/5
Ann Kidman (*née* Warren) 1955–1966
Phyllis Konsievitz, customer
Shelley Lockwood, customer
Isabella Mead, customer
Jim Neale, customer
Lisa Newman 1988–91
Susan Nunn (*née* Fakes) 1959–68
Stephen Perry 1967–80
Veronica Perry (*née* How) 1968–73
Becky Proctor 1992–93
Janet Rayner (*née* Hornsby) 1964–70
Richard Reynolds 1981 to date
Sheila Reuben (*née* Howe) 1956–60
David Robinson 2005 to date
Stephen Robinson, great-grandson of William Heffer
Vanessa Rule (*née* Phillips) 1960–62
Katia Sagovsky 1969–72
Rosemary Sanders (*née* Crouch) 1955–64
Julian Sedgwick 1991–2003
Marcus Sedgwick 1991–93
Helen Siedel, customer
John Skelton 1973–76
Geoffrey Smallwood, fountain pen customer
Eve Stafford 1949–70
Thomas Taylor 1995-2000
Sandra Thompson (*née* Hornsby) 1963–64
Catherine Turner (*née* Hastings) 2001–02
Robert Webb 1975–79
Amy Wilkerson 2003–08
David Wilkerson 1972–74; 1981–85; 1989–2003

ACKNOWLEDGEMENTS AND PERMISSIONS

Completing my doctoral thesis in 2015, meant I finally had the time to focus on what may be described as the less 'academic' endeavour of writing a social history of Heffers of Cambridge. Certainly, this book is nothing like the thesis (much to the reader's relief, no doubt) although I must confess that both projects have been a labour of love. Whilst writing about Heffers, although I applied similar techniques to the doctoral research, such as conducting bibliographic searches, checking sources and interviewing people, it was never my intention to produce an academic treatise on the firm. Hopefully, through a narrative that blends the findings of the desk-top research with the voices of those who shared their memories, I've managed to convey something of the extraordinary Heffers story, culture and legacy.

In February 2016, the Heffer archive at the Cambridge County Records Office was sent away for cleaning, just as the research was getting underway. This meant that I did not have access to, for example, the company minute books (apart from the first, which the Heffer family had not donated to the Records Office). However, many sources were readily available via the Cambridgeshire Collection, including the annual reports for the twenty years to 1999, and a significant archive of press and marketing artefacts. Also, fortunately, the shop and a number of individuals had salvaged material at the time of the Blackwell's takeover, including correspondence, photographs, artwork and twenty years of staff newsletters. In many ways the sources that *were* available readily lent themselves to a social history of the firm.

There are many people I would like to thank, some no longer with us:

Frederick Anstee (1883–1944), my great-grandfather, for his love of books (it must be the blood); my great-aunt, Winifred Anstee (1918–2005), for her love of Heffers; my parents, Triss and Bas Driver, for the Saturday morning routine of visiting Heffers Children's Bookshop (which I describe in a February 2014 blog post, *Choosing books, living life*), for their encouragement, support, and access to Winifred Anstee's Heffers archive; and my husband, Trevor Bounford, for his unstinting faith in me, and for his superb editing and design skills.

The Heffer family, for putting their trust in the stranger who turned up out of the blue, declaring they're writing a book about their family firm; David Robinson and Richard Reynolds at Heffers today, who responded so positively to the project; Jenny Collieson who continued to support the project after the sad loss of her father, Frank, in May 2016.

Robert Webb, for responding to the 2014 blog post and picking up on a shared interest in Heffers, for his encouragement and his invaluable assistance with the research and the writing; Chris Elliott at the *Cambridge News*, for helping to publicise the plea for stories (and the plea for an answer to the mystery of the bust of William Heffer – yet to be solved); Derek Smiley and his Facebook Group, *Cambridge in the Good 'Ol Days in the 1960s* for sharing the plea for stories and for sharing their memories; Hilary Cox Condrun and Shelley Lockwood at The Museum of Cambridge, for hosting a great memory café in February 2016, for making a super film of the event starring Bunty Heffer, and for their interest in the project; Mike Petty, for his wisdom and guidance; and the Cambridgeshire Collection team at Cambridge Central Library – Mary, Celia, Myles and Chris, for their knowledge and superb service.

The most enjoyable and rewarding aspect of researching and writing a social history is meeting people and listening to their stories. A special 'thank you' goes to all those listed, who so generously shared their memories and mementos of Heffers.

PERMISSIONS

Every effort has been made to verify source material. Any copyright query can be addressed to the publisher, Gottahavebooks. Material is reproduced with the kind permission of the following (if only the page number is given, all reproductions on the page are credited to this source):

Alison Blair-Underwood: 19 (bust of William Heffer); 79 (the 1958 Penguin Books catalogue); 93 (first edition of Alan M Turing by his mother, Sara Turing, published by Heffers in 1998).
Audrey Coleman: 63; 151.
Bounford.com: 7 (Heffers in the twenty-first century)
The Cambridgeshire Collection at Cambridge Central Library: 20, 21 (George Heffer) 22 (Ernest Heffer, Arthur with Mary & Reuben Heffer), 23, 29, 31 (The Recorder banner), 31-32 (extract from The Recorder) 38, 39, 40, 55, 65, 71, 101, 102, 109, 110, 112-115, 120-122, 123 (the Performing Arts, the Art & Architecture and Central & South America catalogues), 128 (Heffers by post catalogue), 132 (Books for Christmas catalogue 1978), 133-134.
Cambridge News: 19 (extract from Cambridge Independent Press), 21 (Harry Heffer), 27, 31 (The Discount Bookseller advertisement), 33, 43, 48, 60, 68 (queue outside Petty Cury), 129 (wartime created new advertising themes, as seen in these 1939 examples from the Cambridge Daily News), 140, 141 (managers at Rustat House), 156 (staff with coaches and staff on a river trip), 185 (the Wilkerson family dressed up), 188 (the queue in Trinity Street for the Margaret Thatcher signing event).
Catherine Turner: 75 (photograph bookmark).
Claire Brown: 117.
Clare & Nigel Day: 103.
Clive Cornell: 53, 66, 69 (the new shop, 'like an ocean liner'), 72,141 (bibliographical researchers at work in Rustat House).
Clive James: 9.
Dudley & Marion Davenport: 41 (staff, with Felix Askem standing second from right), 157 (employees enjoying an ice-cream; staff sitting on the beach).
Fonz Chamberlain, Cambridge Historian: 18 (The Forester public house), 28 (Fitzroy Street in the early 1900s).
Gerald Criddle: 61, 62.
Historic England: 81.
Isabella Mead: 83.
ITV Anglia, courtesy of East Anglian Film Archive (University of East Anglia): 64 (policeman directing traffic outside Sidney Street shop).
Jenny Collieson: 70, 84 (advertising slogan by Frank Collieson), 88, 99, 131, 161, 164, 178, 181, 182, 197.
Julie E Bounford: 87, 123 (Going to the Fair catalogue), 179.
Kathy Benton: 136.
Margaret (Bunty) Heffer: 42, 25, 26, 42, 159 (Stephen Heffer), 168, 186.
Mr Doggett: 170.
Museum of Cambridge: 36 (dictograph machine from Heffers: CAMFK:132.68).
National Portrait Gallery: 18 (The Reverend Edward Tucker Leeke, vicar of St Andrew the Less).
Nicholas & Zillah Heffer: 15, 76, 159 (centenary bookmark), 163.

ENDNOTES

1   Chrimes, N. (2012) *Cambridge: Treasure Island in the Fens – The 800-year Story of the University and Town of Cambridge, 1209–2009*, Hobsaerie Publications, Cambridge.

2   Oldfield, M. (April 1944) 'Cambridge and its Stationers: An Unbroken Tradition of the Stationery Trade', *Stationery Trade Review.*

3   F. Brittain (1893–1969) Lecturer in Medieval Latin Literature and Keeper of the Records, Jesus College, Cambridge.

4   Stated by Frank Collieson in an interview with Christopher Andrew on BBC Radio Cambridgeshire, 1985.

5   Heffer, S (1952) *William Heffer 1843-1928.*

6   Actually in Lower Park Street, the house is still there, part of the terrace of workers' cottages along Lower Park Street towards Jesus Green.

7   Clement Court was a courtyard of fourteen households off Park Street, between Round Church Street and Portugal Place, directly behind the Maypole public house, where the Park Street multi-storey car park is now.

8   The Cambridge press article appeared on 13th August 1928, the Monday after William's funeral which had taken place on Saturday 11th.

9   Ernest wrote his own account of the family and the firm's early years that was never published.

10 Named by her brother Sidney because he could not, as a child, pronounce 'Emma Louise'.

11 Mann, S. (2005) *A Wonderful Thing for Cambridge: The Evelyn Hospital – 1921 to 2003*, Grant Editions, p87-98.

12 Founded 1878 in London by the bookseller Quaritch, the Sette today remains a small social club dedicated to book collecting, printing history, and bibliophily.

13 Welch, J. (2004) 'Heffer, Reuben George (1908–1985)', *Oxford Dictionary of National Biography*, Oxford University Press.

14 *The Cambridge Review (A Journal of University Life and Thought)*, was first published in 1879.

15 Published in *The Cambridge Review*, 1986.

16 Turner, R. and M. (July 1979) 'Family Businesses in Cambridge: An Interview with Mr John Heffer, Chairman of the Heffer Group of Companies', *Cambridgeshire, Huntingdon & Peterborough Life*, Vol. 13 No. 145.

17 *W. Heffer & Sons Present with their Compliments, A Few Photographs of their Premises, A Brief Outline of their Business History, A Concise Catalogue of the Articles which may be Procured at each Department* (1909).

18 It was occupied by butcher, Charles Marsh, in 1911.

19 *The Bookseller* has been the business magazine of the book industry since 1858; incorporating the earlier *Bent's Literary Advertiser*, established in 1802.

20   McKitterick, D. (2004) *A History of Cambridge University Press: Volume 3. New Worlds for Learning 1873–1972*, Cambridge University Press.

21   Wilson, J. (2010) *Cambridge Grocer: The story of Matthew's of Trinity Street 1832–1952*, R.A. Wilson.

22   *Cambridge Independent Press & University Herald*, 8th January 1892.

23   Established in 1890, *The Clique* was at that time the official organ of the Antiquarian Booksellers' Association.

24   A web-based prices and inflation calculator, www.thisismoney.co.uk was used to estimate monetary worth at today's value. The aim is to provide an approximate indication only.

25   Bradley, S. (ed.) (2008) *The British Book Trade: An Oral History*, British Library.

26   Proceedings of the OLD BAILEY: London's Central Criminal Court, 1674 to 1913 https://www.oldbaileyonline.org/browse.jsp?id=def1-384-19040418&div=t19040418-384#highlight

27   The complete New English Bible (Old and New Testaments) was jointly published in 1970 by Cambridge University Press and Oxford University Press.

28   In his speech at the formal opening of the Trinity Street shop Reuben stated he was first approached by Dr Bradfield, Bursar of Trinity, who suggested it would be good for Heffers and for Trinity College if the shop was moved from Petty Cury to Trinity Street.

29   Now held at the Visual Arts Data Service, a web resource hosted by the University for the Creative Arts.

30   *Cambridge Evening News*, 17th February 1970.

31   *Cambridge Evening News*, 22nd September 1970.

32   *Cambridge Daily News*, 6th April 1957.

33   Black, M. (2011) *Learning to be a Publisher: Cambridge University Press, 1951–1987, Personal Reminiscences*, Cambridge University Press.

34   *The Times*, 16th November 1977.

35   *Cambridge Daily News*, 10th March 1919.

36   *Cambridge Daily News*, 15th October 1920.

37   Bradley, S. (ed.) (2008) *The British Book Trade: An Oral History*, British Library, p51.

38   Isenberg, Steven L. *Lunching on Olympus: My meals with W. H. Auden, E. M. Forster, Philip Larkin, and William Empson*, The American Scholar, 28th January 2010.

39   Hansard, HL Deb 29 July 1964 vol 260 cc1186–200.

40   *Cambridge Evening News*, 25th February 1987.

41   Frederick Brittain, a renowned author of several books published by Heffers and good friend to the firm in earlier years, had written a history of Jesus College, in which he gave a description of the life of Tobias Rustat, the founder of the Rustat scholarships in 1671.

42   'Stock-taking leaving firm out for the count', 4th April 1984.

43   *Cambridge Independent Press*, 25th September 1914.

44   F. Collieson (May 1986) 'Remembering Reuben', *The Cambridge Review*.

45 John Welch, 'Heffer, Reuben George (1908–1985)', *Oxford Dictionary of National Biography*, Oxford University Press, 2004.

46 *Cambridge Evening News*, 8th November 1974.

47 *Cambridge Evening News*, 18th June 1987.

48 *Cambridge Evening News*, 28th June 1976.

49 *Cambridge Evening News*, 1st July 1976.

50 *Cambridge Evening News*, 1st June 1993.

51 *The Times*, 22nd July 1985.

52 F. Collieson (May 1986) 'Remembering Reuben', *The Cambridge Review*.

53 Frank Stubbings, in his 1991 ABC of *Bedders, Bulldogs and Bedells*, gives this description of 'freshmen':

FRESHMAN, colloquially FRESHER. A first-year undergraduate. Since the increase in the number of women undergraduates through men's Colleges becoming co-educational, the form *fresher*, has grown more usual, presumably to avoid using *freshman* of a woman (though in the U.S.A. it is, we are told, a 'unisex' word). *First-years* also seem to be increasingly common.

54 Bradley, S. (ed.) (2008) *The British Book Trade: An Oral History*, British Library, p49.

55 Feinstein, E. (2001) *Ted Hughes – The Life of a Poet*, Norton, p21.

56 ©The Pembroke College Winnie-the-Pooh Society 2000. Reproduced with the kind permission of Owen Barritt of the Pembroke College Winnie-the-Pooh Society.

57 Faulks, S. (2008) *Engleby*, Vintage Books, p256.

58 Foreword to Bradley, S. (ed.) (2008) *The British Book Trade: An Oral History*, British Library.

INDEX

Gottahavebooks

Other Gottahavebooks publications now available via www.gottahavebooks.co.uk

DAYS OF SORROW, TIMES OF JOY

"An extraordinary story of an extraordinary family"
Michael Wood, Historian & Broadcaster

'Readers of this impressive and enjoyable book will surely long remember the vivid scenes in which one family's commitment enabled its members to play a part in events that helped to shape our world.'
Professor Anthony Bradley

New extended 2016 edition with a foreword by Michael Wood, new photographs and an afterword by Fran Clemmow.

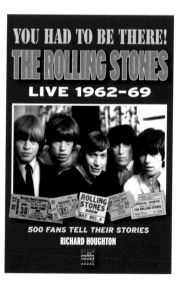

YOU HAD TO BE THERE:
THE ROLLING STONES LIVE 1962–69

This book draws on over 500 first-hand accounts from fans, supporting musicians and backstage staff, giving a unique insight into the period. Through the eyes of their fans the book charts the group's rise from an early rehearsal in a London jazz club through to the Hyde Park concert that became a memorial for Brian Jones.

'This book is a fabulous reminder of those heady days of the early '60s' (*Amazon review*)

'I really love this book. It conjures up my youth so well.' (*Amazon review*)

About the author

Dr Julie E Bounford, a sociologist and writer, hails from a Cambridge 'town' stock of booksellers, bakers and college bedders and lives with her husband, Trevor, in a Cambridgeshire village. Julie spends her time on research and writing, and on running Gottahavebooks, the Bounford's small indie publishing operation. She is available for talks on Heffers and commissions in qualitative academic and social history research and writing. Julie regularly publishes a blog on her website at http://jebounford.net and can be contacted via julie@gottahavebooks.co.uk